DEMAND THE IMPOSSIBLE

ALSO BY ROBERT L. TSAI

Practical Equality:
Forging Justice in a Divided Nation

America's Forgotten Constitutions:
Defiant Visions of Power and Community

Eloquence and Reason:
Creating a First Amendment Culture

DEMAND THE IMPOSSIBLE

ONE LAWYER'S PURSUIT OF EQUAL JUSTICE FOR ALL

ROBERT L. TSAI

W. W. NORTON & COMPANY
Independent Publishers Since 1923

Copyright © 2024 by Robert L. Tsai

All rights reserved
Printed in the United States of America
First Edition

For information about permission to reproduce selections from this book, write to Permissions, W. W. Norton & Company, Inc., 500 Fifth Avenue, New York, NY 10110

For information about special discounts for bulk purchases, please contact W. W. Norton Special Sales at specialsales@wwnorton.com or 800-233-4830

Manufacturing by Lakeside Book Company
Design by Patrice Sheridan
Production manager: Julia Druskin

ISBN 978-0-393-86783-1

W. W. Norton & Company, Inc., 500 Fifth Avenue, New York, N.Y. 10110
www.wwnorton.com

W. W. Norton & Company Ltd., 15 Carlisle Street, London W1D 3BS

1 2 3 4 5 6 7 8 9 0

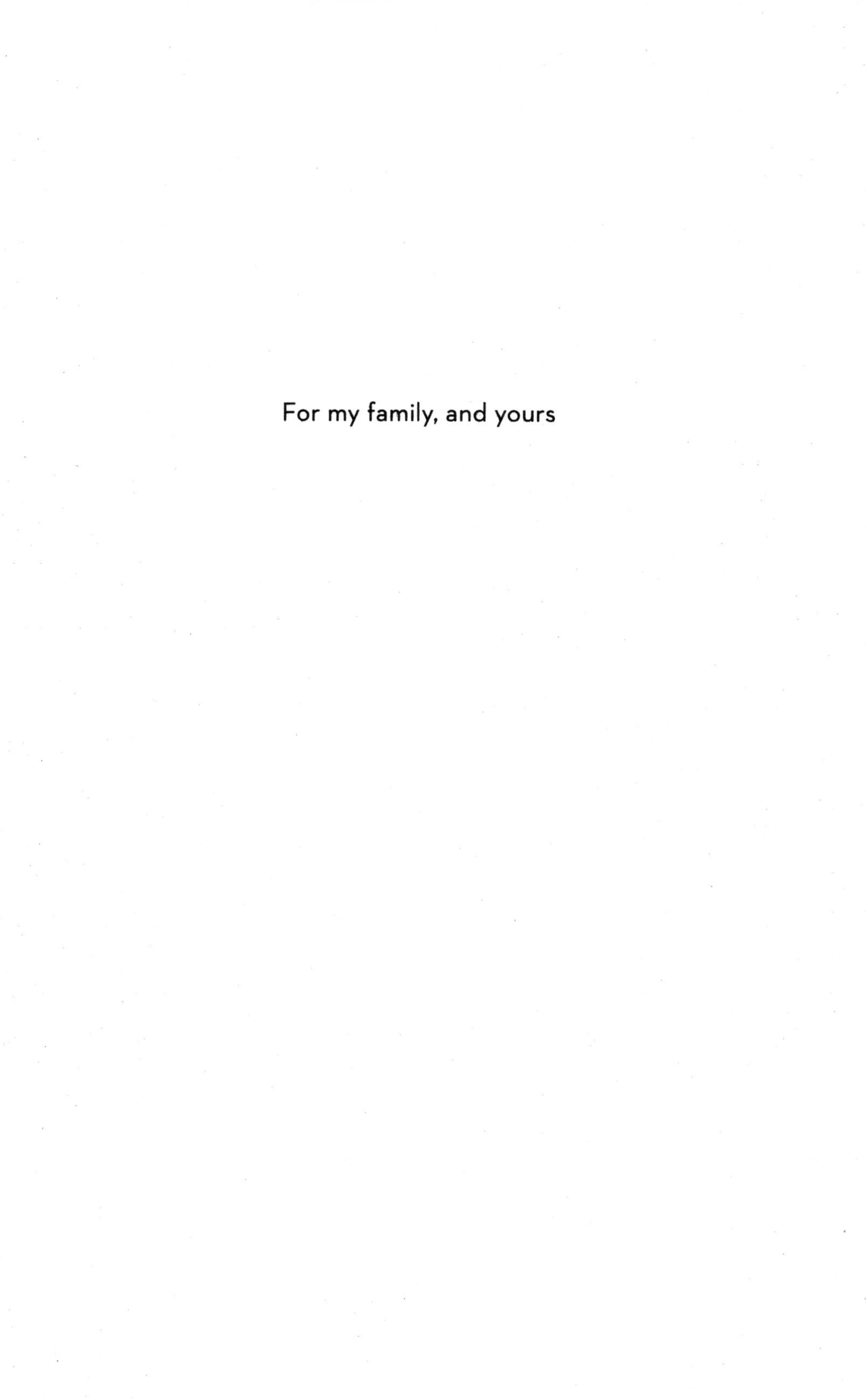

For my family, and yours

So, after all, maybe the South,
the nation and the world are in dire need of creative extremists.

—Martin Luther King, Jr., April 16, 1963

CONTENTS

INTRODUCTION 1

PART I SMOKING GUN
Amadeo v. Zant 27

PART II POVERTY AND REFORM
Snyder v. Louisiana 71

PART III DEMOCRACY AND RACE
Foster v. Chatman 109

PART IV INTELLECTUAL DISABILITY
McWilliams v. Dunn 147

EPILOGUE 179

ACKNOWLEDGMENTS 193

NOTES 197

INDEX 213

DEMAND THE IMPOSSIBLE

INTRODUCTION

On the morning of April 24, 2017, Stephen Bright arrived at the most powerful court in the nation for the fourth time in his career. His client's life was at stake. Three times before, Bright had argued in front of the U.S. Supreme Court, and all three times he had won. Could he pull it off one more time?

"We'll hear argument first this morning in case 16-5294, *McWilliams v. Dunn*," announced John Roberts, Chief Justice of the U.S. Supreme Court, promptly at 10 a.m. As the presiding justice, he sat in the center of a raised bench carved from mahogany, with the other eight justices fanning out in either direction. Constructed in 1935 in classical Corinthian style, the building was designed to be an awe-inspiring testament to "equal justice under law," a phrase that is emblazoned above the main entrance.

Bright, who represented James McWilliams, stood up and buttoned his jacket—one that he had picked out in a thrift store. For thirty-five years, Bright had led the Southern Center for Human Rights (SCHR), a nonprofit based in Atlanta that rendered legal aid to people under death sentence and pursued the reform of incarceration policies. Bright had spent decades trying to fulfill the promise of *Gideon v. Wainwright*, the landmark 1963 Supreme Court decision that established the right of counsel for poor people. It was a worthy and ambitious vision, but one that had never been fully realized. Bright's work had focused on improving the criminal system of the Deep South, where the politics of mass incarceration had exacerbated the legacy of slavery and Jim Crow, producing a dehumanizing form of unequal justice.[1]

America had changed so much since Bright's first Supreme Court argument back in 1988. Then, he could work with the remnants of the fabled Warren Court, a series of legal precedents established between 1953 and 1969 when Earl Warren oversaw the Court's work. President Eisenhower appointed Warren, former attorney general of California, to the Court at a crucial historical juncture: his liberalism and statesmanship helped break a logjam over the constitutionality of racially segregated schools. With Warren at the helm, the high court not only produced *Brown v. Board of Education of Topeka* and supervised the dismantling of legal apartheid, but also issued decisions protecting the right to vote and ensuring that people charged with a crime would be treated fairly.

Even as the Court lurched to the right over the years, Bright still achieved a remarkable win rate as a cause lawyer. Each of the previous times he argued in the highest court of the land, he had persuaded enough of the justices to come together and give a condemned man another chance. When it came to reading the shifting sands, Bright displayed an instinct for discerning the most attractive arguments that could be used to cobble together a consensus. He knew that compromise was unavoidable, given the generally cautious nature of most judges. Flexibility over strategy was essential because saving clients had to be the priority—human beings were not just means to an end. Yet he also cared about pushing the law in the direction of justice so other people in desperate straits could also benefit.[2]

While Bright was certainly skillful in front of appellate judges, those who knew him best felt that it was before a jury that he "truly thrived." Bright had a knack for conveying how broken people could fall through the cracks in the criminal justice system, and his barely contained sense of outrage and fierce attention to detail earned him the respect of judges and adversaries alike. He had earned his reputation by taking cases that no one else wanted, representing clients that society had long ago discarded. By plunging himself into his clients' whole life and pulling out all the stops, he had won cases few lawyers would dare tackle.[3]

Even so, McWilliams's appeal faced long odds. Unlike his past trips to the Supreme Court, Bright did not have a compelling story about official misconduct to tell. There was not a racist district attorney who manufactured unrepresentative juries. Instead, in representing McWilliams, Bright was pleading for the life of an intellectually disabled Black man convicted of killing a convenience store clerk during a robbery. These kinds of cases were made even more difficult because bigotry and suspicion rendered the issue of intellectual disability volatile. There was no telling whether a judge or juror would see such a condition as a reason for mercy or instead as an excuse to treat a person more harshly. Did it make someone less morally culpable or was it proof that the individual represented a future danger?

Bright had come to Washington to tell the justices that even when someone has been found guilty of a brutal and senseless crime, an accurate sentencing process still mattered: whenever evidence suggests that a defendant might have brain damage, basic fairness requires he be given a mental health expert.

As his time ticked away at oral argument, Bright realized he had to somehow hang on to the liberal justices—who had dwindled to just a handful—and find a way to convince someone else to join the fold. If he could manage that, he might still eke out a ruling that would extend his client's life for a few more months and help other people with a potential intellectual disability. If he failed to scale that mountain, then brain damaged or not, McWilliams would lose his life.

* * *

STEPHEN BROOKS BRIGHT ENTERED the arena of death penalty politics at a critical moment in American history. Bright came of age during the tumult of the late 1960s and early '70s. As a teenager, he heard the pleas for justice at home and abroad, as fellow citizens spilled into the streets to demand an end to racial segregation and students occupied campus buildings to protest American imperialism in Southeast Asia. At first, his tool of choice consisted of social activism. But as America's conservative mood deepened, Bright became disillusioned with electoral politics and instead became a convert to legal liberalism, believing that judges had to curb democracy's excesses by enforcing individual rights. Trained as an advocate for the poor, he took up the cause lawyer's primary instrument: harnessing the power of the courts to spur social change.

In that respect, he resembled radical lawyers like Thurgood Marshall, William Kunstler, and Bryan Stevenson. Like his counterparts, Bright sought to unleash social change by representing unpopular clients, reviving legal principles from within the political order, and leaving behind organizations to carry on the work.

Bright and his allies began their fight for equality under the law at a time when headwinds were the strongest and changes in criminal justice policy were widening existing inequities. Regardless of party, most politicians in the 1980s and '90s proved to be largely indistinguishable in their demands for more statutory offenses, longer sentences, and expansive use of the death penalty. Democrats like Ed Koch and Bill Clinton sounded exactly like Republicans Rudy Giuliani and George H. W. Bush, as they worked across the aisle to push ever-harsher criminal laws. The War on Crime turned into the War on Drugs, and the War on Drugs eventually rolled seamlessly into the War on Terror. In the crusade against a seemingly endless stream of social misfits, legislators and judges found novel ways to limit access to justice. Often working in tandem, elites built an imposing jurisprudence of dread—a set of laws, doctrines, and concepts based on outsized fears of strangers and intended to facilitate severe punishment policies.[4]

America's incarceration rate exploded in these decades, as the country became the world's leader in using criminal laws to deal with a wide range of social ills. Resort to capital punishment also expanded. Jonathan Simon has described the political sentiment that drove policies as "lawmaking without pity," reflecting an overinvestment in penal laws, prisons, and the rise of a "waste management" model of handling human beings convicted of criminal offenses. The death penalty represented the ultimate means of disposing of unwanted lives.[5]

Through most of the twentieth century, the prison population hovered around 200,000. But starting in the mid-1970s, the incarcerated population leapt to over 1.5 million. Today, America accounts for 22 percent of the entire world's prisoners, even though it makes up only 4 percent of the world's population. The United States is unlikely to be the most crime-ridden country in the world, but for the last fifty years, its policies have been driven by a perception that social disorder lurks around every corner.

Bright emerged on the scene as a cause lawyer just as these cascading policies crashed hardest on poor people and racial minorities. Although America has been killing its own people since the colonial period, capital punishment was refashioned into a tool of racial control. Eager to preserve White order, slaveholding states made the rape of a White woman a capital offense. And between 1930 and 1972, 89.1 percent of the people executed for rape in the United States were Black. Nearly all of these sentences were carried out by former Confederate states. Even after explicitly racist death penalty laws were struck down by courts or repealed by legislatures, significant racial and regional disparities remained.[6]

Like many Americans, Bright had not spent much time thinking about capital punishment because he assumed that the Supreme Court's 1972 decision in *Furman v. Georgia* striking down death penalty laws as "arbitrary and capricious" had ended the punishment once and for all. Yet within the next few years, thirty-five states responded to *Furman* by enacting new death penalty statutes.[7]

Then came the anguished pleas for help from incarcerated people after the Supreme Court reinstated the death penalty in its 1976 decision, *Gregg v. Georgia*, deeming the practice permissible so long as a state enacted procedures to constrain sentencing decisions over life and death. State officials wheeled back out electric chairs that had been decommissioned and covered in dust; some prosecutors rallied to the pro–death penalty banner as a way of making a name for themselves. Death warrants stacked up high, few attorneys had any real expertise trying capital cases, and volunteers who kept an eye on these troubling developments scoured the country for anyone brave enough to lend a hand.[8]

Bright took on three cases right away. What he saw infuriated him: inexperienced lawyers appointed for the poor presented little or no mitigation evidence to try to convince juries to spare their clients. In a number of cases, defendants were tried and sentenced to death in a day or two. The brief filed in a subsequent appeal might be bare-bones, lacking arguments or even citations to key cases, all evidence of a slapdash effort. Bright's experience scrambling around the country trying to obtain stays of execution for people who had been wronged by their own lawyers would lead him to embrace the correction of these problems as his life's mission.[9]

These days, cause lawyers are thought to be advocates who run to court and demand injunctions to halt abortion restrictions or immigration policies. That misconception is more likely due to the fact that by the mid-twentieth century civil rights activism had splintered, with some of its most visible activities outside of the criminal justice realm, rather than because the definition of cause lawyering inherently excludes criminal matters.

Few today remember that the NAACP had originally been established in the wake of race riots in Springfield, Illinois. A White mob tried to lynch two Black men detained in a local jail and, when their plans were thwarted, began a rampage throughout the city. Appalled, suffragists, labor reformers, socialists, and clergy came together to promote a "new abolition movement" to "eradicate caste or racial prejudice" and "securing justice in the courts." In 1910, the NAACP handled its first major legal case by defending Pink Franklin, a Black sharecropper sentenced to death for killing a police officer in South Carolina. Franklin had gotten into a shootout after police came to arrest him for failing to show up to work. He and his wife had to escape a lynch mob before the NAACP arrived to help.

The NAACP continued its anti-lynching efforts in the 1920s, and in the 1930s represented Black defendants accused of serious offenses against White victims where the sentiment for mob justice ran high. Only as the organization's resources grew did more of its energies go toward dismantling segregated workplaces and schools.[10]

Called to the South in 1982 and believing himself to be working in this tradition, Bright threw himself against the gears of a restarted killing machine. If the rush to incarcerate and execute were not reversed, he believed, the many injustices would eventually delegitimate the legal system and bring the entire thing crashing down. What Bright lacked in pedigree and powerful patrons, he made up for through a punishing work ethic, a wicked sense of humor, and keen insight into the human condition.

He went on to become one of the greatest lawyers of his generation: arguing four times before the U.S. Supreme Court, reviving a dormant organization established by ministers during the civil rights movement called the Southern Prisoners' Defense Committee and renaming it the Southern Center for Human Rights, and shining a spotlight on a host of unconstitutional practices.

Most striking of all, Bright's devotion to legal liberalism fostered the development of a distinctive method of cause lawyering—one that could be passed on to the next generation. It all came back to the central idea of human dignity. This concept has many meanings in the law, but in Bright's hands the idea meant, first and foremost, that state-sanctioned killing and mass confinement of human beings raise moral questions. If a system of punishment consistently marks the poor or other disenfranchised groups for punishment, then that system cannot be reconciled with our nation's fundamental values. A truly humane approach to punishment, by contrast, enfolds the values of equality, fairness, proportionality, and rehabilitation. As Bright would often say, such a system of justice "treats a person accused of a crime as more than the worst thing he has ever done."[11]

The Brazilian educator Paulo Freire once observed that a person "is solidary with the oppressed only when he stops regarding the oppressed as an abstract category and sees them as persons who have been unjustly dealt with . . . when he stops making pious, sentimental and individualist gestures and risks an act of love."[12]

For Bright, an ethical model of lawyering counteracted the dehumanizing aspects of the American criminal justice system. He felt that the lawyer-client relationship could be transformed into an act of self-discovery for both parties to it—and, more ambitiously, that that connection could be an engine for social reexamination. If the adversarial process was central to our nation's deepest values and indeed represented a key method of contesting those very values, then a trial could, in the right hands, serve an agonistic function by affirming those principles for all to see.

In this sense, fearlessly demanding justice on behalf of the whole person and pursuing an end to unjust punishments went hand in hand, for the two projects together helped build a broader culture of equal respect. Treating despised members of society as worthy of a vigorous defense restored their dignity. In turn, laying everything on the line to show a community that a person was more than the sum of bad things he did in his life was the greatest act of love a lawyer could muster.

This was why nothing enraged Bright more than hearing about incompetent lawyers and indifferent judges. Where others would indulge excuses, he saw violations of constitutional rights, a stain on his profession, a continuation of the age-old pattern of the wealthy getting their way and the poor getting the shaft. He collected such betrayals as if they were America's scars, true stories of sleeping lawyers, drunk lawyers, lawyers who despised their own clients so much they did almost no work on their behalf and begged jurors to put them out of their misery. And he railed against judges who had become so numb to the daily grind of processing cases that they were no longer capable of distinguishing between inconvenience and injustice.

* * *

Born in 1948, Steve Bright grew up on a farmhouse in Danville, Kentucky, with his three siblings. Their father, Robert, who had inherited the farm from his father, raised cattle and grew tobacco. Patricia, their mother, made sure that the children were fed and cared for. In his spare time as a teenager, Steve Bright wrote for the local newspaper, *The Advocate-Messenger*. The job allowed him to "get into everything." It also gave him his first taste of the political world.[13]

Bright had been fascinated by politics since he was a child. He loved everything about it: the energy of the crowds, the soaring oratory of the most practiced speakers, and the way that well-formed sentences could move people to action. He was energized by the first political rally he attended at age fifteen, when Democrat Edward "Ned" Breathitt spoke at the Danville courthouse during his campaign for governor. Breathitt, an underdog who offered a progressive view on civil rights, went on to win that race.[14]

After finishing at Boyle County High, Bright traveled down to Lexington to attend the University of Kentucky. It is difficult to overstate just how hopeful many young people felt at this time. Starting in 1961, brave Freedom Riders had descended upon southern states. A biracial coalition of students led the way through freedom rides, as organizations such as CORE and SNCC organized sit-ins and demonstrations to help galvanize the country to see the inherent brutality of racial segregation in America. All of this had sparked a moment of moral reckoning, leading Congress to enact the landmark Civil Rights Act of 1964. After defeating conservative Barry Goldwater for the presidency in a landslide, Lyndon B. Johnson promised to build the Great Society.[15]

Yet many Americans—especially the older generations—grew weary of the upheaval associated with the rapid pace of legal transformation. Involvement in Vietnam also increasingly divided the country, as young people were forced to bear the brunt of Cold War policy in a faraway land.

Bright had entered college with a plan to become a journalist. By his sophomore year he decided to shelve his original plan. He switched to political science and threw himself completely into student government. After being branded by the school paper as an individual "with a very unenlightened attitude," Bright lost his bid for the student government vice-presidency in the spring of 1969. A year later, he campaigned on a platform for "radical change in student government," earned the endorsement of the paper, and won the presidency going away.[16]

He made an early misstep by supporting the playing of "Dixie" at sporting events, but also publicly urged additional integration efforts. Although the university had desegregated after *Brown v. Board of Education*, it remained a mostly white institution into the early '70s. Bright had always understood this issue more intimately. In Danville, his parents had participated in efforts to desegregate schools and businesses.[17]

As a member of Sigma Nu, Bright gave speeches to persuade the fraternity to admit Black members, but his efforts fell short against a traditional selection process that allowed a single objection to keep someone out. The truth was hard to swallow: it would take more than a few speeches to do anything about systemic racism.[18]

Everything changed for Bright and so many other members of his generation when the National Guard opened fire on unarmed students at Kent State University on May 4, 1970. President Nixon said of the killings that "when dissent turns to violence it turns to tragedy," while his pugnacious vice president Spiro Agnew blamed "tomentose exhibitionists" on college campuses. The administration's callous response to the Kent State massacre, coupled with its extensive efforts to undermine anti-war protests, sparked additional marches and sit-ins throughout the country. At the University of Kentucky, students occupied an administrative building while university trustees met, calling on school officials to denounce the Nixon administration's undeclared war in Southeast Asia.

For as long as possible, Bright sought to play a bit of both roles: as a mediator to facilitate dialogue and defuse crises, but as an activist when it came to voicing the grievances of his generation. Yet he would learn that the ground could shift under your feet during a struggle for social justice. When that happened, you might have to take one side or another—or else get out of the way.

After an Air Force ROTC building on campus was set ablaze during a protest, Governor Louie B. Nunn declared martial law on the campus of University of Kentucky. State police cleared campus grounds and imposed a curfew. The next day, guardsmen in riot gear deployed tear gas against students and arrested several protest leaders—including Bright. Governor Nunn justified his crackdown as part of an effort to resist "the paralyzing effects of violence, intimidation, and anarchy" in American society. "The dangerous people here are not the students," Bright declared. Instead, he criticized Nunn for "exploiting the students to save a dying political career." A majority of voters backed the governor's strong-arm tactics.[19]

Bright lent his name to lawsuits that challenged the governor's emergency order and university policies, but lost in court. In turn, the university filed disciplinary charges against him and several others, seeking to expel dissenters. Only by obtaining the services of a talented third-year law student did Bright escape being drummed out of school.[20]

Bright's encounters with the state radicalized him. He could not stop the university from rewriting the disciplinary code to make it easier to sanction students, but he castigated school officials for failing to "recognize the student as a human being" and rejecting trials "by one's peers." Feeling powerless, he told trustees that "when we deny the rights of a few, we have denied everyone their rights."[21]

"I want to get out of the South for awhile," Bright told people. His goal as a student leader was to "make the university treat students as human beings rather than machines." He had learned to confront power, winning some battles and losing others. He also now knew how to mend political relationships that had frayed. Most important of all, he had started to formulate a critique of the state: how law and politics can degrade human beings and lock everyone else into a cycle of recrimination and violence.

A possible career in politics became far less attractive to Bright when Democrat George McGovern lost his bid for the presidency in 1972. After entering law school, Bright had taken a leave to work for McGovern's campaign. McGovern wasn't just an anti-war candidate; at the time he had seemed like the best hope for a national revival of humanistic politics. But his resounding defeat by Nixon led Bright to turn to the prospect of pursuing social change through the courts—the inspirational radical lawyering of William Kunstler and Leonard Weinglass loomed larger as political heroes waned. As much as he found law school out of step with the needs of the times, Bright returned to the University of Kentucky and completed his legal education.

After a stint at the Appalachian Research and Defense Fund advocating for the poor, Bright relocated to Washington, D.C., to work for the Public Defender Service for the District of Columbia. Originally operating as a legal aid society, PDS was charged with a new mission in 1970: to satisfy the Constitution's guarantee of providing defense counsel for people who cannot afford an attorney. In three years, Bright worked his way up from misdemeanors to felonies. Most of his clients were African American, as were the jurors in the cases that went to trial. He learned the stark differences between urban poverty and the kinds of deprivation he had seen in rural Appalachia. Bright discovered that what truly mattered in changing his clients' lives was doing the grueling social work, especially in getting youthful offenders into the right program rather than incarceration.[22]

In a place filled with incredibly personable and dedicated attorneys, Bright built a reputation as a talented and well-prepared public defender. When he had a trial, word would spread like wildfire through the courthouse. Attorneys and staff would fill the back of the room to watch him in action. These years didn't offer the chance to litigate complicated constitutional issues, just the occasional search-and-seizure question. Critically, however, Bright did have the opportunity to hone a brand of client-centered lawyering instilled in him by his colleagues.

In court, Bright focused on ensuring that a client was treated as a human being in front of others. He demanded that people charged with crimes be allowed to wear regular clothes, not be forced to appear in orange jumpsuits or shackles. He artfully used physical contact and proximity—a hand on the shoulder, a pat of the elbow—to convey that he cared about his clients, signal that they deserved to be treated fairly and with dignity, and protect them from the forces that sought to reduce them to the worst things they had done.

Bright built rapport quickly with clients, especially streetwise youths. "I'm here to beat the rap," Bright would say cheerily. He had a preternatural ability to get judges and jurors to see things from a new perspective. During one bail hearing, a state's witness had testified about the number of out-of-wedlock children a detainee had, calling it antisocial behavior. But Bright shifted attention from the man's conduct to his relationships, telling the judge that he had many "community contacts": people would surely miss him if the state kept him locked up; the people counting on him could also help him stay out of trouble if he was let out on bail.[23]

Bright became a tireless advocate, but his single-minded devotion to clients could exact a high price. He paid that price by neglecting regular exercise, eating well, vacations. While working late one evening during a trial, at the age of thirty-one, he experienced fast and irregular heartbeats. Because he was hospitalized for several days, the judge declared a mistrial. At the time, Bright was supervising another PDS attorney, Ellen Kreitzberg, who had her first juvenile trial. He called Kreitzberg from the hospital and left a message asking how things went for the first day, wanting to know if she wanted to discuss anything in preparation for the next day. She shook her head at the phone. "The client always came first to Steve."[24]

* * *

BRIGHT'S FIRST EXPERIENCE WORKING a death case changed the trajectory of his career. Patsy Morris, who had founded the Georgia affiliate of the ACLU with her husband, minister John B. Morris, was seeking legal representation for Donnie Thomas, who faced imminent execution. Bright, who had left PDS to work at Law Students in Court, agreed to take on Thomas's case. It turned out that Morris had already spoken to two other attorneys, George Kendall and Russell Canan. The trio would stay on that case to the very end.

When Thomas's legal documents showed up at Bright's door, everything fit in a single envelope. Bright imagined there would be several boxes of documents and exhibits, but it dawned on him that there was so little paperwork because of how quickly Thomas had been tried for an infamous crime and sentenced to death. The brief filed in his appeal was eleven pages long, shorter than what a first-year law student might complete as an assignment for an imaginary case. Because Thomas's appeal had been denied, he would soon be slated for execution if no other lawyer could be found.

From that moment on, Bright was drawn into a lifelong commitment to serving the needs of incarcerated people, gradually at first, then all in a rush. Thomas's plight was followed by those of James David Raulerson, J. C. Shaw, William Anthony Brooks. Bright even began calling on attorneys he knew to take capital cases, providing a crucial new hub for Morris's recruitment efforts.

Bright soon found himself recruited by a minister named Joe Ingle to resuscitate a prisoners' rights organization founded by clergy who had been active in the civil rights movement. In 1976, members of the Southern Prison Ministry, the Southern Coalition of Jails and Prisons, and the Mississippi Prisoners' Defense Committee met at a farm owned by Will Campbell, a whiskey-sipping "bootleg preacher." Lacking a church pulpit, Campbell nevertheless preached the gospel of radical inclusiveness through his itinerant activism. He was the only White founding member of the Southern Christian Leadership Conference established by Martin Luther King, Jr., and other civil rights leaders to resist segregation nonviolently. Campbell participated in sit-ins of Whites-only businesses while seeking to convince Klan members to give up their ideology of hate. At a time when politics encouraged people choose sides and stick to them, he spread an unpopular message: "If you're gonna love one, you've got to love 'em all."[25]

At Campbell's home in Mt. Juliet, Tennessee, this group established an organization with a mission to offer direct legal representation to people incarcerated in Deep South states. The new organization was named the Southern Prisoners' Defense Committee. After a few years, it struggled to stay afloat, losing two staff attorneys and dealing with more expenses than income. After thinking it over, Bright told his close friends he believed that reviving the organization was what he was meant to do.

When Bright arrived in Atlanta in 1982, the only lawyers representing poor people charged with death penalty crimes in any organized fashion were the NAACP Legal Defense Fund and an Atlanta-based organization called Team Defense. Established in 1976, Team Defense originally planned to provide trial-level aid to people charged with death-eligible offenses in Georgia. But that sensible goal became overwhelmed by the deluge of cases.

Once Bright settled into his new home, the first task was to stabilize the organization and sort out its budget. That first year, as they searched for funding, the Center's budget was $180,000. Salaries were the same for everyone, starting at $8,500 and increasing to $16,000. They were basically poverty lawyers who were themselves living in poverty. Several of the attorneys shared an apartment and, later a home, when the Center had gained better control of its finances. Reflecting the radical ethic of service, many would open their homes to others who wanted to lend a hand on the Center's cases. People needed to get around all over the South to visit clients, hunt down witnesses and documents, and attend hearings in faraway courthouses. To do so, they relied on a used Plymouth Duster donated by the Open Door Community, which ministered to homeless people in Atlanta.

The initial group of SCHR lawyers had mostly been public defenders or legal aid lawyers, or had worked with Bright on cases in the past. As time passed, other staff attorneys were hired straight out of law school, a clerkship with a judge, or a fellowship. Among the early crop of such recruits was Bryan Stevenson, who called Bright "the first person committed to indigent defense" he had ever met. From the start, both SCHR and Team Defense welcomed women lawyers at a time when women rarely played leading roles in the law. In the late 1970s and even through much of the '80s, there were few women in southern courtrooms as either lawyers or jurors.[26]

A few years later, the organization changed its name to the Southern Center for Human Rights. The Southern Prisoners' Defense Committee was "quite possibly the worst name in the history of NGOs," a lawyer working at the Center noted. "Everyone despises the South, everyone hates prisoners, no one likes defense, and we all despise committees." The new name better captured the organization's mission to serve poor people throughout the region most affected by tough-on-crime demagoguery, as well as an emerging ethos that matters of criminal punishment presented a struggle of human concern and international scope.[27]

When it came to litigation strategy, Bright's approach represented an evolution in what Millard Farmer, founder of Team Defense, had pioneered. Farmer had coined the term, "conflictioneering," predicated on the belief that "the government wants the death penalty to be a cheap, easy political fix." By contrast, capital defense attorneys "want it to be a big, expensive political nightmare." Over time, Bright figured out how to perfect the theory, "doing it way more thoroughly" than it had been done in the past and "taking it to another level." Bright's approach, which may have been less flashy than Farmer's, centered on highlighting the institutional pathologies in legal representation that arise from the absence of adequate resources. It would emerge as an effective way of providing effective indigent defense in a fully bureaucratized yet broken system—at least until people in charge saw fit to dismantle it.[28]

In those early years, Bright believed that he and his colleagues were engaged in a form of legal "triage": trying anything within the bounds of the law to keep people alive for as long as possible. "There is no great issue that's going to save people on death row," he told them. Through trial and error, they tried to help "whoever was most desperate" by seeking stays of execution, but they were often saddled with a trial record containing mistakes by others.[29]

By the mid-1980s, it became apparent that a handful of lawyers focused exclusively on handling the most desperate postconviction cases did not represent a viable model for the long run. They would burn out. Not enough people could be rescued from gruesome ends. Errors made during trial were too hard to get overturned later. Moreover, politicians began to demand reforms that would make it harder for advocates to engage in last-minute maneuvers. Judges had also started to extend procedural doctrines to stop individuals from raising issues their lawyers had failed to raise earlier.

Advocates for the poor needed to find ways of getting involved in cases earlier, before egregious mistakes were made. They needed better focus in litigating issues. Bright had to raise an army of lawyers willing to lend time and expertise. Volunteers had to be trained in legal strategies and mitigation techniques. The media needed to hear about the deficiencies of the justice system. In time, the Center would attract enough staff to concentrate knowledge and expertise about the history and practice of southern justice. This allowed the staff to work with volunteers who had been vetted for experience and commitment.

During the early days, a great deal of the Center's work was performed at a frantic pace. Lawyers often met a client for the first time once an execution date was set. Everything was time-consuming. Working on Kaypro computers with no backups, they had to edit briefs by physically cutting and pasting new sections of argument into a document and hurriedly retyping entire pages if they cited new cases. Waiting for a last-minute stay of execution meant standing next to the fax machine or pacing near a telephone plugged into the wall.

In those days, the U.S. Supreme Court did not accept electronic filings or faxes. If someone wanted a case reviewed, legal papers had to be hand delivered. SCHR staff would often put a brief on a Greyhound bus, praying there would not be a traffic jam and nervously counting the hours until the bus arrived. More than once, they sent a brief by airplane, arranging for someone to pick up the documents and get them filed on time.

In 1987, SCHR won the first in a series of cases involving racial discrimination by prosecutors during jury selection. Clive Stafford Smith, an Englishman who joined the Center after an internship with Team Defense, argued the cause of Willie Gamble, Jr. before the Georgia Supreme Court. An all-White Emanuel County jury had sentenced Gamble, a Black man, to die in the electric chair for the slaying of the wife and son of a prominent optometrist. The prosecutor had used all ten of his allotted peremptory strikes to remove ten African Americans from the jury pool.

This was the first time the Georgia Supreme Court had occasion to apply the U.S. Supreme Court decision *Batson v. Kentucky*, which held that the Equal Protection Clause is violated by the race-based removal of a juror. Under *Batson*, if a defendant objects that a juror is excluded because of race, a prosecutor must give a nondiscriminatory explanation. Asked why he had removed a particular Black person from the jury, the prosecutor in Gamble's case said that "he appears to have the intelligence of a fencepost." His reason for striking another Black juror was that "he looks a little like the defendant."[30]

During oral argument, Justice Hardy Gregory, Jr., appeared hesitant to second-guess the trial judge overseeing jury selection, asking, "How can we decide the strike question when we were not there to see it?" Stafford Smith retorted, "You are never going to get another case like this" where the racial bias is so obvious.[31]

On July 9, 1987, the Georgia Supreme Court issued a unanimous decision ordering a new trial for Gamble. Black citizens comprised nearly a quarter of the panel of forty-two people, but zero African Americans wound up on the jury that heard Gamble's case. That discrepancy alone was "more than sufficient" to demonstrate that the state's strikes had a discriminatory effect. Justice Gregory concluded that several of the explanations given for removing particular Black jurors were "suspect" because "similarly situated white jurors were not challenged."[32]

After that major victory, the Center started devoting more resources to jury composition issues. Bright believed not only that these represented worthwhile issues to pursue, but also that the demographics of a jury would be essential to reflecting the "conscience of the community." That so many Black people were excluded meant that they were denied civic participation and that the accused were being denied equal justice.[33]

Once Bright and others exposed these and other legal inadequacies, the Georgia Supreme Court began to look more closely at death penalty cases and reverse for serious errors. It helped that the Georgia courts themselves were slowly changing. By 1992, the court had two Black justices and two women. But it was also true that advocacy by the tiny public interest community during these years started to identify persistent problems in the criminal justice system.

Of course, there were dark days. Multiple death warrants signed, extended road trips to beg judges for stays of execution, restless nights in dingy motels, hearings one after another. These were "all hands on deck" moments. They were also periods of lonely suffering.[34]

In a span of a few weeks, Bright lost two clients: J. C. Shaw on January 11, 1985, David Raulerson on January 30. He attended both executions, believing it important to bear witness to state violence and "to be there in that final moment when they don't have anyone else." A lawyer juggles multiple, exhausting roles during a client's final days: litigator, counselor, friend, witness.

Bright was devastated by the human toll, the stripping away of each man's dignity in "a modern day equivalent of burning at the stake." He felt himself overcome by waves of anger, then futility. "I think sometimes the only service I provide my clients is knowing them and comforting them," he said at the time. "We lurch from crisis to crisis. I get real sad." No group conversation about the emotional aspects of such traumatic events took place. There had been no playbook for that. Each person was left to grieve and cope in his own way.[35]

In quieter moments, Bright and his colleagues would share with each other "the challenges of doing this kind of work in this kind of world." They had to find meaning in the relationships created through their representation of desperate clients. And they had to make peace with the reality that personal rewards would always be intrinsic in nature, and never come from fame or fortune. When advocates for the poor did their job to the best of their ability, the fight itself constituted an affirmation of life.[36]

At the beginning of their struggle, Bright believed that they should choose their words carefully when speaking about state officials to the media because "we have to do business with these people." They should maintain a sense of decorum and civility between repeat players. But after observing the execution of their clients, Bright and his allies swore they would tell the world the truth about exactly what happens inside the machinery of death.

* * *

IF THE DEATH PENALTY was confidently yet chaotically restarted across the country in the late 1970s, today it is rarely inflicted, its many flaws exposed for all to see. Drawing on Bright's career, this book traces the history of the ideas that have brought the practice to heel: racial equality, human dignity, competent representation. As Leah Ward Sears, the first African American woman to serve as chief justice of the Georgia Supreme Court, put it: "We need to understand how to get more people like Steve— We've got to get the recipe." But our task is to discern the man behind the myth, to understand Bright as a historical subject in political time. Thus, this book is not just an investigation of one person's life. Rather, it is a history of the methods and ideas that influenced Bright's cause lawyering, and in turn were reshaped through his advocacy. It is also about an extended effort by lawyers and activists to rescue legal liberalism from itself.[37]

Demand the Impossible is organized around the four cases Bright argued in the U.S. Supreme Court. These cases serve as milestones in his career, through which we can trace his long fight for equal justice. Bright's approach offers an inspiring model of legal advocacy as a component of collective action, illustrating how progress can be made even in a challenging political climate.

Of course, constitutional principles do not emerge fully formed from the minds of judges. Instead, they are forged against the backdrop of broader social and political conditions, refined through advocacy and resistance, and tested over time. Most of Bright's contributions to constitutional law came from a defensive posture to protect the hard-won gains of past achievements—what Harvard Law professor Mark Tushnet has called "defensive crouch liberalism"—given the zeal for punishment and the increasingly conservative nature of the federal judiciary. These were the structural conditions no one could change overnight, and so the arguments Bright made had to account for the increased hostility towards the rights of the accused.

Part I delves into *Amadeo v. Zant*, Bright's first major case in the U.S. Supreme Court. This legal battle taught SCHR lawyers that, despite an inhospitable climate for transformative change, inroads could still be made by paying attention to jury selection procedures. *Amadeo* startled the world by showing that death penalty enthusiasts might cut corners by rigging unrepresentative juries. It also showed how indifferent judges could be part of the problem.[38]

A major casualty of the War on Crime has been access to justice. It was a Democratic president—Lyndon Johnson—who on March 8, 1965, first called upon the nation to mobilize to fight "a thorough, intelligent, and effective war against crime." His Republican successor, Richard Nixon, criticized Johnson for lacking zeal as he wrested the issue from the Democrats to benefit his own party. During these years, the goal of speeding executions served as the tip of the spear in tough-on-crime politics. Bright played a valuable, yet largely unsung, role trying to fend off harsh changes to the law of habeas corpus in Congress. He warned that closing the courthouse doors would exacerbate racial and economic inequities in the justice system.[39]

As the Supreme Court handed down decisions making it harder to challenge racial inequality, and many citizens showed less interest in the possibility of redemption, Bright and his allies chose to double down on equality. Bright shifted tactics, disturbing the status quo by going aggressively after unethical prosecutors and "hanging judges" believed to be perpetuating unequal justice.

Part II tells the story of Bright's second trip to the nation's highest court. This time, he resolved to save the life of Allen Snyder, a Black man who was sentenced to death by an all-White jury. Prosecutors inflamed jurors by comparing Snyder to O. J. Simpson, reminding them that "the perpetrator in that case . . . got away with it." *Snyder v. Louisiana* raises troubling and persistent issues about how peremptory strikes undermine both democracy and equality.

Part III recounts the case of *Foster v. Chatman*, Bright's third oral argument before the Supreme Court. Once again, the issue was whether an American citizen may be put to death after prosecutors removed every single Black juror from the pool. The ease with which prosecutors manufactured an all-White jury, and the extent to which judges still routinely fail to stop racial discrimination during jury selection, suggest more drastic reforms are necessary.

Finally, Part IV finishes the tale of *McWilliams v. Dunn*. This legal dispute dramatized the plight of people with intellectual disabilities, who face a heightened risk of being misunderstood and judged unworthy to live. The value of effective legal representation and access to a mental health expert were at stake in Bright's most difficult argument in the Supreme Court.

Bright's relentless pursuit of equality and fairness in his four Supreme Court cases exposed how far prosecutors and judges were willing to go to secure a death sentence. His efforts—not just in those specific controversies but also in his speeches and writings outside of courtrooms—laid bare the structural conditions of unequal justice and produced ringing affirmations of the Bill of Rights.

Paraphrasing James Baldwin, Bright once told a class of graduating law students that "the impossible is the least we can demand if we are to make good on a promise broken for centuries. For justice has become impossible for so many." Bright spent most of his time in courtrooms, but he never lost the critical consciousness he acquired during his youth. Instead, he became a cause lawyer so he could help complete the unfinished work of the civil rights movement, in the places that the movement had largely bypassed: southern courthouses, jails, and prisons. Traveling to faraway corners of former slaveholding states, he demanded that judges and politicians honor the Fourteenth Amendment—that monument to equality and fairness constructed by those who won the Civil War.[40]

We still grapple with the unforgiving institutions and practices built during decades of mass incarceration, but Bright's example teaches us another way to live.

PART I

SMOKING GUN

Amadeo v. Zant

"I CAN'T BELIEVE IT," Christopher Coates said to himself. He held up the piece of legal paper in the light for closer inspection. It bore no caption, signature, date, or stamp from the clerk's office. Yet the contents of the document were explosive. Below the heading, "Result," someone had scrawled figures for how many African Americans and women should be placed on master jury lists if one wanted to underrepresent their numbers on juries.

Coates had been in the Putnam County clerk's office doing archival research for an ongoing civil rights lawsuit challenging the county's at-large voting procedures. That's when the document slipped out.[1]

Coates asked the clerk about the origins of the handwritten document he discovered. He was informed that it had come from district attorney Joe Briley. Locals knew Briley, a tobacco-chewing throwback who oversaw the Okmulgee Judicial District, as "Death

Row Joe" for his enthusiastic pursuit of death sentences. Briley had sought the death penalty over thirty times during his career—more than any other prosecutor in the state.

Coates immediately introduced the explosive memo into the record of his lawsuit. Appalled, Judge Wilbur Owens, Jr., ordered county officials to halt further use of the master jury lists until they had been reconstituted. These lists, which were used by county officials to create the jury pools for trials, now appeared to be completely tainted by bias.

Located in a quiet part of Georgia's Piedmont region, Putnam County once contained cotton plantations. Despite its large population of Black citizens, or perhaps because of it, the place had a long history of racial segregation. Black people were barred from voting in the Democratic primary until courts struck it down in the 1940s. Uncowed, the county's leaders responded by abolishing the primary and imposing literacy tests. That strategy to cling to white power worked—not a single Black citizen was registered by the county to vote before 1948. Well into the 1970s, the county maintained separate lists for Black and White voters.[2]

When Briley's memo surfaced, talk in civil rights circles eventually turned to the people whose court cases may have been affected by the county's jury-rigging practice. One person's plight stood out: Tony Amadeo, a White marine, who sat on death row.

Amadeo was eighteen when he committed the crimes that led him to stand before a Putnam County judge, who pronounced sentence upon him: "You shall be submitted to the punishment of death by electrocution. May the Lord have mercy on your soul."

Amadeo had gone AWOL from Camp Lejeune near Memphis and engaged in a drug-induced binge along with three other men. They had driven from Tennessee through Alabama, where they robbed a store clerk; they wound up in a parking lot near Eatonton, Georgia. There, Amadeo tried to rob James Turk, Sr., when he climbed out of his pickup truck. Amadeo shot him dead.

Because Amadeo was too poor to hire his own lawyer, the county appointed one for him. Amadeo was tried on a Monday, he was convicted and sentenced to death by the end of the day Tuesday. The same court handled two other capital cases that same week.

* * *

COATES, WHO HAD DISCOVERED Briley's memo, advised Amadeo's volunteer lawyer to amend his appeal to add the jury composition issue. But the Georgia Supreme Court refused to hear it, ruling that "his challenge comes too late." He ran back to the trial judge to ask for a new trial on the issue, but relief was refused. At that point, Palmer Singleton and Robert McGlasson of SCHR got involved. They filed suit in U.S. district court challenging Amadeo's conviction, petitioning for a writ of habeas corpus. Because the vast majority of criminal cases are resolved in state courts, and because the U.S. Supreme Court rarely takes a direct appeal, a habeas petition is usually the first time a federal judge has an opportunity to review a criminal trial for compliance with the Constitution.[3]

The writ of habeas corpus—known as "The Great Writ"—can be traced all the way back to English common law, predating the Magna Carta. Americans inherited this practice to protect their basic liberties, and judges have since issued writs of habeas corpus ordering the release of everyone from free Black people wrongly detained as runaway slaves to loyal Japanese Americans illegally interned during wartime. By the 1980s, however, habeas corpus had emerged as a new front in the War on Crime, as judges and politicians imposed more restrictions on its availability.

In asking for Amadeo's conviction to be set aside, SCHR lawyers argued that the jury-rigging scheme deprived Amadeo of his right to an impartial and representative jury. The jury was once so cherished that the Framers mentioned it in the Constitution three separate times, more than any other right. John Adams called the right to vote and the right to a jury trial "the heart and lungs" of "liberty and security."[4]

For the habeas suit Amadeo drew Wilbur Owens, Jr., a former federal prosecutor with a reputation for being firm but fair as a judge. Even more important, he was already intimately familiar with Briley's memo. More good news soon came down the pike: Judge Owens ruled that the DA and jury commissioners had manipulated the master jury lists to deliberately underrepresent Black citizens and women. Ignoring the constitutional violation would amount to an "miscarriage of justice," Judge Owens declared. He ordered a new trial for Amadeo. Unwilling to comply, the state appealed.

The Eleventh Circuit overturned Judge Owens and instructed him to conduct a full hearing to determine whether the county's method of selecting jurors "was so devious and hidden as to be nondiscoverable." At the subsequent hearing, Judge Owens heard testimony from Amadeo's original attorneys, who explained why they had no reason to go rummaging around looking for such documents earlier. He then reaffirmed his earlier decision granting Amadeo relief.

Georgia's attorney general appealed to the Eleventh Circuit a second time. Once again, the federal appeals judges backed the state. In a shocking opinion, the judges on the panel said they were bound to "preserve the integrity of state judicial procedures." They found that Amadeo's lawyers "were aware that minorities were probably underrepresented" on juries in the county but had "elected not to pursue the challenge for various tactical reasons." In addition, if counsel had "elected to examine the jury lists, they would have found the memorandum."[5]

Because one of the three judges on the Eleventh Circuit dissented, Amadeo's odds of getting the U.S. Supreme Court's attention improved. A stay of execution from the high court temporarily blocked the state from electrocuting Amadeo, buying time for the justices to consider Amadeo's petition.

Inside the U.S. Supreme Court, Amadeo's appeal had to overcome not only the fact that the justices were granting review in fewer cases, but also that they did not like to get involved in criminal matters unless there was an issue of national importance or a split among the various circuit courts about how to deal with an issue of federal law. In fact, Chief Justice William Rehnquist's law clerk circulated a pool memo recommending that Amadeo's appeal be rejected. Acknowledging "this case is a close one," he observed that it "seems to present for the first time the issue of under what circumstances the discovery of new evidence after trial will enable a petitioner to raise a claim at habeas even though the trial attorney made a 'tactical decision' not to raise the claim initially."

The law clerk's framing of Amadeo's appeal showed he was inclined to accept the state's view of what happened. As a result, he advised that "this issue is not particularly certworthy" because it required getting too much into the facts rather than presenting a clean legal challenge to "the approach" of a circuit court when new evidence is discovered.[6]

One of Justice Harry Blackmun's law clerks, Emily Buss, strongly disagreed with the pool memo's recommendation to duck the case. "Boy, this one's tough," she scrawled on the memo. "The underlying issue, regardless of how infrequently it comes up, appears to be a very important one." She noted that the findings of fact by the appeals court "is inappropriate in itself" and should not prevent the Court from reaching the issue. She went on: "All tactical decisions are made with reference to some perceived sense of the big picture—and the state in this case distorted the big picture by changing expectations about jury panels."

Buss made a note on the pool memo recommending that Blackmun provide the fourth vote to grant review if three other justices showed interest. Further conversations between the clerks and independent determinations by the justices overcame the pool memo's recommendation to deny certiorari. On October 19, 1987, the Supreme Court agreed to hear Amadeo's appeal.[7]

Amadeo's new team decided that Steve Bright would plead his case before the justices. With review granted, Bright believed he could count on the votes of Thurgood Marshall and William Brennan, who had publicly announced their unswerving opposition to the death penalty. But he would still need to garner at least three more votes. Most promising were Blackmun, John Paul Stevens, and Byron White, all of whom voted to reinstate the death penalty in *Gregg v. Georgia* but continued to wrestle with its unequal and haphazard application over the years.[8]

Bright didn't know it at the time, but someone else was in play. It wasn't Blackmun who provided the crucial fourth vote to grant Amadeo's appeal—it was Sandra Day O'Connor who did so. Despite his own law clerk's entreaties, Blackmun had actually voted with the Chief, White, and Scalia to deny review. Only eight justices voted because Powell had retired and the Senate was in the process of considering—and eventually rejecting—Robert Bork's nomination to replace him.

Buss did not give up. She followed up her note with a twenty-one-page memo advising Blackmun to vote to overturn Amadeo's conviction. Buss asked Blackmun to see the big picture: "This case calls a larger, societal interest in the just administration of the criminal laws into question." She said that "society has an interest in ensuring that his conviction and death sentence do not rest on such an offensive, county-wide scheme of racial discrimination."[9]

Buss also directed attention to a friend-of-the-court brief filed by the NAACP Legal Defense Fund, which argued that jury manipulation is "a direct affront to all Black citizens of this country." That brief put Putnam County's effort to undermine democracy in historical context, as part of a pattern "stretching back to 1880, of the refusal of state officials to recognize the rights of Blacks to be free of racial discrimination" in the administration of justice. Buss urged Justice Blackmun to order the state to give Amadeo a new trial "free of the racist taint of the current verdict."[10]

After absorbing Buss's memo, Justice Blackmun jotted some notes on the eve of oral argument. His final thoughts in shorthand stood out: "Defendant may well be guilty. But all of society is hurt by this kind of thing. Just go back and make them do it right."[11]

Unless he did something foolish at argument, Bright would have O'Connor and Blackmun listening intently. But nothing was assured.

TOE TO TOE WITH JUSTICE SCALIA

Amadeo's case landed in Washington, D.C., at a time when the conservatives on the U.S. Supreme Court were consolidating their influence, and the liberals hunted for creative ways of preserving what remained of Warren Court legacies on matters of equality and rights for people charged with crimes. Reagan's appointees often joined Nixon's appointees to curtail defendants' rights, especially those believed to be technicalities that impeded law enforcement objectives. Promoting states' rights and facilitating the war on drugs remained the priorities of the political class.

This was Bright's first appearance before the U.S. Supreme Court—a nerve-wracking experience for even the most experienced lawyer. The justices might let an advocate get a few sentences out before peppering him with questions from all sides.

During oral argument, Bright zeroed in right away on the prosecutor's misconduct. "At the start of the penalty phase of Mr. Amadeo's trial, the district attorney said that you probably couldn't find a fairer jury anywhere in the State of Georgia than you could find in Putnam County." But this was a lie, Bright argued: "Of course, he was the only one who knew at the time he made that statement that he had earlier that same year directed the jury commissioners in Putnam County to underrepresent black people and women in the master jury lists."[12]

The jury-rigging scheme required someone who knew the law well enough to pull it off. As Bright explained, someone tried to make "it appear that racial discrimination had been eliminated" in the local jury pools "while actually perpetuating racial discrimination and discrimination on the basis of gender."

Bright was referring to the finding of Judge Owens that county officials had sought to keep the number of African Americans and women on Putnam County juries low, but not so low as to raise suspicions. In a 1965 case called *Swain v. Alabama* the U.S. Supreme Court held that no one had a right to be tried by a diverse jury, but only a right to have a jury whose demographics had not been artificially suppressed on account of race. A jury composition challenge could go forward only if a defendant could show systemic discrimination. Worse, in that case the Court let stand juries that were underrepresented by 10 to 15 percent, saying that without more, such a disparity didn't show intentional discrimination. *Swain* was a tragic decision that rejected the claim of a Black man sentenced to death even though no Black person had served on a jury in that county since 1950. The Court's overriding concern was to "insulate from inquiry" a prosecutor's prerogative.[13]

In his ruling in Amadeo's case, Judge Owens found that Briley had acted purposefully by conspiring with jury commissioners to evade the Constitution's guarantee of equality. But they had tried to keep the numbers close to those in *Swain* so their misconduct remained difficult to prove.

Standing before them, Bright wanted the justices to appreciate that it was only sheer luck that had kept his client alive. "Ten months after Mr. Amadeo's trial this scheme came to light when another lawyer in another case inadvertently came across it."

Justice Sandra Day O'Connor, known for her law-and-order leaning, wanted to know whether the failure by Amadeo's lawyers to flag the issue earlier could be explained by trial strategy. If staying mum was a tactical choice, then Amadeo should be barred from raising the jury issue now.

"Did he not deliberately bypass the constitutional challenge to the composition of the master jury list?" she asked. Wasn't it the case that "defense counsel considered challenging the jury list, thought they could win such a challenge but chose not to raise it in order to preserve what they thought was a favorable jury?"

Although O'Connor's support for capital punishment dated back to her time as an Arizona legislator, she was open to fairness arguments. She had authored the 1984 *Strickland v. Washington* decision, which endorsed the idea that effective representation "is critical to the ability of the adversarial system to produce just results"—especially in cases where execution was on the table. But she also counted herself as a defender of states' rights and a stickler for rules.[14]

Bright returned to Judge Owens's findings. The Eleventh Circuit had disagreed with him on appeal, but the rules of civil procedure require that an appeals court defer to the factual findings of a trial judge who has had a chance to evaluate the witnesses unless they were clearly erroneous. Bright emphasized the record wherever he could to illustrate that the appeals court had violated the rules of federal procedure by substituting its own understanding of the facts. Because no one could have known about Briley's secret plan to manipulate the jury pool until discovery of the "smoking gun" evidence, the failure to object earlier should not be held against Amadeo. His court-appointed lawyers would have brought the claim if they had even an inkling of the scheme.

Justice Antonin Scalia then weighed in: "You had explicit testimony by the lawyer saying that we like this jury, we didn't think we could get a better jury. We like it because it had, what, . . . eight or nine women, which they thought was highly desirable." Scalia, appointed by President Reagan in 1986, was already a darling of the conservative legal movement. But, according to Bright, what actually happened was that Amadeo's lawyers obtained the names of prospective jurors drawn from the master list, noticed a few names who were likely women and black citizens, and so didn't see a basis for objecting to the jury's composition. "Of course, that's exactly what the district attorney's scheme was designed to accomplish."

Years after Amadeo's trial, one of his original lawyers recalled that they had been generally pleased with the jury. But Bright pointed out that "of course, they didn't know they had this claim." And of course, another lawyer testified, "it would have been a great issue, I would have raised it if I'd known about it."

Justice Blackmun sounded convinced. "If this is true, I think it utterly destroys this talk" about whether the issue was waived. "I think there is a complete answer to it in the record."

Bright could tell that he was making some headway. He added that "once the prosecutor's actions here were discovered, it was immediately presented to the state courts." The lawyers "basically did what they could possibly do." It was not realistic, nor would it be fair, to have expected them to do any more at the time.

Anthony Kennedy, a California Republican, had joined the

Court after Bork's failed nomination, and just in time for oral argument in Amadeo's appeal. Justice Kennedy asked Bright whether Amadeo's original lawyers were "not credible." If so, that might justify the Eleventh Circuit's choice to disregard some of their testimony. Bright rejected that reading of the record, saying that Judge Owens had every right to find the witnesses credible. After all, the state deliberately hid evidence of its own wrongdoing. Bright then made a plea for the equities lining up in Amadeo's favor rather than against him. "Really, the fundamental question, it seems, is who put this case in the posture that it is today?" he asked. "And the answer to that has to be the district attorney in this case."

It would be deeply unfair to bar Amadeo from raising this constitutional issue, without considering the government's role in creating the dilemma in the first place. Briley was the one who had cheated. "He could have stood up at arraignment and said, 'I just want to put on the record I have instructed the jury commission to underrepresent black people and women in the master list,'" Bright told the justices wryly. "And once everyone recovered from the shock," the county could have "stop[ped] trying people for criminal cases until you revise your jury list there."

At that point, Justice Scalia pushed the questioning in another direction. "Mr. Bright, this was a white defendant, right?" Justice Scalia wanted to know whether the jury Amadeo wound up with "was indeed quite satisfactory to this white defendant."

"Well, it's not implausible," Bright replied, "but I think what we know now which we didn't know at the time is that this basically was a jury selected through a clearly unconstitutional and illegal scheme."

Scalia wouldn't let the point go. "There was some evidence, was there not, of prior offenses that this individual had committed against blacks which might indeed cause him to prefer a jury with fewer blacks rather than more?"

Bright had to concede that this was on the minds of Amadeo's lawyers. Yet he noted that they couldn't have truly believed this was the best jury Amadeo could get, because they actually filed a motion seeking a venue change, arguing that Amadeo couldn't get a fair trial in the county. They also asked for a delay to try to "put together some sort of statistical challenge."

Intrigued, Justice John Paul Stevens wondered how employees of the clerk's office knew which jurors were black and which were white? "They maintained the lists separately by race," Bright explained. "The numbers here were very explicit." The DA told the clerk "to put 101 black people on the grand jury," and "an exact number of how many blacks were to go on the traverse jury, and even figured out the percentage to make sure" that they could avoid a legal challenge.

The questions eventually turned to the actual discovery of Briley's memo. Justice Scalia flashed irritation. "I can think of things that are not concealed but may not be readily discoverable. Doesn't 'concealed' require some affirmative action on somebody's part?" This colloquy piqued Justice Kennedy's interest. "Well, there's no finding that the memorandum was hidden. In fact, just the opposite isn't it?" The document was "delivered promptly when anybody requested it."

But Amadeo's lawyers "had no earthly reason to go over there," Bright responded. They should not have been expected to hunt "for a needle in a haystack over at the clerk's office."

At last, Bright sat down. Virtually all the justices' questions had been about obscure procedural rules such as whether a legal issue had been waived. Throughout, Bright had tried to keep Briley's wrongdoing front and center so the justices could not avert their eyes from injustice. He felt in his bones that executing a man whose jury had been rigged was legally and morally wrong. If enough justices also saw the merits of the issue the same way, surely they would find a way to deal with the legal hurdles that stood between their sense of outrage and the right outcome.

Susan Boleyn stood up. As assistant attorney general, she had a wealth of experience on death penalty cases. Her strategy entailed arguing that Amadeo's trial lawyers could have figured out there was a jury underrepresentation problem and were obliged to raise it earlier. If they had gone to the clerk's office years ago, they might have discovered Briley's memo. Her fallback position was this: If they didn't know about the memo's existence, "it has no relevance in this case because it was not a basis for the trial attorneys' deliberate decision." Amadeo's new lawyers led by Bright "were reaching for straws," Boleyn argued.

It didn't take long for Justice Stevens to lose patience. "Well, do you think this is a straw issue? Isn't this a rather serious issue?"

"I think the allegations and the nature of the memo are very serious," Boleyn started to answer, before Stevens interrupted again.

"*This actually happened*," Justice Stevens snapped. "Often, we get complaints alleging things and we assume them for purposes of trial. This is a case in which the evidence discloses an intentional program of rigging the jury by the prosecutor's office. And they even used jury lists that were segregated by race."

Justice Stevens tried again: "But do you seriously think that the district attorney's office wanted that document to be found?" Boleyn had to concede that she did not.

Yet Boleyn doubted there was ever a plan to create demographic limits along the lines outlined in the memo. "All that is inference and speculation because there is no direct evidence in the record on that."

"No, but the percentages do fit, don't they?" asked Justice Stevens. "And the District Judge was persuaded by that." Boleyn tried another tack: playing down the degree of underrepresentation. Whatever the prosecutor's office and the jury commissioners were doing, their efforts resulted in "minimal disparities . . . minimal even if you are trying to discriminate."

"Just a little bit pregnant," Justice Stevens shot back. Laughter broke out in the chamber.

Things kept going downhill for the state, as Boleyn suggested that a true racist would act in more obvious ways. "Is that all it is, speculation?" Justice Byron White inquired about who, in fact, sent the memo to the jury commissioners. "He sent it, though, didn't he?" Boleyn stuck to her guns in trying to relitigate earlier questions. "The prosecutor never testified. We don't know if he sent it. All the clerk said is, it came from his office."

"Well, it just didn't create itself," Justice White replied. "So it came from the prosecutor's office."

"That's right, your honor."

"There has never been an action against the prosecutor?" Justice White asked. This amounted to the best sign yet that White was bothered by the jury-rigging effort and might be edging toward Amadeo's position. "No, your honor," Boleyn answered. Even Justice Scalia sounded peeved by this entire exchange. "I thought this had been determined in an earlier case that it was indeed malicious."

As the state's time wound down, Bright felt he had done what he could. He had hammered the theme that harsh application of a procedural rule would leave discrimination unremedied, and hoped the justices would see things the same way.

THURGOOD MARSHALL WRITES

Throughout the argument, Thurgood Marshall had remained curiously quiet. But given his stature on matters of racial equality, his colleagues paid close attention to how he came down in cases involving such claims. He certainly had the most personal experience with extreme forms of southern justice. When he served as founding Director-Counsel of the NAACP Legal Defense Fund, he handled a series of death penalty cases. Marshall learned firsthand about local efforts to rig jury trials. In 1951, he won retrials for two Black men under death sentence for the rape of a White teenage girl. In a rush to convict, prosecutors had categorically excluded Black people from the jury and the judge had allowed the trial to proceed under mob-like conditions.[15]

On May 28, 1988, the Supreme Court issued its decision in Amadeo's case. It was a wipeout, as the justices voted 9–0 for Amadeo. Behind the scenes, the justices had voted 8–1 to reverse right after oral argument, with only Rehnquist wanting to leave Amadeo's death sentence in place. As the most senior justice in the majority, Justice Brennan had assigned the opinion to Marshall to write. Each of the other justices then read a draft of Marshall's draft and offered suggestions. Once they joined it, one after another, the Chief relented to make it unanimous.[16]

Bright's approach had paid off. Justice Marshall's opinion did not go out of its way to excoriate Briley. However, the Court's disapproval of his misconduct was unmistakable. Accepting Bright's framing, Justice Marshall leaned heavily on Judge Owens's original findings, starting with the fact that Amadeo had been "indicted, tried, and sentenced by unconstitutionally composed juries."

He first concluded that ample evidence supported Judge Owens's finding that the scheme to underrepresent women and African Americans had been concealed. The "physical characteristics" of Briley's memo "strongly belie the notion that the document was intended for public consumption." Additionally, that the memo was not the first page of a set of documents but left "in a stack of materials" strongly suggested it was not meant to be readily discovered.

Justice Marshall next took up the Eleventh Circuit's conclusion that Amadeo's lawyers had deliberately given up the jury issue. While Judge Owens could have been more precise about why Amadeo's lawyers did not object to the composition of his jury earlier, there were several possible reasons to excuse that lapse: his original attorneys could have believed they were giving up only a statistical challenge to the jury's composition rather than a claim based on "direct evidence of intentional discrimination," or Judge Owen could have rejected some of the attorney's post-trial explanations for their conduct as "not credible." After all, Justice Marshall said, Amadeo's lawyers had just lost a murder trial, and a different lawyer, Coates, had uncovered evidence of a serious constitutional violation. They had "significant incentive to insist that they had considered every possible angle."

In disagreeing with Judge Owens, who conducted the hearing on Amadeo's habeas petition, the Eleventh Circuit had "substituted its own factual findings for those of the District Court," a violation of the rules governing how appeals are handled. Amadeo won a new trial—for a third and final time.

The Supreme Court's decision provided a powerful rebuke of judges who are too quick to block scrutiny of official misconduct. According to the ruling, an individual need only show that a factual or legal basis for a claim "was not reasonably available" at the time or that "some interference by officials made compliance impracticable." Amadeo's situation, Justice Marshall said pointedly, "fits squarely, indeed almost verbatim, within our holdings." Judge Owens was prepared to enforce the Constitution and grant Amadeo a new trial, and the circuit judges should not have stopped him from doing so.

Even so, the unanimous opinion obscured some likely tradeoffs on criminal justice policy. For liberals, some of whom had strong reservations about the constitutionality of the death penalty, justice was done in Amadeo's case by halting his execution and denying to the state the fruits of its racist practice. They also cheered the fair application of the rules that regulated access to federal courts when state courts fail to cure the violation of rights.

For conservatives, the calculus must have been more complicated: ruling for Amadeo denied cover to intentionally racist conduct, and Putnam County had been caught red-handed. Conservatives subscribed to a narrower concept of equality than liberals, but they drew the line at overt mistreatment. Granting Amadeo a retrial also vindicated the integrity of legal institutions and the rule of law. Overturning Amadeo's conviction was a one-off for an extraordinary situation, compatible with their long game to remake legal rules so they facilitate tough-on-crime policies.

ANOTHER SKIRMISH IN THE GEORGIA COURTS

AMADEO'S STORY DID NOT end with a victory at the U.S. Supreme Court. As expected, Putnam County promptly reindicted him. Briley stayed on as prosecutor to get another crack at Amadeo. But in a staggering development, the trial judge overseeing the retrial kicked Bright and the rest of Amadeo's team off the case. He then appointed two inexperienced attorneys as their replacements, claiming that Georgia law allowed him to insist upon local lawyers.

Bright now had to take on the combined forces of the local and state governments just to get back on Amadeo's case. Ruth Friedman, fresh out of law school, dashed to the library and began scouring the law books in search of useful precedent. After hours of work, she located the perfect decision. The problem was that the case came out of California, so they could urge its logic on Georgia judges, but not claim that they were bound by it. Because America's constitutional order is based on federalism, each state gets to decide its own laws, and that includes the rules in court.[17]

The California controversy had involved several members of the Symbionese Liberation Army, who had kidnapped Patty Hearst. The trial judge refused to appoint the defendants' preferred lawyers and instead picked "total strangers." But the California Supreme Court reversed, concluding that the trial judge had abused his discretion given the "trust and confidence developed over a substantial period of time" between the defendants and their previous attorneys. Based on this reasoning, Amadeo's lawyers would have a similarly strong argument to stay on his case given the relationships they had forged and their superior knowledge of the intimate details of his case. Armed with this decision, Friedman penned a brief asking the Georgia Supreme Court to reinstate the SCHR team. Everyone crossed their fingers.[18]

On October 5, 1989, the court gave its answer. Justice Willis B. Hunt, Jr., wrote a resounding decision vindicating Amadeo's right to counsel. While recognizing that a defendant does not have an "absolute" right to an attorney of his own choosing, he acknowledged that "it has become apparent that special skills are necessary to assure adequate representation of defendants in death penalty cases." Justice Hunt explained that a trial judge can consider the availability of local lawyers, but "must also consider the prior experience of the available lawyers when choosing counsel in a death penalty case."

Justice Hunt also invoked *Harris v. People*, the case Friedman had cited to the court, embracing its framework for Amadeo's situation and whenever the issue might arise in the future. As for Amadeo, the "relationship of trust and confidence with prior counsel," as well as the "legal and factual complexities of the case," which Bright's staff had already mastered, weighed heavily against the judge's rash decision. He was ordered to appoint them to Amadeo's case for the retrial. In the press, Bright applauded the Georgia Supreme Court's decision to ensure that the "scandalous" type of "hometown justice" Amadeo received during his first trial "will not happen again."[19]

This seemed like proof that Georgia's Supreme Court had gotten the message: time to give Amadeo a clean trial. But not everyone was happy. District Attorney Doug Pullen groused, "They're as bad as the old Warren Court, dreaming up policy and rights where there is none in the law."[20]

Back on Amadeo's case, Bright filed a stack of motions, including one that tried to turn the tables on the state. Bright now demanded that Joe Briley be barred from retrying the case because of his documented disdain for the principle of equality. He cited not just Judge Owens's finding that Briley had participated in a scheme to underrepresent minorities and women on juries, but also the reversal of Amadeo's death sentence for this reason by a unanimous U.S. Supreme Court.

Legal ethics experts and members of the bar filed a brief to support the move to disqualify Briley. They argued that the district attorney's "misconduct is shocking to the conscience" and violated his obligation to ensure that "all citizens" in the community "stand on equal footing before the law." Disqualification was "required to protect the integrity of the adversary system, to assure public confidence in the administration of justice, to assure that the past misconduct does not interfere" with Amadeo's retrial.[21]

On the day of the hearing on Bright's motion to disqualify Briley, witnesses were lined up and ready to go. Briley observed, "This is worse than being electrocuted."

"Well, why don't we try it out and see," Bright fired back, without missing a beat.[22]

Just before the hearing was to start, Briley offered a surprise deal. He would take the death penalty off the table if Amadeo pleaded guilty to murder and promised not to seek parole for at least twenty-five years. Briley also conditioned the deal on the defense lawyers forgoing any legal fees. Bright believed this to be a "legally dubious" request but took the deal anyway with "a young man's life at stake." His objective was simply to extract a promise that the state would not kill his client.

Why would Briley risk his reputation by demanding that Amadeo's lawyers work for free? Bright had an inkling: "It was a way for the prosecutor to go back to the citizens who elected him and say he saved them tax dollars." Although the prosecutor was ready to wave the white flag, the provision was a "face-saving device."[23]

As the Georgia Bar later admonished, however, it is patently unethical for a prosecutor to make a lawyer's fees a condition of a plea bargain because it "creates a conflict of interest for the defense attorney, who is torn between the need for compensation . . . and the duty to protect the freedom, sometimes even the life, of the client." For those concerned about equal justice, "this impossible position" gives already underpaid lawyers even less incentive to do a good job for their clients. A prosecutor who asks for the waiver of fees violates his "duty as a 'minister of justice' to seek justice, and not merely convict."[24]

This public rejection of Briley's methods was frosting on the cake. For Amadeo, getting off death row represented a miracle. It was also a testament to Bright's tenacity. "As long as I had a breath of life before they pulled that switch, he was still giving it 110 percent. To me, that man walks on water."[25]

Far away from the swirling politics of death playing out in the rest of the country, Amadeo made the most of his new lease on life. His years in prison somehow didn't break him, even though he had been locked up since 1977.

But Amadeo was a model inmate even before Bright helped liberate him from a death sentence, earning a Bachelor of Science from Mercer University summa cum laude. He also learned cabinet- and furniture making from a vocational school. Amadeo took responsibility for his crimes and showed remorse for the wreckage he caused. In 2011, the State of Georgia paroled him. After spending thirty-eight years in prison, including thirteen on death row, Amadeo was released.

Some years later, Amadeo penned a letter to Bright. He had moved to Texas, where he worked on a ranch. He served as operations manager for the entire eight-hundred acres of land, overseeing the needs of 274 head of cattle, many cows, and white-tail deer. "Life does take some unusual twists and turns," Amadeo mused. "If you would have told me ten years ago what I'd be doing today I would have laughed and said you were out of your mind." "Every day I count my blessings," he wrote. "God bless, and thanks for my life."

CLOSING THE COURTHOUSE DOORS

THE WRIT OF HABEAS had been instrumental in keeping Amadeo alive and securing a remedy for a blatant violation of his constitutional rights. Yet he would not have gotten a shot at redemption if certain politicians and judges had their way. Restricting access to the federal courts had become a vital component of the War on Crime. Early on, conservatives objected to having to give *Miranda* rights before interrogating someone or making an arrest. Then, in the 1980s, speeding the execution of people on death row emerged as the rallying cry. To do so, conservative reformers called for not only the curtailment of substantive rights, but also the enactment of structural changes that made it harder to assert rights in federal court.[26]

Centrist leaders of the Democratic Party, eager to defuse the GOP's accusation that Democrats were soft on crime, also warmed to the idea of "habeas reform." Many became convinced that defense lawyers were doing nothing more than gumming up the legal system with frivolous claims. For example, President Reagan's attorney general William French Smith publicly made racking up executions a primary goal for reforming access to the courts. "Thirty-six states currently authorize capital punishment, and there are over one thousand prisoners under sentence of death," he wrote in a 1992 Department of Justice report. "Remarkably, however, only five executions have been carried out since 1967." Smith expressed contempt for "public interest organizations" like that run by Bright, which he said had "fully exploited the system's potential for obstruction." According to Reagan's Justice Department, "there is no justification . . . for the availability of federal habeas corpus as a routine means of review of state criminal convictions."

Smith led a task force, which proposed that Congress enact a law to funnel all relevant fact-finding to state judges, prohibit federal judges from holding hearings on facts "fully expounded and found in the state court proceeding," and impose a three-year limit for habeas petitions. These proposals, as Professor Larry Yackle explains, valorized "the ascertainment of guilt in criminal cases and placed comparatively less emphasis on the observance of procedural safeguards."[27]

Once the goal became limiting access to justice, the major issue that arose was the right to counsel. This issue split death penalty supporters. Those who believed in equal justice knew that restricting habeas corpus raised the stakes of the quality of representation a person received during trial. If errors took place, and a person was given subpar legal assistance, restricting the writ of habeas corpus might leave manifest injustice during a trial unremedied. But reformers gripped by the desire to speed executions felt differently: access to lawyers must also be restricted to protect the legal system from abusive litigation.

In 1986, the Department of Justice opposed Senator Howard Metzenbaum's proposal to furnish attorneys for indigent death-row prisoners seeking federal review. The Supreme Court had earlier held that a person had a constitutional right to a lawyer only for his initial appeal and not for any subsequent challenges, such as when someone seeks a writ of habeas corpus. Lawmakers could do more to protect equal justice if they wanted. Yet subsidizing attorneys for already convicted felons would "frustrate the overwhelming public will supporting capital punishment," wrote John R. Bolton. In the administration's view, giving an individual more than a single chance to get a federal court's attention was a "pervasive abuse of process." This became the overarching reform idea: one bite at the apple.[28]

Once upon a time, the Supreme Court treated the writ of habeas corpus as so sacrosanct that it admonished President Abraham Lincoln for unilaterally denying Confederate soldiers the right to challenge their detentions. In a case called *Ex Parte Merryman*, the justices vindicated "the great importance which the framers of the Constitution attached to the privilege of the writ of habeas corpus to protect the liberty of the citizen." Now, a very different set of justices enabled War on Crime policies by actively curtailing access to justice. Rehnquist had been a fierce supporter of habeas reform since his days as a lawyer in the Reagan administration. As Chief Justice he appointed Justice Lewis Powell to chair a committee on habeas corpus, which included only judges from Florida, Texas, and other Deep South states. These jurisdictions, the most enthusiastic practitioners of the death penalty, also all happened to be former slaveholding states.[29]

In 1989, Powell's committee produced a set of recommendations, which Senator Strom Thurmond introduced as legislation. In support of the bill, Thurmond denounced "frivolous" and "delaying tactic[s]" by defense attorneys. He cited the fact that federal district courts had received 9,880 habeas petitions in a single year, though he didn't mention that the prison population in America had also jumped exponentially during the War on Crime. What might have been seen as signs of desperation and legitimate efforts to test the constitutionality of intricate new crime laws were instead treated as extra work for judges and prosecutors.

Aides on Capitol Hill had a nickname for the project: "Fry Them Faster." A macabre joke circulated among staffers: certain elderly justices had gotten fed up with being awakened in the middle of the night by prisoners trying to halt their execution. In February 1990, Bright joined a coalition trying to head off proposed legislation. He agreed to appear before the U.S. Senate's Judiciary Committee chaired by Joe Biden. Kicking off the hearing, Senator Biden said, "There is perhaps no legal action in our system of law more venerated than habeas corpus. . . . It is the only writ expressly mentioned in our Constitution."[30]

Even so, Biden, like many Democrats, was willing to restrict state prisoners "to a single round of Federal habeas corpus legislation" so long as it was "truly complete and comprehensive." He noted that his own past votes against the death penalty were not out of religious objections but because of the "undue risk of permitting execution of innocent persons." Biden offered his own bill built on principles of fairness, which accepted restrictions but also codified a right to a lawyer for a habeas proceeding, even though that had never been required by the Supreme Court. Although extending the right to counsel was a nonstarter for most Republicans, Democrats controlled both houses of Congress at the time.[31]

Justice Powell testified first. He explained that his committee wished to facilitate the enforcement of federal drug laws, which imposed the death penalty for certain drug-related offenses. His committee's report repeatedly emphasized capital punishment. "Studies of public opinion establish that an overwhelming majority of our citizens favors the death penalty," the very first line of the report read. "The relatively small number of executions, as well as the delay in cases where an execution has occurred," the judges diagnosed ominously, "makes clear that the present system of collateral review operates to frustrate the law of 37 States." Similarly, Senator Charles Grassley stated that limiting federal review of state convictions "is pivotal to law enforcement at every level and may well determine the ultimate outcome of the fight against drugs and crime."

When it came time for Bright to testify, he chose to highlight the problem of inadequate representation. "I can think of cases in both Georgia and Mississippi where the lawyer's first trial verdict was a capital case." In the Mississippi case, "half the witnesses were examined by a third-year law student" and his poor client got the death penalty. Often, these are "downright incompetent lawyers," he explained. "I think the last place where a litigant should be punished for the conduct of their counsel is in the area of capital punishment."

Bright objected to a time limit on habeas petitions. His concern was that "some person is going to be denied any review in the federal process because of negligence or incompetence on the part of a lawyer." If such an ironclad provision had been in effect for Amadeo, he would have been killed long before the state's plan to underrepresent Black people and women could be uncovered. Bright wanted the Senators to see the connection between the assortment of restrictions on the table and the quality of justice. Thurmond's bill represented a "draconian remedy," he said, "a meat-ax approach" to problems. If the restrictions were enacted, they would push the ideal of equal justice further out of reach.[32]

"There are 20,000 homicides in this country every year," Bright reminded them. "We pick out about 270 people to get the death penalty." The question was whether there is "evenhanded justice."

Bright stressed the random nature of the process by which someone was deemed worthy to be killed—"You could shuffle the facts and the background of the offenders and you couldn't pick out who got death and who didn't"—which he had once likened to "death by lottery."

For his comments, he drew from an article he had written for the *West Virginia Law Review.* In that piece, Bright quoted an unnamed law clerk for the U.S. Supreme Court who, after a year of reviewing pleas from people under death sentence, concluded that "the death penalty frequently results from nothing more than poverty and poor lawyering." Bright denounced *Wainwright v. Sykes*, a decision by Justice Rehnquist that adopted the "cause and prejudice" rule, which prohibited state prisoners from making federal constitutional claims that had not been raised earlier. This was the exact rule that prevented Amadeo's rights from being considered until the Supreme Court stepped in at the last possible moment. Bright did not believe these rules should apply when a life was at stake: federal judges should never ignore legal errors "that were the result of ignorance, neglect, or incompetence by defense counsel."

Sykes undermined *Fay v. Noia*, in which Justice Brennan had declared that an "unimpaired" right to habeas review affirmed the principle that "in a civilized society, government must always be accountable to the judiciary for a man's imprisonment." Yet conservatives opposed that broad vision of liberty, and Justice Rehnquist took aim at "the sweeping language" in Brennan's decision. Besides asserting federalism and judicial efficiency, he raised the specter that defense attorneys "may take their chances on a verdict of not guilty in a state trial court with the intent to raise their constitutional claims in a federal habeas court if their initial gamble does not pay off." This was pure speculation—it boggles the mind to think that any decent lawyer would throw a trial on the mere possibility of winning in front of a federal judge somewhere down the road.

Justice Rehnquist's procedural bar was just one of several judge-created restrictions that Powell's committee wanted to codify into federal law. But in Bright's view, such a rule locked in egregious mistakes by incompetent lawyers, malicious conduct by prosecutors, and bad decisions by inattentive trial judges. He decried the fact that executions had been carried out after courts refused to examine valid constitutional issues.[33]

An attorney for the accused would have to keep abreast of legal developments around the country and assert any issues that might be percolating just in case the law later developed in a favorable direction. Failure to do so would be held against the attorney's client. Bright found such an expectation ludicrous. "Unfortunately, the poor person accused of a capital crime is seldom, if ever, defended by a constitutional scholar possessing this extraordinary depth and range of knowledge." Instead, most poor people accused of serious crimes received far less diligent representation. Bright told senators on the Judiciary Committee about the case of a "fellow named Richardson" executed by Alabama last year. His lawyer didn't file a brief in the appellate court. "So he went through these stages" in the state courts but "he really had no review." And in another Alabama case, "the clerk of the court sent the brief back because it did not cite one single case." The clerk begged the indigent man's lawyer, "Please cite one or two cases in the brief."

A court-appointed lawyer in Florida didn't know there were two stages in a capital trial and had to have the judge explain it to him. And in Georgia, a lawyer who had tried several capital cases was asked to name all the criminal law cases he knew. He could name only two cases, *Miranda* and *Dred Scott*, and one of those wasn't even a criminal case. Finally, Bright alluded to the racism to which he bore witness on a regular basis. He told senators about one of his own clients, George Dungee, whose original lawyer referred to him using the N-word during closing argument.

You could hear a pin drop as Bright spoke. The entire chamber was riveted. Most hadn't the faintest clue how most criminal trials were conducted, much less what might pass for justice in distant parts of the country.

Why would the capital defense bar be in such a troubled state? Bright explained that asymmetries in funding had a lot to do with it. But it was also true that death penalty enthusiasts were willing to cut corners and tolerate unequal justice. In several communities, the people in charge wanted defense lawyers to be bad. "It increases the chance of the death penalty being imposed because a bad lawyer is not going to put up much of a fight." In the end, "cases in which there is the worst lawyering" get the least careful review by higher courts.

Bright pointed to Amadeo's ordeal to counter the argument that stricter procedural rules would in fact lead to more efficient disposition of a case. "We spent 3 years on just the procedural question of whether or not the litigant could get around *Wainwright v. Sykes*" but "we could have reversed that case, gone back and had a retrial by now." He summed up: "The system we have should encourage the States to provide good lawyers, and to provide constitutional trials."

Ed Carnes, chief of Alabama's capital litigation division, testified in favor of habeas restrictions. He attacked the ABA's recommendations about the appointment and compensation of counsel for capital cases incorporated in Biden's bill. He warned that establishing standards would "result in a worse backlog." Carnes raised the specter of "constant litigation over whether the attorney was effective and did a constitutionally permissible job" even when someone "does such a good job that even Mr. Bright, for the first time in his professional career, doesn't raise an ineffective of assistance of counsel claim."[34]

Despite strong calls for reform, at the time Bright's testimony helped blunt the momentum for change. According to Victoria Nourse, Special Counsel to the Judiciary Committee, Bright's tales of lawyerly incompetence "stunned the Republicans on the committee." Decades later, his account of the lawyer who was high on cocaine at the time of the trial and another about the attorney jailed the night before trial and let out for purposes of representing his client remained burned into her memory.[35]

Justice Powell pushed hard for reform, calling senators to support Senator Thurmond's bill. Even so, Bright's outspoken defense of the downtrodden proved critical to counter the lobbying by federal judges. His testimony made it easier for Nourse to negotiate with GOP counterparts to keep the right-to-counsel provision in the bill.[36]

The Senate enacted a watered-down version of habeas reform several months later, the House passed a different version, and the matter was dropped in the conference report. When Congress revisited habeas reform in 1994, Joe Biden played a central role in minimizing the damage, even as that law expanded the number of death-eligible federal crimes. He wanted three things during negotiations over the Crime Bill: The Violence Against Women Act, funding for 100,000 police officers, and habeas reform to be stricken. He got what he wanted. Disaster had been narrowly averted again.

In the meantime, as legislation went nowhere, Chief Justice Rehnquist returned to creating more restrictions on access to courts by exercising the Court's own authority. Following the collapse of habeas reform in the early '90s, the Supreme Court prohibited successive habeas petitions by expanding the definition of "abuse of the writ." The justices also invoked federalism to justify ignoring constitutional claims in a habeas petition if a state court's judgment also rested on an independent and adequate state law rationale.[37]

Everything changed when Timothy McVeigh bombed a federal courthouse in Oklahoma City on April 19, 1995. Bill Clinton, the first Democrat elected president since 1976, called for habeas reform, citing the act of domestic terror. Justice should be "certain, swift, and severe," Clinton said on *60 Minutes*. He urged Congress "this year to reform the habeas corpus proceedings."[38]

Clinton had positioned himself as a different kind of candidate than the last Democratic candidate, Michael Dukakis, whose support cratered after his weak answer about how he would feel about the death penalty if his wife were raped and murdered. During the 1996 campaign, Governor Clinton repeatedly set execution dates for inmates on Arkansas's death row even when they had not exhausted all legal remedies. He returned to his home state to turn down clemency for Ricky Ray Rector, who was missing a large section of his brain.

After President Clinton's remarks on television about McVeigh, his own aides realized that "the habeas train is coming down the track and is unstoppable." At first, they tried to "salvage" the counsel competency standards. But Democrats had little leverage given Clinton's priorities and the political reality on the Hill. For the first time in forty years, Republicans seized control of both houses of Congress during the 1994 midterm elections. Among the provisions in Newt Gingrich's much-touted Contract with America were "effective death penalty provisions" and funding to build more prisons.[39]

Congress now teed up a harsher set of habeas restrictions than what had been considered before. Where Reagan's proposal once envisioned a three-year statute of limitations, the Anti-Terrorism and Effective Death Penalty Act (AEDPA) now gave prisoners one year to seek a writ. Among the other byzantine conditions: a person now hoping to be heard in federal court had to demonstrate that his conviction "was contrary to, or involved an unreasonable application of, clearly established Federal law." Had this law been in force when Amadeo desperately sought federal review of his constitutional claim, Judge Owens might have been prevented from ordering a new trial, forced to accept the state court's finding that the jury issue was raised too late or conclude that Putnam County's actions did not violate "clearly established" law.[40]

"There will be many injustices which will not be corrected" because of this legislation, Bright warned in the press. No matter—President Clinton signed what landed on his desk. Yet there was a disjunction between what politicians said and what they did. They had talked a lot about people who committed heinous offenses, but the new federal law curtailed the rights of anyone who might need the Great Writ, and did so without doing anything to improve the quality of counsel for the poor.[41]

DOUBLING DOWN ON RACIAL EQUALITY

As Congress was restricting access to federal courts, another project was well underway. The U.S. Supreme Court had been employing its authority to interpret the Constitution to narrow the concept of equality, making it especially difficult to challenge the administration of criminal laws. In a series of cases starting in the late 1970s and stretching through the '80s, the justices began to limit the reach of the principle of equality to situations where specific wrongdoers could be identified.[42]

The most notorious ruling may have been *McCleskey v. Kemp*, a 1987 decision that made it virtually impossible to bring structural racism claims against the justice system when a policy makes no mention of race. For months, a team of experts led by the NAACP Legal Defense Fund had gathered and analyzed statistics on death penalty proceedings throughout Georgia. University of Iowa law professor David Baldus had run sophisticated regression analyses on over 2,000 murders since the reinstatement of capital punishment. Among his discoveries: Georgia prosecutors sought the death penalty more often in crimes involving Black defendants and White victims than in crimes involving White defendants and White victims or even Black-on-Black crimes.[43]

Yet by endorsing a 5–4 vote, a bitterly divided Court in *McCleskey* rejected the equality claim. Justice Powell's decision held that the mere risk of racial bias in the administration of the death penalty was not enough. A defendant had to show exactly who was responsible for discrimination in a complex system.

Why did the Supreme Court work so hard to insulate the criminal justice system? The five justices in *McCleskey* worried that the defendant's equality argument would open the floodgates to equality claims based on every kind of disparity—leading Justice Brennan to accuse the majority of displaying "a fear of too much justice." Bryan Stevenson, who had just joined SCHR out of law school, recalled this as an incredibly demoralizing moment. "Most of us were just unbelievably heartbroken," he said. He could not wrap his head around the fact that the most powerful court in the land "could be talking about the inevitability of racial bias in the administration of the death penalty."[44]

Bright similarly believed *McCleskey* to be "an everlasting blight on the Supreme Court and a badge of shame for the state of Georgia." But after reading the opinion closely, he told SCHR's entire staff: "There's language in here we can do something with." The proper response, he said, was to identify every single situation where a judge or prosecutor might have acted out of bias and "litigate the hell out of it."

At that moment Bright realized a new model would be needed. His colleagues observed that "he talked more about race, and class, and power." Instead of giving up on racial equality claims, Bright encouraged everyone to double down on proving racial bias. With Bright leading the charge, they vowed to go county by county, prosecutor by prosecutor, and judge by judge if necessary to ensure their clients got a fair trial.[45]

They had uncovered a plot to exclude racial minorities in the Amadeo case, but now the campaign for equal justice would have to expand to other discriminatory practices such as the creation of jury pools, prosecutors' charging decisions and tactics during jury selection, and to judges who might be prejudiced against their clients. SCHR attorneys began demanding the recusal of prosecutors with a record of racial discrimination, such as Briley, or judges who exhibited bias. This was "the kind of litigation most people ran from," Stevenson explained. "But Steve embraced it."[46]

SCHR held events at Black churches to create "a consciousness that there was an obligation to serve" on juries. Bright or Stevenson would warm up the crowd by talking about a case they had in that county. Then a prominent civil rights figure like C. T. Vivian or Dr. Joseph Lowery would take the stage and tell the story of how he was beaten when he marched and had gotten back up for the right to vote and serve on a jury. "Now when you get summoned for jury service, I want you to walk to the courthouse like we walked to the courthouse in 1963, like we walked across the bridge," he would say. "Don't wait until it's *your son* sitting in a courtroom filled with White people and an all-White jury." These tactics tried to turn a sense of frustration and exclusion into democratic engagement. Black citizens began showing up for hearings in SCHR's cases.[47]

Bright and his staff continued to draw attention to the makeup of juries, arguing that the exclusion of racial minorities and poor people threatened not just the legitimacy of criminal justice policy, but also democracy itself. "There were no Black prosecutors, no Black decision makers, and the only opportunity for a Black person to play a role was on the jury," Stevenson painfully observed. "We'd routinely go to these counties where the county was 30% Black, the jury pool would be 20%, if the county was 20% Black, the jury pool would be 10%."[48]

What Stevenson described was more sophisticated than what was uncovered in *Amadeo*—an interlocking set of racist practices used by the state to game the rules, create all-White juries, and thereby dramatically increase the odds of securing a death sentence. But there was more than one way to manipulate a jury pool. After ratification of the Reconstruction Amendments, states that wanted to keep racial minorities from voting or serving on juries found facially neutral ways of doing so—for instance, by turning to literacy tests or discretionary evaluations of a citizen's moral character. Any remaining undesired citizens could then be excluded by a prosecutor through peremptory challenges during jury selection, which traditionally did not require an explanation.[49]

One of the more successful displays of SCHR's new approach to confront racism in the justice system occurred in the case of William Brooks. The Columbus jury that sentenced him to death had been all White, even though African Americans made up 30 percent of the community. The case against Brooks was brought by an office where all ten prosecutors were White men. The lead prosecutor, Mullins Whisnant, told jurors during closing argument that Georgia's crime rate had risen since 1964, the date of the last execution in the state. He called jurors "soldiers" in the "war on crime" and urged them to send Brooks to the electric chair.[50]

The writ of habeas corpus was instrumental in securing Brooks a new trial. In his retrial, the legal team filed a flurry of pretrial motions trying to block the death penalty. They flagged the jury composition issue. More aggressively, they moved to recuse Judge John Henry Land, arguing that Brooks could not get a fair trial before him. They were prepared to delve into the judge's family history to show that his father had participated in a lynching and that Judge Land had done something similar by giving Brooks "two uncaring lawyers" and allowing the prosecutor to rig an all-White jury. Unwilling to endure what a recusal motion required, Judge Land stepped off the case.[51]

Brooks's team lost most of the motions. But they convinced the new judge, Hugh Lawson, to order the district attorney to turn over any documents that might be relevant to the racial discrimination claims. This extraordinary development allowed Bright to show that since the death penalty was reinstated in 1976, prosecutors for the Chattahoochee Judicial District had pursued twenty-seven capital cases, twenty-one involving White victims. In those cases, prosecutors exercised peremptory challenges fifty-nine times (85.5 percent) against Black jurors, and only ten times (14.5 percent) against White jurors. They argued that the entire prosecutor's office had been violating the rights of Black defendants for years.[52]

Ruth Friedman, Mary Sinclair, and several investigators had spent the summer months leading up to Brooks's retrial studying the case files of District Attorney Doug Pullen. They went through every file, coding them for factors that could conceivably be relevant to the exercise of prosecutorial discretion such as prior offenses, the number of victims, and so on. They found an expert who calculated there was less than 1 in 1,000 chance that Pullen's office could be striking Black jurors at such a high rate randomly. The NAACP hailed these efforts as "a model of new defense strategies" to satisfy the more stringent standard for proving discrimination demanded by the Supreme Court.[53]

Judge Lawson refused to bar the death penalty. Nevertheless, SCHR's vigorous litigation of racial equality and fundamental fairness issues led to a jury seated with nine Black citizens—a far cry from what had happened the first time around. For the first time, Brooks had a fighting chance in front of a mixed-race jury.

The district attorney told jurors that Brooks deserved to pay with his life for cutting Carol Galloway's life short—a death for a death. Because of his actions, she would never grow old or get married. Some people are "just plain mean," Pullen said.

When his turn came, Bright told jurors that Brooks "had been punished his whole life." He grew up in a violence-filled home, and his alcoholic father would throw their mother and the kids out of the house. His parents were constantly "threatening to kill everybody and threatening to kill themselves." When his mother remarried, Brooks's stepfather beat him mercilessly with a belt buckle and harassed him because of a speech defect. Things got so bad that Brooks's mother fired a gun at her husband after he slapped her in front of the crying children.

"All of us human beings have different frailties, weaknesses, strengths," Bright reminded the jurors. Brooks was "endowed with below-average intelligence," struggled with a stutter, tested as "educable mentally retarded" as an eighth grader, and as an adult he still read "at a third-grade level." In prison he posed no problems and had shown remorse for his crimes. "I ask you to sentence him to the rest of his natural life in prison," Bright implored. "Let this rough and difficult journey go on there until it ends."[54]

The jury deliberated and returned with a life sentence. Brooks sighed deeply. Bright whispered "Thank you" as the jurors filed out.

HORTON V. ZANT

BRIGHT SOON GOT INVOLVED in another case that raised the issues of jury manipulation and substandard representation. One night, Jimmy Lee Horton and Pless Brown, Jr., both Black, were burglarizing an apartment when Sherrell Grant came home with her date and surprised them. A shootout ensued with the man accompanying Grant. Her date was killed, though no one could tell who fired the lethal shot.

Everything changed when the dead man turned out to be Don Thompson, the district attorney of Macon Judicial District, Georgia. People were so outraged that Joe Briley was brought down specially to secure death sentences even though it wasn't his circuit. Briley scoffed at charges that capital punishment was racist. Once, he was asked about a lawyer who used a racial epithet in open court to describe his own client. His reaction: southern lawyers have "freed many a Black man by getting up and denigrating (him) and getting the jury to feel sorry for him."[55]

Brown, who wound up with a mixed-race jury, received a life sentence. By contrast, Horton was sentenced to die by an all-White jury. His court-appointed lawyers did no investigation and presented no evidence on his behalf as to why he might deserve mercy. In his remarks to the jury, Horton's own lawyer called him "a worthless man" and praised the prosecutor's closing, saying, "Mr. Briley has admirably told you just exactly why it is that Jimmy Lee has got to die. . . . I find my task virtually impossible."

In a stroke of fortune, Judge Owens was assigned to consider Horton's habeas petition. Andy Lipps, a PDS veteran in private practice, deposed Briley. During the deposition, Briley denied striking jurors on account of their race. When Lipps asked about his role in manipulating jury pools in Putnam County, the prosecutor got up and stormed out.[56]

Bright and Lipps returned to Judge Owens, who was none too pleased about Briley's behavior. He sent federal marshals over to Briley's office with an order requiring him to sit for another deposition.

Bright deposed Briley the second time. Under withering questioning, Briley finally took responsibility for the memo that had proved decisive in Amadeo's case. But Briley gave an explanation that no one had heard before: he was doing his best to *rectify* constitutional problems rather than trying to get away with them. It was actually a judge, Briley claimed, who instructed him to bring the levels of non-White representation to a tolerable level without the jury commissioners having to "redo the box." That judge had since passed away.

On October 18, 1989, Bright handled the hearing for Horton's habeas petition. The first witness he called was Briley. The memo he prepared for the county became evidence in Horton's case, as Bright argued that it was not an isolated incident but rather evidence that the prosecutor had a history of racially discriminatory behavior. "The issue is who is the person behind this discrimination?" Bright reminded. He knew that if the proof of discrimination wasn't in the record, if he could not identify someone responsible for purposeful discrimination in his client's case, then Horton couldn't benefit even if there was inequality somewhere in the system.[57]

There was something else. To get a judge to find a prosecutor responsible for racial discrimination, Bright had to shake their presumption that prosecutors always tell the truth—a tall task. "You're not going to win or lose based upon that one incident," Judge Owens reminded him. Bright took the hint and moved straight to a study compiled by SCHR staff on Briley's peremptory strikes over his career. Just as they had done in Brooks's case, the staff had hunted down old case files, reconstructing the twists and turns of jury selection in Briley's cases across eight different counties since 1974. They charted 25 capital and 159 noncapital cases of Briley's and then cross-referenced that information with county voter registration lists to identify each juror's race.[58]

Displaying the document in his hand, Bright asked Briley about a case he prosecuted in 1977 in Jasper County: "In that case you used seven of your peremptory strikes against seven Black people; is that correct?"

"If that's what the record shows," Briley shrugged.

"You're not able to recall any reasons why you struck those people?"

"No sir," Briley responded. At that moment the state's lawyer, Paula Smith, stood up and objected to the line of question on relevancy grounds. "Under *Swain*, reasons in a particular case are not necessarily even required," she argued.

"If he recalls a reason he can certainly give it," Judge Owens replied.

Bright turned back to Briley: "It is your testimony that the fact that all seven happened to be Black people is just coincidental?"

"Yes sir," Briley answered.

The prosecutor's strategy was to deny any recollection of why he rejected so many Black citizens as jurors and hope that the silence in the record would be enough to satisfy tolerant judges. After leading him through the exhibit and getting Briley to admit to the disturbing pattern of jury strikes over many years, Bright turned to his client's case. "And in Mr. Horton's case you used nine out of ten strikes against Black jurors?"

Again: "If that's what the record shows."

On cross-examination, Paula Smith asked Briley to describe the process of jury selection in Georgia. He explained that "you've got to have all twelve jurors to vote for the death penalty because if one of them votes against the death penalty . . . it is a life sentence. So it takes a perfect score."[59]

Bright stood back up on redirect, slapping his legal pad down on the podium. He tried to lock down what the patterns showed. "You used ninety-six of your hundred and three strikes, 94% of your strikes, against Black people. Do you know why these reasons you have tend to fall so heavily upon Black people?"

Briley said weakly, "No sir, other than the reasons I have already given, I don't know why that would be." At this point, Bright had the experienced prosecutor squirming in the witness chair and everyone in the room knew it.

Next, Horton's lawyers called Gary Liberson, a PhD in mathematical statistics. Liberson had worked for the EPA to analyze their programs. Liberson testified that he examined Briley's juror strikes on a county-by-county basis to see whether they were "consistent with the ratio or percentage of Blacks in the population for that particular county." He testified that the probability the prosecutor's decisions reflected the random selection of jurors who happened to be Black was infinitesimal. In his expert opinion, there was "a very strong racial component to the strikes."[60]

On cross-examination, Smith got Liberson to admit that "the most your analysis would reveal is that the numbers do not show what one would expect if the prosecutor struck at random." She tried to suggest that any number of subjective factors not considered by the expert could explain the disparity. That is where Liberson stopped her. If there were other factors that were strongly correlated with race, they would dampen the results; they would not make the results "non-significant."

The state's lawyers called to the stand Joseph Katz, the very statistician Georgia had retained in the *McCleskey* case to rebut the Baldus study. Katz disputed Liberson's conclusions but didn't offer any alternative study or explanation, saying "some things don't easily reduce to numbers." Under cross-examination, he conceded that Liberson's methods were "appropriate." He also acknowledged that if you were a Black defendant, Briley was more likely to use his strikes to eliminate Black citizens during jury selection in your trial.

After all the witnesses and exhibits were entered into the record, Bright rose and addressed Judge Owens. What the evidence showed was that "Mr. Briley has a remarkable history of striking Black people from juries." In capital cases "90% of the time he used his strikes against Black jurors." The "only time he changes," Bright argued, "is when he has White people on trial." He urged Judge Owens to find that the state had "deprived members of Mr. Horton's race of participation in the judicial process."[61]

Smith stood up and gave her final remarks. She conceded that Horton had shown that the state "has struck a higher proportion of Black jurors than White jurors," but said that still didn't violate the Constitution. The petitioner's burden was to prove "historic systemic exclusion," she insisted.

Judge Owens broke in, giving Horton's team hope. "What information have we gotten from Mr. Briley that would explain his strikes on any grounds other than" race? "You'd better point them out." Smith responded that reasons didn't matter, just that some Black jurors "actually served and it is along the same percentages you would find in the general population."

Judge Owens sounded dumbfounded by this statement. "So what you are saying is if Mr. Briley in a hundred minor felony case lets Blacks serve and over here in fifty death penalty cases uses his strikes and does not let them serve, *Swain* has not been violated?" Bright felt optimistic about their chances. While prickly, Judge Owens had earlier shown little tolerance for prosecutorial misconduct.

The next spring, on April 12, 1990, Judge Owens dashed those hopes. In a forty-three-page opinion, he refused to disturb Horton's conviction. On the most promising claim, Judge Owens concluded that Horton "did not show that the prosecuting attorney has historically and systematically excluded Blacks from serving on trial juries." Judge Owens made quick work of Horton's remaining claims.[62]

Over the next several months, Bright and Lipps worked on Horton's appeal. Their mood brightened when they heard they had drawn judges Frank Johnson, Stanley Birch, and Joel Dubina. Frank M. Johnson, Jr., born thirty years earlier than Bright, was the intellectual and moral leader of the Eleventh Circuit. Like

Bright, Johnson had grown up on a farm. Most important, the two men shared an outlook as southerners who fiercely rejected their ancestors' old ways when it came to race relations. Indeed, Judge Johnson had repeatedly clashed with his close college friend turned governor, George Wallace, over the integration of Alabama's public institutions.[63]

One sunny day the next September, Lipps got a call while in his Washington, D.C., office. Bright's voice boomed through the receiver: "Andy, we won!"[64]

Frank Johnson wrote the opinion reversing Judge Owens. Birch and Dubina joined the opinion, making it unanimous. This would be one of Johnson's final rulings before taking senior status, and it was a tour de force.

Judge Johnson began by observing that the penalty phase of Horton's trial was "extremely short" and that his lawyers "called no witnesses and offered no evidence in mitigation." He first took up jury selection. Although the Supreme Court in *Batson v. Kentucky* made it easier for a defendant to challenge jury strikes, Horton could not rely on that decision because his trial took place before that case was decided. Instead, he was bound by *Swain*.

In *Swain*, Justice White had said that the fact that in a single trial every Black person was removed from the jury would not be sufficient to overcome the presumption that a prosecutor is acting in good faith "to obtain a fair and impartial jury." The only way to defeat that presumption is to prove that "the prosecutor in a county, case after case, whatever the circumstances, whatever the crime, and whoever the defendant or the victim may be," removed qualified jurors on the basis of their race. The Eleventh Circuit applied *Swain* stringently and had not found a violation of a defendant's rights even when a prosecutor struck every Black juror in six trials during a single week.[65]

Judge Johnson then delivered the good news: Horton had met

that high burden. "Mr. Briley's hardball tactics clearly do not comport with the prosecutor's obligation to 'do justice,'" he admonished. It was the first time the Eleventh Circuit declared a *Swain* violation in a Georgia case.[66]

Citing the *Amadeo* case, Judge Johnson pointed to Briley's role as the "author of a now infamous memo" designed to underrepresent Black people, women, and young people in Putnam County's juries. Even if Briley's effort to pin the blame on a deceased judge were true, a prosecutor had a duty to do justice and to "not engage in the subsequent cover up." The compelling evidence of Briley's jury strikes sealed the deal.[67]

The outrage wasn't reserved for the prosecutors alone. Judge Johnson also concluded that Horton's court-appointed lawyers were constitutionally deficient. They had put on absolutely no mitigating evidence to persuade a jury that their client's life should be spared and "performed hardly any investigation." Horton's own lawyer "attacked his client's character and separated himself from his client." By praising the prosecution's case, he had sent jurors the message that it was appropriate to kill his own client.[68]

At last, the state was held to account. This was a resounding legal victory that exposed prosecutorial misconduct, continuing racial inequality, and the subpar quality of legal representation for poor southerners. Because the nature of the constitutional defects went directly to the quality of justice, they had earned Horton a new trial. The media called it "yet another rebuke" of Briley "for keeping Blacks off juries." Bright told a reporter, "The chickens have come home to roost."[69]

Faced with the prospect of having to retry the case after all these years, this time against Bright and his staff, the state agreed to a plea deal that assured a life sentence for Horton. For Lipps, the entire experience demonstrated that once Bright had a grasp of someone in danger, "he never lets go."[70]

One life saved had led to other lives saved. Success in *Amadeo* had created legal precedent on fairness and equality, an invisible lifeline that linked one man's plight to another, Amadeo to Horton, though the men might never meet. Just as important, a tenacious and imaginative style of lawyering ran through all three cases: *Amadeo*, *Brooks*, and now *Horton*. Innovative tactics to prove racial discrimination that were only partially successful in *Brooks* led to a judicial rebuke in *Horton*. Like conductors along the Underground Railroad, different sets of attorneys had ferried each man to safety. In the end, three executions were avoided.

The Eleventh Circuit's surprising ruling gave advocates a valuable precedent. *Horton v. Zant* could be leveraged to force a second look at other cases handled by the same prosecutor on the theory they were also tainted by racial bias. Through relentless advocacy, Bright and his staff had pried open the death penalty system like a tin can, and even some people who supported capital punishment began to recoil at the unsavory mess they saw inside.

PART II

POVERTY AND REFORM

Snyder v. Louisiana

Concerns about rising crime and the prevalence of crack cocaine reached a fevered pitch during the 1990s, as civic leaders across the country called for additional crime control measures. Even racially diverse cities with Black leaders pressed for draconian punishments. In 1994, Congress passed the Violent Crime Control and Law Enforcement Act, the largest crime bill in history, adding sixty new death penalty offenses to existing federal law and funding the construction of more prisons. The day he signed the bill into law, President Clinton conjured the memory of the "half a million Americans [that] have been killed by other Americans" and praised the bipartisan support to "roll back this awful tide of violence."[1]

In the meantime, far away from Washington, D.C., ordinary Americans continued to struggle with love, jealousy, domestic strife. Mary and Allen Snyder had been married for eight years and had three children together. Yet their relationship was tempestuous as fights turned physical. When she'd had enough and a chance to get away materialized, Mary grabbed the kids and moved to her mother's home. Allen, despondent, kept trying to reconcile during the separation.

Hoping to reach his wife the evening of August 15, 1995, Allen Snyder waited for Mary outside her mother's home. The hour grew late, yet he remained. Around 1:30 a.m. the next morning, he spied Mary being dropped off by a man. Enraged, Allen approached the vehicle, opened the car door, and repeatedly stabbed Mary and her companion. She survived, but Howard Wilson perished from his wounds. When police officers went to arrest Allen, they found him curled up in a fetal position, mumbling to himself.

No one doubted that Snyder was responsible for the attacks. The excruciating question for a jury would be the appropriate punishment. Did he deserve to die because of the brutal nature of the slaying or could he be safely confined for the rest of his life in prison because he had committed a horrific crime in a fit of jealousy? A former marine with no significant criminal record, he had a decent chance of being spared.

Yet the timing of Snyder's trial could not have been worse. Two months after his arrest, on October 3, 1995, a California jury acquitted former NFL player O. J. Simpson of murdering his ex-wife and another man—a verdict that split the country sharply along racial lines. Louisiana itself was racially polarized: although the state was enormously diverse, David Duke, a former Grand Wizard of the Ku Klux Klan, still had a significant following there. He was elected to the state legislature and then, in 1991, ran for governor as the Republican Party's nominee.

According to Snyder's court-appointed lawyers, James Williams, the lead prosecutor, "was all over two parishes" telling people that the Snyder trial was his O. J. Simpson case. Alarmed by the prosecutor's effort to whip up bloodlust and racial animus, Snyder's attorneys asked the judge to order the prosecutor not to make any references to O. J. Simpson in front of the jurors. They filed a separate motion to prohibit Williams from making such statements in the media. "Sixty-something percent of all white people in America think that O. J. Simpson got away with murder," Snyder's attorneys told the judge. Such comments prevented their client from getting a fair trial. They pointed out that the jury pool was 95 percent White.[2]

The prosecutor groused about his "First Amendment" rights but promised not to mention the Simpson case. After hearing from both sides, the judge denied the defense motions based on the prosecutor's representations as an officer of the court.

Jury selection then got underway. Randomly selected panels of thirteen prospective jurors were called for questioning by both sides. The trial judge ruled on any challenges for cause, such as bias or hardship. Among the eighty-five prospective jurors called to serve, nine were African Americans. The judge permitted four Black jurors to be removed for cause. This left only five Black citizens in the pool. After asking some questions of Jeffrey Brooks, the first of the remaining Black jurors, prosecutors deemed him acceptable.

Prosecutors then struck the next two African American jurors: an engineer and a ship foreman. At that point, Snyder's lawyers noted their race for the record but did not raise a *Batson* challenge. Under the leading case, *Batson v. Kentucky*, if a party objected to the removal of a juror and could demonstrate that the strike was made on account of the prospective juror's race, a race-neutral explanation must be given and the judge must make a ruling. But Snyder's lawyers hesitated, doubtful they could convince the judge that race was the reason for their removal. After all, prosecutors had accepted one Black juror and objected to two others.[3]

When prosecutors tried to remove Elaine Scott, a Black finance clerk, the defense finally objected, pointing out that she was "the third African American struck." Now "there has been a pattern," Snyder's lawyers informed the judge. Because the defense had objected, the judge paused and asked the prosecutors why they had moved to exclude Scott. Although Scott had said she could impose the death penalty, the prosecutors told the judge she was "very weak on her ability to consider" it. The judge nodded, overruled the defendant's objection, and excused the juror.

Prosecutors then returned to Jeffrey Brooks and "backstruck" him. In Louisiana, as with a handful of other states, either side in a trial may go back and remove a juror that has already been deemed acceptable. Statistically it has been shown that backstrikes in Louisiana were used disproportionately to remove Black jurors when a case was brought against a Black defendant. Challenged by the defense to explain their backstrike of Brooks, prosecutors in Snyder's case said that Brooks looked "very nervous" and wanted to "go home quickly" even though they hadn't raised that concern earlier. The trial judge accepted these reasons.[4]

Prosecutors also challenged the sole remaining Black juror, Loretta Walker, asserting that she seemed willing to impose the death penalty for only very limited circumstances. The judge allowed this strike too, over an objection by the defense.

In the end, the judge overseeing Snyder's capital trial had no problem with the state eliminating every single Black juror from the pool, even though African Americans made up 20 percent of the local population. A murder trial in which the state sought to kill a Black defendant went forward before an all-White jury.

Once the jury found Snyder guilty, the sentencing phase of the trial began. His lawyers immediately objected the moment the prosecutor told jurors that the facts of Snyder's case "made me think of another case, the most famous murder case in the last, in probably recorded history."

"He's going to mention the O.J. Simpson trial," Snyder's lawyer asserted. "I object to that." James Williams responded, "Your Honor, based upon what he did in this case, where he sat for about 12 hours, he huddled and pretended to kill himself, just like O.J. did and just like O.J. got away with it. I think that's fair."

"That's ridiculous," Snyder's lawyer replied. But the judge waved away the objection and allowed the prosecutor to proceed. Turning back to the jury, Williams resumed his argument as to why Snyder should die for his crimes: "The most famous murder case, and all of you all have heard about it, happened in California, very, very similar to this case." That perpetrator "claimed he was going to kill himself as he drove in a Ford Bronco and kept the police off of him, and you know what, *he got away with it*."[5]

The obvious message to the all-White jury: Remember O.J.?, don't let *this* Black man get away with murder.

On August 30, 1996, after two and a half hours of deliberation, the jury returned with a verdict: death by lethal injection. For the next several years, Snyder's lawyers raised issues of prosecutorial misconduct during his trial, but those claims went nowhere. Court after court reviewing the record found ways of rationalizing the prosecutor's behavior. But that extended period of legal activity also meant that the state could not take Snyder's life.

On a 4–3 vote, the Louisiana Supreme Court narrowly rejected Snyder's *Batson* claim that the state's use of peremptory challenges violated the Fourteenth Amendment's Equal Protection Clause. At that point, the U.S. Supreme Court suddenly showed interest and granted review. Aware of Bright's success in *Amadeo v. Zant*, Snyder's lawyers asked Bright to plead the condemned man's cause. Bright had recently been diagnosed with a rare health condition: he had a heart that beat too fast. Bright had undergone surgery to have a defibrillator implanted in his chest. When the call for legal help came, he instantly seized the opportunity to do something meaningful again. In the opinion of a close colleague, Harold Koh, Bright returned to serving the hopeless, treating his body "as a vehicle for doing justice" once his carburetor had been replaced.[6]

After he had pulled Amadeo back from the brink of execution, Bright's national reputation shot through the roof. He was invited to teach at Yale Law School as a Skelly J. Wright Fellow in fall 1993, and returned year after year, adding stints at Harvard, Georgetown, Georgia State, and Emory. The first Skelly Wright Fellows had been Marian Wright Edelman and Peter Edelman, long-time advocates for children and poor people. Bright's new post at one of the nation's top law schools, and his association with these social-justice giants, enhanced his credibility whenever he spoke out about impoverished individuals caught in the wheels of justice.[7]

Bright's time at Yale allowed him to develop the themes of individualized justice, systemic indifference, and the constitutional right to counsel in sustained fashion. In 1994, the *Yale Law Journal* published Bright's article "Counsel for the Poor," which became one of the most cited law review articles published that year. Drawing on his own experiences and observations, Bright provocatively argued that the defendants selected for the ultimate punishment by our nation's courts were condemned "not for the worst crime but for the worst lawyer."[8]

He started by telling the story of an Alabama woman, Judy Haney, who had arranged to have her abusive and adulterous husband killed. By the age of sixteen she had married a man whose own brother called him crazy, who broke her nose and ribs during beatings and threatened to kill her and their children. Haney had been sentenced to death after being saddled with a drunk lawyer because she was too poor to afford a good one. As Bright told it, "The next morning, he and his client were both produced from jail, the trial resumed, and the death penalty was imposed a few days later." He posed a question: Why was Haney sentenced to die while so many similar defendants are spared?[9]

Bright's answer: she had received shoddy legal representation. Not only did she have an inebriated lawyer; neither of her attorneys did adequate work to prepare for trial. They did not bother to retrieve hospital records that would have corroborated that Haney's husband had physically abused her and her daughter. A defense expert didn't even meet Haney until the evening before the trial.

Bright then pivoted to the Constitution's promise contained in the Sixth Amendment right to counsel. He quoted Anthony Lewis, author of the best seller *Gideon's Trumpet*, which documented the odyssey of a prisoner whose handwritten petition led to a landmark U.S. Supreme Court decision guaranteeing the right to counsel for indigent people. *Gideon v. Wainwright*, Lewis explained, tried to bring to life "the dream of a vast, diverse country in which every person charged with a crime will be capably defended, no matter what his economic circumstances." Cases like Haney's showed that the project of effective representation articulated in *Gideon* "remains uncompleted, the dream unrealized."

What Bright was describing was the human toll of the economics of death. A major reason why the quality of representation was so bad in many parts of the country had to do with "the wages of death" paid to appointed lawyers, whose fees were often capped. In Alabama, which limited compensation to $1,000, a defense lawyer might make only four or five dollars an hour. A court-appointed lawyer simply could not make a living taking such difficult cases and would naturally give them low priority compared to higher-paying work.

Bright also castigated judges who intentionally appointed inexperienced and overwhelmed attorneys to defend poor people accused of serious crimes. On top of that, judges often refused to grant defense counsel's requests for experts or permitted only paltry expenditures when they did authorize experts. In other words, the political system initially mistreated the poor by creating a long list of crimes and then providing inadequate resources; the legal system compounded the problems through judicial indifference, offering "little protection to the poor person stuck with a bad lawyer."[10]

"Counsel for the Poor" was a hard-hitting exposé—one that reframed the abstract question of the morality of capital punishment as a gritty examination of how fallible human beings actually wielded the power of life or death over other morally flawed human beings. Seen in that light, disparities in the administration of justice were obstacles that an enlightened society should want to overcome. Bright's article presented his own life's work as an effort to not merely preserve but rather to extend the Warren Court's legacy of concern for equal justice.

Arguments grounded in fairness and the right to counsel had another upside: they might attract centrists and the occasional conservative who believed that the rule of the law embodied basic notions of fairness. Such people might abhor broad rationales that reflect excessive pessimism about the rule of law or seem to undermine institutions, but can still be moved to do justice based on the circumstances before them.

In many ways, Bright's gambit resembled the kinds of arguments made by pragmatists, who insist that moral and political disputes cannot be solved at a high level of abstraction but rather through rigorous confrontation of facts on the ground. He may not have been self-consciously invoking their example, but his humane and empirical approach to criminal punishment would surely be approved by devotees of the method.

And on that terrain, Bright was at his best. Instead of treating shocking episodes of injustice as outliers, he insisted that procedural irregularities could be found in every death penalty jurisdiction in America. He documented the escapades of sleeping lawyers, inattentive lawyers, grossly inexperienced lawyers whose clients wound up on death row. These sorts of things would never happen to a well-heeled person charged with a serious crime. As he reminded readers, each year about 250 out of approximately 20,000 homicides wind up as death penalty cases, and whether death is imposed "frequently turns on the quality of the counsel assigned to the accused."[11]

Of course, there were tradeoffs entailed in Bright's arguments. It put to one side universalist approaches and the possibility of clear moral answers, concentrating on narrower guarantees such as a fair shot in front of a diverse jury, competent representation, and access to experts. One could certainly seek broad reforms, or even abolition of capital punishment, based on a sense that basic fairness required them, but stronger steps didn't have to follow if people felt that the outrages identified were rare or just part of the unfortunate cost of doing business.

Seeming to understanding this, Bright opted to go big. You did not solve these problems just by granting relief to individuals after they had been wronged, he insisted; you had to reform the system that tolerated, and even encouraged, such errors in the first place. "Inadequate legal representation does not occur in just a few capital cases," Bright observed. "It is pervasive in those jurisdictions which account for most of the death sentences." Accordingly, he encouraged defense lawyers to "litigate aggressively the right to adequate compensation, to the funds necessary to investigate, and for the experts needed to prepare and present a defense." He also exhorted them to build on violations identified in discrete cases by bringing "systemic challenges to indigent defense systems."

Throughout, Bright urged lawyers to not be complicit in unjust systems, but to record the inadequacies they observed—to "bear witness to the shameful injustices which are all too routine in capital cases" and even to resist wherever they could. "Where these problems make it impossible for attorneys" to fulfill their obligations, they "should frankly declare their inability to render effective assistance." Advocates for the poor "must refuse unreasonable caseloads and insist upon the training and resources to do the job right."[12]

RETURN ENGAGEMENT

Snyder's case presented Bright with a chance to further test the ideas he had sketched in "Counsel for the Poor." It also offered an opportunity to make headway on the use of peremptory strikes for race-based reasons, as uncovered in cases involving SCHR clients such as Brooks and Horton.

Could arguments rooted in the principles of equality and fairness break through the emerging conservative consensus? The Supreme Court had become even more hostile to the rights of the accused than when Bright argued Amadeo's case, with a second generation of jurists hand-selected to complete the conservative revolution begun by Nixon's appointees. Clarence Thomas, appointed by George H. W. Bush, had replaced Thurgood Marshall, the liberal stalwart who wrote the *Amadeo* decision. Thomas, a more devoted originalist than even Justice Scalia, was willing to turn the clock on the Constitution back to 1789, when it came to the power of the federal government, and to 1868, when it came to individual rights. According to the theory of originalism, the Constitution's meaning was fixed at the moment each of the provisions was written and ratified; judges should not try to update these historical understandings but merely try to enforce them.[13]

Since Thomas's elevation, Republican presidents had also been able to add John Roberts as chief justice, and Anthony Kennedy and Samuel Alito as associate justices. There certainly had been a few surprises involving the death penalty over the years. Dramatically, on February 22, 1994, Justice Blackmun announced that the uneven quality of legal representation of people facing capital punishment had turned him into an abolitionist. He concluded that "the death penalty experiment had failed" because the project of trying to ensure fairness since *Gregg v. Georgia* had disintegrated into judges propping up "the mere appearance of fairness" and that the system inevitably "must wrongly kill some defendants." Although Blackmun had vowed to no longer "tinker with the machinery of death," he too, was long gone by the time Snyder's case landed in the high court. The rest of Blackmun's colleagues, including his replacement, Stephen Breyer, still believed that the death penalty could be administered in constitutional fashion.[14]

Despite the Court's lurch to the right, could an emphasis on procedural fairness and the gritty facts of jury selection be enough to convince a Court predisposed against the condemned to give Snyder a new trial? The case involved something that Bright had exposed effectively in his representation of Brooks and Horton: how historical racism and the drive to secure death sentences can warp jury selection, even in racially diverse communities.

On December 4, 2007, Bright arrived in Washington, D.C., to plead for Snyder's life. Nineteen years had passed since he argued Amadeo's appeal, but to Bright it felt like the blink of an eye. Of course, some things *had* changed: Bright's co-counsel worried about his defibrillator suddenly going off during oral argument. The defense team came up with a plan in case it kicked in and caused him to pass out.[15]

Bright was prepared to argue that the Louisiana Supreme Court erred when it affirmed Snyder's conviction. According to their brief, the state's highest court failed to consider "the totality of the relevant facts when it reviewed the state's use of peremptory strikes removing all the Black jurors. Once he had manufactured an all-White jury, the prosecutor "played the race card" by referring to O.J., "catching the court and counsel by surprise." His blatant refusal to keep his word should have been taken as evidence of his racial bias.[16]

On the day of oral argument, Justice Alito proved to be an especially lively questioner. Alito, a former federal prosecutor and experienced judge on the Third Circuit, had been nominated by President Bush to replace Sandra Day O'Connor when she retired in 2005. Alito was an avowed originalist who produced conservative rulings that often preserved the power of police. Yet in his very first opinion, he had joined a unanimous Court in reversing a conviction where the judge had barred the defendant from introducing evidence that someone else had committed the crimes. Alito's choice to do so suggested that, in the right case, he might be willing to sift through the facts.[17]

"Suppose there's a case where it's perfectly clear that certain strikes were not racially motivated," Justice Alito said. "Let's say the prosecution has the strategy of striking every lawyer who's on the panel. It strikes every white lawyer and it strikes every black lawyer." He asked Bright whether there was any legal significance to the fact that some African American lawyers had been removed from the jury pool.[18]

Bright answered, "There's a common reason." Under the scenario presented by Justice Alito, the fact that some of the excluded jurors happened to be Black would not be dispositive because the state would have a race-neutral explanation.

Alito was thinking aloud about what significance should be given to the fact that a prosecutor exercised a peremptory challenge against a Black person. Did it always mean something nefarious was afoot? In the hypothetical where race wasn't the motivating reason for removing the juror, the fact that the lawyers happened to be Black didn't seem relevant at all. Bright's answer suggested that things weren't always so clear as to a prosecutor's motivations, and you had to scrutinize both the pattern of strikes and the consistency of the explanations given.

Did it matter that Snyder wasn't challenging the constitutionality of some of the strikes of Black jurors? Justice Alito asked, "What is the relevance of strikes you do not even claim were racially motivated?"

"They struck all the blacks they could in this case," Bright replied. "There were only five." He meant that the pattern of conduct should help the defense demonstrate that race was on the mind of prosecutors. A recent ruling by the Supreme Court held that a curious pattern "unlikely to be happenstance" should be counted as a factor supporting the defendant's allegation that racism was involved. When that case, *Miller-El v. Dretke*, came down, Justice David Souter announced the decision from the bench, a technique to ensure maximum coverage of conduct the Court felt was distasteful or illegal. Miller-El's case had gone up and down the entire federal judiciary twice, with the Fifth Circuit finding no problems with the prosecutor's exclusion of Black jurors.

"We again reverse the judgment of the Fifth Circuit," Justice Souter said on that occasion. He explained that prosecutors had removed African American jurors who gave similar answers to White jurors who were not removed, which made the state's explanations fishy. And "there were other indications of racial discrimination by the prosecutors," including describing the death penalty "in graphic detail to black panelists more often than to others to weed out the black panelists by prompting them to express opposition to the death penalty." Prosecutors "also asked manipulative questions about the minimum punishment for murder more often to black panelists." On top of that, the prosecutors had been "trained in a District Attorney's Office that used a manual recommending the exclusion of minorities from juries." The lower court "findings of no discrimination were unreasonable," Justice Souter said sternly.[19]

Miller-El had finally required trial judges to be more active in questioning lawyers when they appeared to exclude jurors based on their race. Bright's interactions with the justices in Snyder's appeal now turned to what guidance that precedent offered. "There were a large number of strikes in *Miller-El*," Justice Alito reminded. "This is a much smaller number." He sounded doubtful about drawing an inference of intentional racism from the pattern of strikes in Snyder's case because there were so few African American jurors in the pool to begin with.

Chief Justice Roberts sounded bothered by something else: Snyder's trial counsel had objected to the removal of some Black jurors but not others. "You want to rely on the fact that these other jurors were excluded, and no objection was made to their exclusion." If a concern had been raised, prosecutors might have offered a race-neutral explanation, he pointed out. "Yet you want them to be considered as evincing racial bias."

Everyone was now deep in the weeds of how to prove racism on the part of a prosecutor and how judges should manage jury selection. It was all so tricky. *Batson* required a person to show that jurors were excluded because of their race before a prosecutor was obligated to give a reason for a jury strike, but there wasn't much to go on except for how jury selection unfolded in the heat of the moment. A defendant couldn't put the prosecutor under oath during jury selection. Seeking access to documents in the moment would also be futile because they are lawyers' work product. For the legal framework to ferret out racism and deter misconduct, judges would have to play an active role by demanding truthful reasons from lawyers and jurors.

Bright painted a vivid picture of how jury selection unfolded in Snyder's case. The fact that Louisiana allowed backstrikes not only complicated the strategic decisions by lawyers but also made it harder to detect racial discrimination against jurors. That's why

Snyder's lawyers hadn't originally objected to the exclusion of two Black jurors—"There's no pattern" yet, Bright acknowledged. Even if they had objected earlier, they probably could not convince the judge that the strikes were based on race.

Justice Ginsburg piped up. "Couldn't counsel at that point have gone back and said, 'Ah, now I see what's going on, so I'm going to challenge . . . the second and third African-American?' "

She was right, but Bright answered: "I think basically the defense was snookered here." Because Snyder's lawyers were thrown off by the backstrike, failing to raise concerns about some of the Black jurors shouldn't be held against their client. It certainly did not absolve prosecutors of responsibility if race was a motivating factor in the elimination of any Black jurors to which the defense did object.

Justice Scalia decided to make his presence felt. The trial judge "is in a much better position" to decide the credibility of a juror or an attorney, he asserted. Scalia confessed he could not tell from a cold record months or years later whether someone was really hesitant to impose the death penalty. Under the case law, prosecutors were entitled to a "death-qualified jury": citizens who were not inalterably opposed to capital punishment and were willing to listen to arguments that a defendant deserved to die. Bright knew that the rule requiring death-qualified juries could be exploited by prosecutors to get rid of Black jurors because that segment of the community tended to have more qualms about capital punishment, but he bit his tongue as Justice Scalia pressed his point. Playing the role of the prosecutor, Justice Scalia told Bright: "If you have one juror who says 'I think I could' and another one who said 'I could,' I'm going to strike the one who says 'I think I could.' "[20]

Bright responded that it would have been very easy to follow up to determine what a juror like Scott meant. Bright's point was that prosecutors had exploited one word in a Black juror's response in order to get rid of her, but they had consistently asked clarifying questions of the White jurors in an effort to keep them on the panel. In fact, they asked all twenty-one of the White jurors what they meant by their responses.

Scalia sounded skeptical. "Did all 21 say 'I think I could'" impose the death penalty?

In fact, Bright replied, all twenty-one White jurors who expressed qualms about imposing the death penalty were asked follow-up questions and said they would vote for a death sentence in certain situations.

Suddenly, Justice Alito broke back in. "Mr. Bright, you make good arguments about comparisons between White jurors and Black jurors." In the clearest sign that he was leaning Snyder's way, he added that Bright had "a good argument" in comparing Jeffrey Brooks to some of the White jurors. Brooks was the Black graduate student who had been backstruck by the prosecution, which later asserted that he seemed nervous and might want to rush through the trial to get back to school.

Prosecutors had initially left Brooks on the jury after a call was made to the dean of his school. That call confirmed that as an education student at Southern University Brooks had graduate teaching commitments and had just started to observe experienced instructors teach before teaching on his own. But the dean also said that jury service would not interfere with his degree requirements so long as the trial didn't go on longer than the week. All this suggested that prosecutors hadn't treated the work concerns of Black and White jurors the same. This kind of close comparative analysis had been the approach in *Miller-El* when the Court ferreted out a racial purpose to a prosecutor's jury strikes.

Scalia interjected again: "I don't understand how the dean could resolve his problem."

"Well, he's the *dean*," Bright retorted. Laughter rippled through the Chamber.

Scalia continued with his line of inquiry, but his questions allowed Bright to show a better command of the facts. "The man's problem, what he's worried about, is that he has to put in a certain number of hours of teaching. And what was it? A couple of months before the end of the term?," Justice Scalia wondered. "No, this was in August," Bright clarified. And at that point, the juror "was just observing someone else teach."

"That wouldn't inspire a great deal of confidence in me" if a dean had answered " 'okay,' " said Justice Scalia. He was suggesting that Brooks still might have been worried about returning to school expeditiously and that any agitation could have been visible to prosecutors, despite the dean's assurances.

Bright kept things simple. "Well, again, it would have only taken one question: 'Mr. Brooks, now that you've heard that your dean said it won't be a problem, do you have further concerns about wanting to get home quickly?' " He then emphasized other evidence that Brooks was treated differently from White jurors: there was consistent questioning of everybody except Brooks about their competing commitments. He was the only African American rejected by the prosecutors for hardship reasons. Bright wanted the justices to see that the fact the prosecutors were initially satisfied with Brooks's willingness and capacity to serve, coupled with differential questioning of the jurors when hardship came up, showed that the real reason they later backstruck him was his race.

The questions soon turned to the trial judge's role in overseeing jury selection. "The judge was quite passive," noted Justice Ginsburg. "Was the judge, in fact, present throughout the entire voir dire?"

Bright confirmed that the trial judge had been present the entire time, before making the most of the opportunity to showcase the problems with judicial indifference. Once a party objected to the elimination of a juror due to race, *Batson* required a judge to assess the explanation given for removing a juror and making a finding on the record. To do the job right, a judge must take an active role during jury selection to ensure respect for the Constitution. How the Supreme Court expected a trial judge to perform this duty could make the difference between a fair trial and one tainted by racism.

To illustrate just how passive the judge had been for jury selection in Snyder's trial, Bright noted that when he finally granted a defense strike for cause, the prosecutor, Mr. Williams, yelled, "Are you crazy?"

"It sounds like the right answer to me," said Justice Scalia, to more laughter.

"It wasn't the right question." With a grin, Bright said he often wondered about that pro-prosecution bias. The audience was enjoying the rhetorical prowess of the participants.

Bright then launched into more evidence of the trial judge falling down on the job in Snyder's case. He pointed out another moment that showed the prosecutor seemed to be running the courtroom rather than the judge. At one point the prosecutor actually instructed the judge how to get through jury selection faster, without inquiring whether each person had a good enough reason to skip out on their civic duty: "Swear all these people to say they've got a valid reason for leaving, and send them all out of here." If the justices came away from oral argument with the sense that the trial judge let the prosecutor do whatever he wanted, Bright reasoned, they would be less inclined to defer to his findings that race played no part in the strikes of Black jurors.

According to Bright, the judge had asked the prosecutor "Well, do I do it individually, or do I do it in a group?" The prosecutor had replied: "Do it in a group." And the judge "goes right along with it." In fact, Bright observed, every ruling the judge made was done in "four or five words: 'I'm going to allow it.' " It was in this exceedingly permissive environment that an all-White jury emerged from jury selection.

At that point Justice Stevens asked his first question. He wanted to know whether the prosecutor's repeated O.J. references were relevant to the constitutionality of the state's jury strikes. Bright responded yes, that alluding to that infamous murder trial broke his promise as an officer of the court not to inject race into the trial.

"So he broke his promise," Scalia stated derisively. "I mean sue him or something, but I don't see how it has anything to do with" whether Snyder had a fair trial.

"It has to do with his credibility," Bright replied, "which is very much what *Batson* is about." He brought the issue of race back to the forefront to emphasize the stakes of the appeal. "What this prosecutor learned from O. J. Simpson . . . is that you don't let blacks on the jury. I think he saw that this racially mixed jury in Los Angeles let him quote 'get away with it' and we're going to have an all-white jury here in Jefferson Parish." With that, Bright's time expired and he returned to counsel's table.

Terry Boudreaux defended Snyder's conviction on behalf of the State of Louisiana. He conceded under heavy questioning that there were not many follow-up questions of prospective jurors, but said that was because the jury was picked fairly quickly. This didn't make Justice Alito any happier, as he told Boudreaux: "The explanation for Mr. Brooks is not terribly convincing on its face." He noted that the facts of the case were fairly straightforward. In fact it turned out to be "an incredibly short trial" as expected—jury selection started on a Tuesday and verdict came in on Friday. So the prosecutors' reason for striking Brooks seemed suspicious. Did they really worry Brooks would refuse to do his civic duty responsibly because he might miss a little observation time?

Justice Souter sounded convinced that the trial judge should have done more. After Snyder's lawyers had objected to the O. J. Simpson remark during closing argument, the judge ruled that the statement was not racially significant because the prosecutor had not mentioned that either O. J. Simpson or Snyder was Black. "Now that is not a critical mind at work, is it?" Souter asked rhetorically. Peals of laughter rippled through the media and observers in attendance.

"I would suppose not, Your Honor," admitted Boudreaux.

"And because you suppose not and I certainly suppose not, we have to consider the O. J. Simpson remark in trying to evaluate what went on."

Boudreaux tried to offer a nonracial reason for bringing up O.J. in connection with violent crimes perpetrated by someone else: the prosecutor simply wanted to point out other factual similarities involving the Simpson case and Snyder's situation, such as a jealous husband who stalked his wife. But Souter would have none of it. "Do you believe that, if there had been a White defendant here, the O. J. Simpson case would have been mentioned?"

"Yes, your Honor, and I believe—"

"I will be candid to say to you, under the circumstances of the record in front of us, I find that highly unlikely," Souter asserted.

Though the prosecutor's fixation with the O.J. trial had barely come up during oral argument, it was now obvious that this fact was not far from the justices' minds. "Do you think the prosecutor would have made the analogy if there had been a black juror on the jury?" Chief Justice Roberts followed up.

Boudreaux let the question hang for five full seconds, as if he wasn't sure how to respond. "I think he would have, Your Honor," he finally said, gamely.

After oral argument, Bright felt relief that the defibrillator had not kicked in, followed by a burst of confidence. A few court watchers told Bright he had an outside shot at picking up Justice Alito's vote.[21]

They were right. On December 4, 2007, the Supreme Court announced that by a 7–2 vote, the trial judge had "committed clear error" when he rejected Snyder's Fourteenth Amendment claim. The prosecutor had excluded one of the jurors because of race: Mr. Brooks, the graduate student. That misconduct with regard to a single Black juror denied Snyder equal protection of the law.

"All of the circumstances that bear upon the issue of racial animosity must be consulted," Justice Alito explained in his majority opinion. That meant the strike of other Black people, such as that of Ms. Scott, should be considered by a trial judge in the future when evaluating the veracity of a lawyer's reasons. In this situation, however, "the explanation given for the strike of Mr. Brooks is by itself unconvincing."[22]

Justice Alito discussed the two reasons given by prosecutors for backstriking Brooks: his allegedly nervous demeanor and his teaching obligations. The record didn't show that the judge actually made a finding about his demeanor at the time, so "we cannot presume" that the judge agreed with the prosecutor that the juror seemed nervous. As for the second reason, Justice Alito observed that forty-nine other jurors expressed concerns that jury service would interfere with other obligations. He said that the prosecutor's reason went from "suspicious" to "implausibl[e]" once you considered that the state was fine with White jurors who had obligations "at least as serious" as the Black juror's. One White juror ran his own business and his wife had just had surgery. "If the prosecution had been sincerely concerned that Mr. Brooks" would favor a verdict with a less serious offense to shorten the trial, "it is hard to see why the prosecution would not have had at least as much concern" about what this White juror might have done.

Justices Thomas and Scalia dissented. They accused their colleagues of "second-guessing" the trial judge. In their view, if the record was ambiguous about why a trial judge permitted a peremptory strike, a higher court should leave things alone. But their dissent merely underscored the importance of Alito's opinion, which reinforced the obligation of judges who preside over a trial as the primary guardians of fairness. A judge has a duty to ensure that the jury's demographics are not being manipulated. If judges tolerate superficial, nonsensical, or inconsistent explanations for eliminating citizen participation, they are contributing to the distortion of the democratic process as well as to unjust legal outcomes.

Justice Alito's opinion made no mention of the most explosive allegations, including the prosecutor's O.J.-inspired call for the death penalty, or even the possibility raised by Bright that prosecutors planned from the start to manufacture an all-White jury receptive to racist appeals about the kinds of people who deserve to die. But vindicating legal rights requires making compromises. Saying less is often the price of securing victories. The key is to get more for the cause of justice than you give up.

In this instance, the ruling might actually be more useful in everyday situations precisely because it didn't rely on the more outrageous accusations for its finding of discrimination. The more egregious the misconduct, the easier Snyder's case could be brushed aside as an outlier by future judges. Although the Supreme Court couldn't reach consensus over the removal of Ms. Scott, that didn't matter. Racial bias in the state's exclusion of a single prospective juror was intolerable.

After twelve years on death row, Snyder would get a new trial. Bright had helped deliver this unlikely outcome by showing that race played an impermissible role during his trial. What the state did the first time around violated the Fourteenth Amendment's guarantee of equal protection of the laws. Satisfied with the lawyers who would continue to represent Snyder in the aftermath of the Supreme Court's ruling, Bright chose not participate in the retrial.

After losing in the U.S. Supreme Court, prosecutors in Louisiana decided not to pursue a death sentence any longer. In a vastly altered political climate, Snyder was tried for second-degree murder, this time in front of a jury with three African Americans. Prosecutors did not make racist appeals. This time, the mixed-race jury convicted Snyder and he received a life sentence without the possibility of parole.[23]

SHAMING GEORGIA'S INDIGENT DEFENSE SYSTEM

Increasingly, Bright felt it important to educate others that outrageous treatment like that received by Snyder was a regular occurrence. He had seen Black citizens excluded from the administration of justice time and time again. But as he explained in "Counsel for the Poor," the real problems were systemic rather than individualistic in nature. The manipulation of juries did not keep happening merely because a few prosecutors hated Black people or distrusted women, but because deep imbalances between the state and the individual on trial tempted even well-intentioned prosecutors to take advantage of the situation. Structural problems required structural solutions.

Gideon v. Wainwright had promised the help of an attorney to anyone charged with a crime who could not afford one. The legal ideal of justice depended on the adversary system, where truth and desert would emerge from the clash between two sides. For the poor, the reality was rarely a fair fight.

Louisiana, where Snyder was tried, had no statewide public defender at the time—that system was established for the first time in 2007. It is also the state with the highest incarceration rate in the United States and one of the highest rates of wrongful convictions. Reliable funding for the representation of the poor has generally been hard to come by in Louisiana, as it is in so many other parts of the country. In some places a judge appoints inexperienced local attorneys to perform the work, often causing resentment, inadequate representation, and legal errors. In other jurisdictions, a contract system is used, where the lowest bidder is awarded the right to handle all the criminal cases involving the poor. These Frankenstein monster–style policies to comply with the constitutional right to counsel create huge disparities between cities and counties that devote resources to the ideal of equal justice and those that do not. Luckily, Snyder's court-appointed lawyers objected to the constitutional violations at the time so he would not be prevented from raising them on appeal. But even in places with a local public defender's office, like New Orleans, caseloads can be so high that there is little time to devote to investigation or quality advocacy.[24]

Back in Georgia, SCHR's exposure of abuses within the criminal justice system embarrassed members of the bar. Bright's capital cases illustrated many legal errors that could be attributed to inadequate representation. But this structural deficiency extended beyond the death penalty context. Many individuals were left to languish in pretrial detention because they could not afford bail or were forced to plead guilty with little help from an attorney. Would those in power finally do something to improve the quality of justice?

One day in December 2001, Samuel Moore, a forty-five-year-old Black man, was arrested by police for loitering. He was told that he was being detained for an outstanding warrant for selling drugs. From that point on, Moore disappeared into the system for the next thirteen months. He sat in a jail in Crisp County, Georgia, never seeing a lawyer or hearing about what was going on with his case.

Nine months into his ordeal, he finally wrote his own motion asking for copies of documents in his case and an attorney because he could not afford one. Surprised to discover Moore still behind bars, the district attorney dismissed all charges three days later. Yet no one bothered to tell his jailer. A month later, a judge appointed Moore an attorney, but he never showed his face. Moore continued to rot in jail, a victim of a broken legal system. "They just forgot about me.[25]

"I felt like I was just nothing," Moore said. "Nobody—nobody—cared about me." That is, until a SCHR investigator visited the jail and was told by another detainee about Moore's plight.[26]

The district attorney blamed Moore himself for the snafu, saying, "It must be wrong to assume that everyone in South Georgia has a brain cell."

A little investigation showed that Moore's predicament was just the tip of the iceberg in Georgia. One poor person in Coweta County complained that he "had been in jail 14 months without a hearing or a bond." Five months after his arrest, a seventy-one-year-old man still had not seen a lawyer. A third individual told SCHR investigators that he had been in pretrial detention "almost 6 months now and do not have a court [-appointed attorney] yet. No one has told me anything that is going on."[27]

The defects of the indigent defense system can be traced to the way it was organized, with the state devolving responsibility to each of the 159 counties. Traditionally, local attorneys, many with little or no criminal law experience, were forced to take court-appointed cases for which they received little pay and on which they spend even less time. The state legislature historically contributed to only a fraction of the costs of defense services for the poor. Counties chose the least expensive route available that resolved criminal cases as expeditiously as possible. Without uniform state standards, strict accountability, or sufficient resources, poor people might wait weeks or months without meeting a lawyer or getting any closer to trial.

War on Crime policies put additional stress on an already fragile system for delivering legal services to the poor, pushing it past the breaking point. Bright saw Moore's harrowing experience and that of so many others as evidence of a setup that incentivized the making of excuses rather than solutions. "Everybody wants to blame everybody else," he diagnosed. "That's part of the problem here." Bright's experience representing people on "death wages" turned out to be a wider phenomenon that affected poor people throughout the criminal justice system. Suddenly, he found himself in a position to practice what he preached in "Counsel for the Poor" and initiate a "systemic challenge" to Georgia's indigent defense system.

By the late 1990s, Bright began to focus his efforts on shaming Georgia's public officials for their roles in delivering unequal justice. SCHR kickstarted reform by issuing a series of reports on the quality of criminal justice in the state and filing lawsuits to document the failures of existing practices. These publications shined light on poor people languishing in jail without seeing an attorney or judge, assembly-line plea practices, outlandish bail procedures, and excessive fees charged to those enmeshed in the legal system (if you were too poor to pay fines you could also be jailed for nonpayment).

When SCHR staff visited Greene County Superior Court one day, they discovered a trial docket that listed 144 defendants, with "so many people there accused of crimes that they filled the courtroom and spilled down the stairs." The contract lawyer used by the county to represent poor people had been appointed to ninety-four of those individuals accused of more than 200 crimes, everything from murder to robbery. According to Bright, "Even Clarence Darrow couldn't be prepared for 94 cases on one day." Plea discussions would take place in the hallway, and anyone who wanted a different attorney was sternly instructed by the judge that an accused could not "pick and choose" their lawyers. Within a few days, all the cases had been disposed of through guilty pleas, with no investigation and minimal contact between lawyers and clients, and zero trials. "It was truly an assembly line," recalled Bright.[28]

By putting the indigent defense system in his crosshairs, Bright did two things at once: he showed the interlocking practices that led to incompetent lawyers for people who wound up on death row and he shined the light on the everyday consequences of mass incarceration for those charged with less serious crimes. Inadequate funding of legal services led to overworked court-appointed lawyers, little or no investigation, rushed guilty pleas, and slipshod trials—to the detriment of people who are in fact innocent or have valid legal defenses.[29]

Bright's reform efforts brought him full circle. His first job as a legal aid lawyer had focused on improving how social services were provided to the poor. He now drew on his knowledge of criminal and civil law to reform how criminal defense services were delivered to the poor—perhaps the most vital service a person could have the misfortune to require.

To Bright, the justice system dehumanized the people caught up in its jaws: "Poor people in this court are being *processed* through this system, not *represented*." The critique of the political system he had begun as a student activist had matured. He now believed that War on Crime politics had corrupted the very legal system that was supposed to serve as a bulwark to protect vulnerable people.

Judges themselves had become active participants in an unequal justice system by allowing poor people to rot in jail, by not demanding better legal representation, and by creating doctrines that rationalized glaring inequities. Callous jurists also interpreted "due process of law" and the right to counsel in parsimonious ways. As Bright pointed out in a law review article lamenting the rationing of legal services for the poor, "courts have held that the lawyer need not be aware of the governing law, sober, or even awake." Such appallingly low standards didn't just lead to the violations of other rights, as Bright's cases showed, they also provided no incentives for anyone to change their ways.[30]

SCHR staff discovered that in the City of East Point, not far from Atlanta, municipal judges never appointed attorneys for violations of traffic laws. Instead, judges insisted that people sign waivers of their rights, imposed sentences, and had them hauled off to jail if they could not pay fines. The county-based system of securing lawyers for the poor, with delays and incompetence forcing individuals to give up their rights, was "a disgrace," Bright told the media.[31]

Earlier federal lawsuits in Georgia seeking to improve the quality of indigent defense got bogged down in details, even though at least one lawsuit produced funds earmarked by the state to improve the delivery of legal services. No major reforms were implemented. The money from the settlement was quickly spent.

Bright had a theory for why previous efforts failed: they had tried to do too much in a single lawsuit against the state. His solution mirrored the Center's shift in strategy when it came to making racial discrimination claims in criminal cases: scale down, target local bad actors, and uncover more outrageous details about how people were being treated. In a political environment in which national solutions were likely to fail, better to target the worst counties, one by one, and force them to deal with egregious conditions or confess they didn't have the money to do the job right. Going after them piecemeal would take more time and resources than a single global lawsuit, but it would also keep stories about unequal justice in the news and create a sense of rolling momentum pressuring the state's leaders to act.

Starting in 2001, SCHR began suing the counties that had the worst track record of delivering legal services to indigent people, arguing that local officials were violating defendants' right to counsel. The first major lawsuit was brought against Coweta County. With the help of prominent cooperating attorneys, Bright and his staff sued the chief judge, the prosecutors, county commissioners, and the contract defender, contending that they were collectively responsible for punishing the poor by not assigning lawyers, setting bond at an amount they could not afford to pay, "forcing them to be taken into custody." They also alleged that judges routinely directed unrepresented people to speak with a district attorney without advising them of their rights. Bright and cooperating attorney Ed Garland organized the effort in Coweta County as a two-front war, with advocates simultaneously demanding reform of unconstitutional court practices and seeking writs of habeas corpus to overturn convictions obtained without a lawyer.[32]

SCHR's commitment to reform indigent defense in Georgia started to raise eyebrows. Nat Hentoff, an influential social critic, called the Coweta County class action "a historic suit" that "should get national attention." Hentoff made the lawsuit the subject of his column in *The Village Voice*. Especially disturbing to Hentoff was the fact that "over half of the poor people found guilty of some offense in the Superior Court of Coweta County in the last two and a half years *were not represented by counsel*."

Ultimately, Bright's team secured a court-approved consent decree to "ensure that indigent persons accused of felony crimes . . . are promptly assigned counsel." The settlement created for the first time an "indigent defense program" in the county that employed at least one full-time public defender and one staffer. Coweta County officials agreed to abide by guidelines established for caseloads and to hire contract defenders "at no less than $30,000 to provide representation in 100 felony cases." The county's new indigent defense program reported to a three-person committee who "agree to vigorously enforce" the agreement.

Bright's team also turned their attention to McDuffie County, which awarded a contract to Bill Wheeler to provide legal services for the poor. He was the lowest bidder. Over a period of five years, Wheeler represented 850 defendants. An investigation found that in the first four years of his contract, he took only three cases to trial and entered 313 guilty pleas. He filed only three motions during this period. Many times, Wheeler met individuals accused of crimes for the first time in open court and entered a guilty plea worked out with the district attorney after a brief conversation. The lack of vigorous representation hit people charged in Toombs Circuit especially hard because judges there handed down longer prison sentences than judges in other parts of the state.[33]

The right to counsel contemplates somebody who confers with a client early in the process and conducts an independent investigation of the state's case, Bright believed. But what was happening in McDuffie County "is fast-food justice," he thundered, "and it's no justice at all." Bristling at Bright's remarks, Wheeler retorted that his clients were "getting their money's worth." He said he did not waste time filing motions because judges were "loathe" to grant them and he did not bother to investigate cases because prosecutors eventually showed him their evidence. Wheeler acknowledged feeling overwhelmed because he had been assigned 172 indigent clients the previous year on top of his regular paying clients from his private practice. But he blamed his own clients: "I suspect a great deal of them lie when saying they're indigent."[34]

After SCHR threated to sue McDuffie County, and the media confirmed how little an overworked contract defender could do, state officials withheld the meager funding available until Wheeler was replaced by a full-time public defender.[35]

A lawsuit against Fulton County, encompassing Atlanta, ultimately led to a consent decree to fund twenty additional public defenders. The County also promised to "expedite" the appointment of defense counsel for eligible poor people and "consult with the defendant in person" within two business days after a lawyer was assigned.

Another legal action, this time against Sumter County, accused officials of failing to inform misdemeanor defendants they were entitled to a lawyer before asking them to plead guilty. Once again, the threat of a lawsuit caused another county to alter its treatment of poor people in pretrial detention. Incremental change was afoot—could it spark more lasting awareness and structural reform?

Reverend Joseph Lowery, who supported these lawsuits along with the NAACP and the Black Leadership Forum, called attention to how a flawed indigent defense system worsened racial inequality. He noted that the uneven quality of justice fell hardest on racial minorities, creating a prison population where two-thirds of incarcerated people are Black. "The indigent defense system in Georgia represents a new form of slavery," Reverend Lowery declared.[36]

SCHR twice sued the entire Cordele Judicial Circuit for failing to hire properly trained juvenile defenders and underfunding the public defender offices. The first time, Bright and his allies challenged a practice where only two part-time attorneys served all four counties within the Circuit. In a given year, each lawyer handled around 330 felonies, twice the number of cases recommended by the Georgia Supreme Court for full-time lawyers. Ten years later, when SCHR sued again, conditions were only slightly better.[37]

The second time, Bright got the attention of the federal government. The U.S. Department of Justice intervened in the case and helped force a settlement that doubled the number of public defenders from three to six and mandated training for lawyers who handle juvenile issues. "The children that come into the court are not beyond redemption," Bright said, praising the deal. "They certainly are often charged with very minor things."[38]

Even more important, SCHR's indigent defense lawsuits attracted the attention of state legislators, who could no longer duck complaints that the justice system's failures were giving Georgia a bad name. Local officials who feared costly lawsuits and the potential involvement by federal authorities begged state legislators for relief.

LANDMARK LEGISLATION

THE NEXT STEP WAS to leverage support in the state bar and among concerned voters to open another front: in the policymaking domain. As chief justice of the Georgia Supreme Court, Robert Benham had appointed a committee to study the fragmented manner of appointing lawyers for poor people in Georgia. Once his tenure as chief ended, he asked Justice Norman Fletcher to take over this responsibility.

Fletcher served on the Georgia Supreme Court for fifteen years, including four years as chief justice. Fletcher was born in Fitzgerald, Georgia, once a sundown town that barred freed Black people from making their homes there. Justice Fletcher threw himself into this work for the next two years, helping to bring the state bar and the judiciary together to lobby for legislation. During his speech to the General Assembly in January 2002, Justice Fletcher called representation for the poor in the state "woefully inadequate." The commission produced a report that called the state's programs for serving the poor overwhelmed, and warned that this dire situation raised the risk of innocent people being wrongly convicted.[39]

Privately, Chief Justice Fletcher tried to persuade Republican governor Sonny Perdue and Democratic Speaker of the House Terry Coleman that legal reform was in their mutual self-interest. As chief, Fletcher also made public comments encouraging the governor to seize a leadership role over indigent reform or, at the least, not actively obstruct it. "Frankly, I was trying to help him have a cause too," Fletcher later revealed. He knew the moment was ripe to push for legislation at the beginning of Perdue's term, for he had no major legislative agenda at the time.[40]

Meanwhile, state trial judges objected to unannounced visits by the Commission and the Association of Superior Court Judges vigorously opposed reform. In response, SCHR staffers mobilized the families of incarcerated people to telephone legislators and enlisted the support of civil rights groups. SCHR also organized people to testify before the commission about their experiences in court. They played video testimony of formerly incarcerated people, putting human faces to the state's legal failures.

By this time, SCHR had grown from a shoestring budget and skeletal staff to a significant budget and twenty staff members. Salaries had been lifted to a level that, while still modest, began to stem turnover. The organization now had experienced people dedicated to media outreach who worked closely with other grassroots organizations in the region. SCHR's footprint would continue to expand so litigation could be leveraged for legislative reform even more effectively.[41]

Bright had also established reliable talent pipelines from the nation's finest law schools. Yale Law School's dean, Guido Calabresi, called him the moral center of whatever community he became a part of, inspiring others to "do good rather than doing well." Bright served as a "pied piper," rousing students to take up causes and pursue career paths they otherwise would not have considered. Moreover, his perch as a law professor proved helpful in gaining the media's attention in highlighting the cracks in the criminal justice system.[42]

Testifying before Chief Justice Fletcher's commission, Bright said he watched individuals processed in court "like a hamburger at a fast-food restaurant." "You don't need a bar card to do that." Causing looks of discomfort among the lawyers and judges in attendance, Bright told them the unpleasant truth: judges themselves had failed to live up to *Gideon*'s promise and they "ought to get on the right side of history."

A number of judges opposed reform for threatening older ways and took umbrage at the criticism. To Superior Court Judge Lawton Stephens, "The idea that a judge would intentionally appoint an incompetent attorney is ludicrous." But Bright shot back: "It may be ludicrous, but it happens all the time."

Chief Justice Fletcher's Commission on Indigent Defense issued its report on December 12, 2002. In the name of "fairness and equal justice," the commission's members called on the state to assume full responsibility for paying for indigent defense services and to establish basic standards for the quality of representation. The report found that while 80 percent of people who wind up in Georgia's courts are too poor to afford an attorney, the state "is not providing adequate funding to fulfill the constitutional mandate that all citizens have effective assistance of counsel." Additionally, the commission found that Georgia "lacks a statewide system of accountability of oversight to provide constitutionally adequate assistance of counsel for indigent defendants."

Mass incarceration was overwhelming Georgia's legal institutions. As a result of a fragmented system that operates with little oversight or standards and with insufficient funding, "well more than half (59%) of the inmates of county jails in the state were arrestees awaiting trial," and "a large number of these arrestees are charged with non-violent crimes." By contrast, a system that complied with the guarantee of a constitutional right of counsel would not lock up so many poor people who have not seen a lawyer or had their day in court.

The report cited several of SCHR's lawsuits and pointed to the fact that the indigent defense system was in such crisis that a few counties were contemplating suing the state for more financial resources. The Commission made several recommendations, including moving away from court-appointed systems to a public defender model with lawyers for the poor "subject to direct supervision and mentoring of senior lawyers with experience and interest in criminal defense work." This was a major indictment of the way legal services were actually delivered. Public defenders would be employees of the state but must also enjoy a measure of independence from the state's prosecutorial imperatives.

On April 26, 2003, the General Assembly finally enacted a state law that required the creation of a public defender for every judicial circuit in the state starting in 2005. Governor Perdue signed the landmark bill on May 22, calling it "much needed reform" to "uphold our moral obligation of providing criminal defendants with adequate legal counsel." Even so, Bright kept his foot on the gas because the question of how to finance the statewide system was deferred until the following year. "Nobody fully appreciates just how bad the situation is," he said, knowing that much still had to be worked out. "It's just a real embarrassment to have such a shoddy legal system."[43]

Squabbling over funding soon boiled over. Several legislators opposed committing general funds to paying for public defenders. Instead, a proposal emerged that would try to raise funds for indigent defense through fees on civil lawsuits, bail bonds, and applications seeking the help of a public defender. Some legislators fought over who would control the funds collected. On the very last day of the legislative session, Governor Perdue sent word to his staff to finish the budget without anything for indigent defense.

Chief Justice Fletcher made a public statement urging him to reconsider and call a special session to deal with unfinished business. Governor Perdue did so. During the special session in 2004, after some high stakes haggling, the General Assembly reached a deal to fund the indigent defense system strictly out of court fees and fines rather than the state's general funds. The financing issue had been decided, but the setup remained precarious. The mechanism was almost certainly not going to meet statewide needs, given the state's ongoing arrest and incarceration policies. Local counties would still have to make up the difference.[44]

Besides the question of financing, there were other shortcomings with the new state-wide indigent defender system: questions remained about how well the system would be managed and funded, and there were not adequate safeguards against political interference if public defenders did their jobs a little too well. Bright emphasized the virtues of independence, fearing that "when judges and executives control programs which continually provide deficient representation to the accused, . . . lawyers are being provided to the poor only to create an appearance of legitimacy to a system that lacks fairness."

Still, for the first time in Georgia's history, there would be a public defender's office in each of the state's forty-nine judicial circuits to run parallel with the organization of district attorneys. Public defenders would be picked by local committees and receive a salary comparable to that of district attorneys—a marked difference from the process of appointing lawyers for the poor completely controlled by an elected judge.[45]

Equally important, Georgia law now established standards for performance by court-appointed attorneys and caseloads. It also created a mental health division, an objective for which SCHR and its allies had pressed. And in perhaps the most notable achievement, the indigent defense act established a statewide capital defender for the first time. That office would take responsibility for a case as soon as a prosecutor anywhere in the state filed a notice to seek the death penalty. This change meant that local judges could not simply saddle a person facing the ultimate punishment with an inexperienced attorney. The office would be able to marshal expertise and bring science to bear early in legal proceedings when doing so can make a difference. Racially exclusionary practices and the railroading of overmatched defendants in capital cases became far less likely. And if a prosecutor was still bold enough to engage in abusive tactics, such as the race-based jury strikes in *Snyder*, they could be caught by competent lawyers because they would be there to protect the vulnerable from the get-go.

These changes addressed the kinds of issues that Bright had valiantly litigated in court, client by client, under the Sixth Amendment right to counsel or Fourteenth Amendment. Yet a comprehensive state law could do much more to relieve conditions of unequal justice by creating standards, institutions, and resources.

Pushing an unpopular cause, one described as having "no political constituency," had led to a landmark piece of legislation. For his advocacy on indigent defense reform, the *Daily Report* dubbed Bright "agitator of the year." Although others brokered the deals and shepherded legislation over the finish line, the legal periodical gave Bright credit for his "prodding over the years—some would say unrelenting agitation" in "bringing the issue to the fore." He was "the most implacable and visible crusader for better legal defense for the poor," bringing "a sense of urgency to the fight for reform." With the same "firebrand style" of his youth, he had finally brought a measure of meaningful legal change. That sort of "uncompromising" approach "inspires some and antagonizes others." As the reporter put it, "Not everyone likes him, but no one ignores him."[46]

PART III

DEMOCRACY AND RACE

Foster v. Chatman

FOR THE FIRST TIME, Georgia had an indigent defense system, at least on paper. But funding remained fragile and nettlesome questions of oversight lingered. In some counties, high caseloads remained a serious problem. One Georgia resident facing the death penalty did become a victim of a cash-strapped indigent defense system in transition.

Jamie Weis was accused of murdering an elderly woman named Catherine King during a burglary. For two years, the case against Weis had stalled because the state refused to pay his court-appointed lawyers' bills. Since he was poor and charged with a serious crime, that also meant he sat in jail without bail waiting until the state could sort out these financial questions. In the meantime, his mother, who the defense expected to call as a witness, passed away.

The state also told Weis's lawyers there was no money for experts, even though his lawyers believed that he suffered from mental illness and wanted him examined. Weis tried to commit suicide three times while awaiting trial.

Inadequate resources for the state capital defender's office became a major problem for Weis's case in part because of a different high-profile murder case, that of courthouse gunman Brian Nichols. That single capital trial, which cost more than $ 3.2 million to defend, threatened to bankrupt the fledgling public defense system. Another ominous step was the legislature's decision to divert $30 million raised from court fines and fees from the indigent defense system to the state's general fund.[1]

Rather than grant a delay because of the funding issue, Judge Johnnie Caldwell, Jr., simply removed Weis's experienced lawyers and ordered two public defenders to take over. In response, the public defenders tried to withdraw from the case, noting that they did not usually handle complicated death penalty cases. On top of that, they pointed out that their crushing workload precluded them from preparing for a capital trial—engaging in precisely the sort of ethical resistance to an unequal system that Bright had recommended two decades earlier.

"Why, out of all the cases, is this young man without counsel?" Bright wanted to know. That someone facing the death penalty must "go even one week without a lawyer is unthinkable." Even noted retributivist Robert Blecker, who believed that capital punishment was morally justified, felt that the dilemma was unfair: "Money seems to have become the issue, and that's what's so troubling."[2]

When Bright heard about Weis rotting in jail, he stepped in to lend a hand for free. The system was certainly showing signs of strain, but Bright could not abide Weis becoming a victim of institutional failure. Working with Atlanta attorneys Ed Garland and Don Samuel, Bright and his colleague Sarah Geraghty demanded that the state dismiss all charges for violating Weis's right to a speedy trial. Separately, they sued Judge Caldwell directly, accusing him of violating Weis's Sixth Amendment rights by replacing his experienced lawyers for no other reason than wanting cheaper lawyers. They filed a writ of mandamus against Judge Caldwell himself—a vehicle to try to force an official to comply with a clear legal duty—and described the judge's behavior as "an unprecedented deprivation of counsel in modern times."

Judge Caldwell reacted defiantly: "I guess the Supreme Court will have to earn their money. And I'll try to continue to earn mine. We're going forward with this case until I get told differently."[3]

The lawsuit against Judge Caldwell was ultimately resolved through an agreement to reinstate Weis's original lawyers; in exchange, those lawyers promised not to seek any further continuances. But the funding disputes continued even after a trial date was set, so Weis's lawyers pressed his right to a speedy trial. Just as Amadeo's litigation after Bright was removed from the case gave rise to a landmark right of counsel decision, Jamie Weis's plight—which now encompassed the matter of adequate funding for legal services—offered the state courts an opportunity to ensure equal justice for the poor. Would the Georgia Supreme Court come through again?

In his speedy-trial appeal, Weis argued that the court should dismiss the charges or bar the state from killing him because it was "a travesty of justice" that he had languished in jail awaiting trial for more than three years after the state stopped adequately financing his defense.[4]

At oral argument before the Georgia Supreme Court, Bright argued that the judge had violated "the most fundamental right a defendant has" by interfering with the continuity of representation. "There was not one cent to pay for Jamie Weis's defense," Bright said with exasperation. When Judge Caldwell put a trial date on the calendar despite the state's refusal to pay his lawyers, he "might as well have said, 'Show up in August and see if you can get nine people together and play the New York Yankees.' It would have been just as fair."[5]

Once again, the unresolved tension between money and justice reared its head. Indeed, Justice Hugh Thompson wondered aloud, "Is this the case that will determine whether the state of Georgia can afford the death penalty?" Even a couple of major death penalty cases at the same time could throw the state's finances into turmoil. At that moment, the state's Office of the Capital Defender did not have enough lawyers to defend the seventy pending death cases.[6]

Things got surreal. Justice David Nahmias suggested that lawyers could be forced to defend Weis for free and given an IOU—to be paid sometime in the future. At another point during argument, Justice George Carley reminisced about getting what he considered to be great legal experience decades before as a young attorney representing criminal defendants for nothing.

Without skipping a beat, Bright replied, "Let's have everybody work for free." Instead of an indigent defense system where a person charged with a crime must beg for the resources needed, Bright playfully suggested that the state instead pool the salaries of everyone involved in the criminal justice system—including the judge and prosecutor—making sure the accused is taken care of first, and only afterward paying everyone else responsible for making the system run.[7]

Meanwhile, the Pike County district attorney told the justices that his office should be held blameless for any violation of Weis's speedy trial right because it no longer had any control over funding. Bright blasted that view, stating, "It's the responsibility of the state of Georgia—the entire state of Georgia—to provide representation."

On March 25, 2010, the Georgia Supreme Court rejected Weis's speedy trial claim by a razor-thin 4–3 vote. Alas, rather than acknowledging ongoing defects in the funding of death penalty defense and forcing the state to make tough choices, Justice Harold Melton's opinion denied there was any "systemic breakdown in the public defender system." He acknowledged that funding became "non-existent" after about eleven months. Instead of holding the state accountable for the consequences of funding shortages, however, the majority myopically blamed Weis himself for refusing to cooperate with the overworked lawyers who knew nothing about his case. The court also faulted his original lawyers for filing a mandamus action to try to get reinstated. It was hard not to feel that judges once again were protecting the legal system at the expense of ensuring a fair trial. The state might nickel-and-dime an indigent person charged with a crime, put up a fight if a defendant demanded more resources, and then evade its duty for months or years. If Weis wanted swifter justice, the court seemed to be saying, he should swallow less effective representation.[8]

Justice Hugh Thompson wrote a furious dissent, joined by Justices Carol Hunstein and Robert Benham, saying that "the majority wrongly places the blame for the delay in this case on the defendant." Jailed while awaiting trial for three and a half years "is too long," "presumptively prejudicial," and "compromises Weis's ability to present an adequate defense," they insisted. "The bottom line here is that the state should not be allowed to fully arm its prosecutors while it hamstrings the defense and blames defendant for any resultant delay." Poor people are entitled to a "vigorous defense," just like people of means, Justice Thompson wrote, and the state "cannot shirk this responsibility because it is experiencing budgetary constraints."[9]

Bright decried the setback as "a significant step away from equal justice for all." Judge Caldwell was trying to give Weis "token representation at a perfunctory trial where the outcome would have been a foregone conclusion." As a result, the Georgia Supreme Court had "abdicated its constitutional and moral authority to protect the right to counsel," Bright said.[10]

Weis's team filed a long-shot petition seeking review in the U.S. Supreme Court, arguing that the state's fiscal problems made "a fair trial impossible." Weis "faces not a 'trial,' as that term is understood as a contest between adversaries," his lawyers argued, "but the fate of those thrown to the lions."

But it was not to be. There would be no showdown in the U.S. Supreme Court over whether inadequate funding compromised the right to counsel. A ruling to this effect might have put pressure on state legislatures to fix unequal patterns of representation. Yet it was apparent that while the justices might be willing to tinker with existing constitutional rules and occasionally grant an individual relief, the days of large-scale reform of institutions led by federal judges were long gone.[11]

Bright stayed on the matter when it returned to Pike County for trial, eager to shepherd a man to safety one more time. Weis's defense team filed a stack of pretrial motions, including one that would ensure the defendant was not in a jumpsuit and leg irons before the judge and his peers. "We're all wearing a shirt and tie," Bright insisted, "and this young man will be wearing a shirt and tie too." Once again, every detail had to be observed so his client would be treated with dignity and respect before the law.[12]

But before Weis's trial could take place, Judge Caldwell abruptly resigned in a handwritten note to Governor Perdue, saying that he wanted to spend more time with his grandchildren. An attorney in a case before Caldwell had accused Caldwell of sexual harassment, which had generated an investigation by the state's Judicial Qualifications Commission. The investigation ended when Caldwell promised to step down and never run again to be a judge.[13]

In a second twist, a new judge selected to preside over Weis's trial, Tommy Hankinson, offered to streamline the process after four weeks of questioning jurors. Weis would have to plead guilty to murder. They would then immediately move to sentencing, where the judge would hear both sides and render a verdict instead of allowing a jury to do it. If Weis didn't like the sentence the judge gave him, he would be allowed to withdraw his plea and ask a jury to determine the proper punishment. The district attorney initially objected, noting there was no procedure under state law that allowed such a thing. But the judge responded that he had used the unorthodox process before many times for other defendants.[14]

While it could be risky to waive a jury trial, Bright agreed to this "blind plea" process, feeling that the judge could be trusted and it was like getting two bites at the apple. The unusual proposal seemed to be a cost-saving measure for the county, and, while Bright didn't want to read too much into the unusual protocol, it also seemed to signal which way Hankinson might be leaning.

Over five years after his arrest, and after funding issues threatened to send him to his death with an inadequate defense, Weis finally had his day in court with Bright at his side. During the sentencing hearing, District Attorney Scott Ballard told Judge Hankinson that Weis had "a rotten soul." He could have left King alive and departed, but instead he struck her repeatedly in the head and then shot her. "That speaks volumes of who he is, what he's capable of doing, what it will take to stop him." Weis deserved to be eliminated from society, Ballard argued. Weis had been "homeless, living in the woods," hungry. Ballard told the judge that a life sentence would be "a reward, not a punishment" because "he'll have a level of medical and dental care that many hard-working law-abiding citizens don't have."[15]

Then Bright's turn came. He told Judge Hankinson that Weis was the son of a West Virginia coal miner. His youth had been difficult because he had been rejected by his mother, who ran around "denying she had any children." That led to custody being granted to his grandmother, who abused him. As an adult, Weis suffered from depression and anxiety. He had found steady work but gotten hooked on drugs—including the highly addictive crack cocaine right before the robbery. An expert witness for the defense testified that Weis likely suffered from some brain damage from inhaling gas fumes as a teenager to get high.

"There's no excuse for what happened, there's no justification," Bright told Judge Hankinson. "But Jamie Weis is more than the worst thing he ever did." He was not "beyond redemption," Bright said, and "has shown remorse."

In the end, Judge Hankinson agreed, sparing his life. Weis would spend the rest of his days behind bars. Yet Weis's entire ordeal illustrated the pressing need for societal reflection on the policies of mass incarceration and whether capital punishment still fit among a community's priorities. Weis got the benefit of underinvestment in the justice system only because one judge cut corners in a way that benefited him without undermining the integrity of the outcome. Few others would get so lucky.[16]

Georgia finally had a framework statute for indigent defense that put the state on a better path toward realizing equal justice. Funding the system adequately now had to be among the highest priorities to restore people's faith in the rule of law. It is not enough to create new bureaucracies; lawyers for the poor need resources if the adversary process is going to work. There always seems to be plenty of money for police, judges, probation officers, but never enough for lawyers and experts for poor defendants. If a community is not going to drastically scale back front-end criminal policies, it may be necessary to abolish capital punishment altogether. That would free up more resources for individuals charged with everyday crimes. But as Weis's plight illustrates so poignantly, something has to give. Until a community finds a way to better address the underlying social ills that lead to crime or dial back its carceral priorities, it will be stuck hoping to catch the most egregious errors one by one, while turning a blind eye to the rest.

FOSTER V. CHATMAN

Bright was wrapping up a final moot court session on a late Friday afternoon in Washington, D.C., in October 2015, preparing to argue his third capital case in front of the U.S. Supreme Court. Out of the blue, the Clerk of Court sent a letter to all counsel informing them that they "should expect questions at oral argument on whether certiorari in this case should be directed to the Supreme Court of Georgia or the Superior Court of Butts County, Georgia, and what significance, if any, that determination may have on the Court's resolution of the case." Because oral argument in the appeal had been scheduled for first thing Monday morning, this last-minute communication set off a frenzy of activity. The justices' odd message raised the possibility they might try to dispose of the appeal without getting to the merits of a tough constitutional issue for which Bright was demanding an answer.[17]

His client, Timothy Foster, a Black man, had been sentenced to death by an all-White jury in 1986 for sexually assaulting and killing a White teacher during a burglary. He was eighteen at the time and confessed to the crime. As in *Snyder v. Louisiana*, the issue involved whether the state violated the Equal Protection Clause by removing Black citizens from the jury pool. During jury selection in Floyd County, one African American was excused for cause because a friend was related to Foster. Prosecutors Doug Pullen and Steve Lanier subsequently used their peremptory strikes to remove all four remaining Black jurors.

During sentencing, Foster's lawyers asked jurors to consider his youth and intellectual disability as mitigating factors, as he had tested between 58 and 80 on IQ tests. His girlfriend, who incriminated him, had been in possession of some of the victim's belongings—Foster's lawyers suggested that she or others may have been involved in the crime. Foster had a troubled background. His parents introduced him to drugs as a child. Foster's own father refused to cooperate when lawyers reached out to him for help to save his son's life. "I could always make another child," he shrugged.

During closing argument before the all-White jury on the question of appropriate punishment, District Attorney Lanier did the unthinkable: he openly appealed to Foster's race and poverty, urging the jury to impose the death sentence "to deter other people out there in the projects."

Foster had been tried shortly after the Court decided *Batson* and reflected troubling questions about how the legal rule would be enforced. Under the rules established by that decision, a defense objection that a juror had been excluded because of race forced the state to give a neutral explanation. *Batson* then required the trial judge to make a finding about the prosecutor's true reason for removing that juror. During Foster's trial, prosecutors responded to the new requirement to justify a peremptory strike when challenged by throwing the "kitchen sink" at the trial judge and daring him to find a problem. When challenged, prosecutors gave between eight and twelve separate reasons for excluding the Black jurors.[18]

How would the Supreme Court deal with such a strategy? Would the justices see the prosecutor's answers as an attempt to evade his constitutional obligations or just a legitimate way of making strategic decisions in a criminal case? The sheer number of reasons was suspicious, Bright thought, and seemed geared to obscure racist motivations and overwhelm a judge's capacity to reason carefully through a prosecutor's explanations. Yet rejecting the state's tactics meant restricting prosecutorial discretion, which judges are loath to do, and potentially thrust federal judges into a greater supervisory role after trials are finished.

Foster's attorneys kept him alive long enough for a major break in the case. After the Georgia Supreme Court upheld his conviction in 1988 and the U.S. Supreme Court refused to take his appeal, litigation moved into the postconviction phase. A few years passed as lawyers battled over whether Foster was too intellectually disabled to be executed in the state courts; that issue was finally decided against him in 2000. Bright took over as lead counsel in 2005, as Foster's legal situation grew more desperate. Representing Foster was particularly challenging because of his intellectual limitations.[19]

As with previous cases, like *Horton*, SCHR staff sought access to the prosecution's files in search of anything that might be useful. As previously noted, those files are the state's work product during a person's trial and appeal, but can be inspected by any citizen under the state's open records act once direct litigation ends.[20]

They hit paydirt. In 2006, SCHR attorneys finally obtained access to the notes maintained by prosecutors during Foster's trial. These documents showed that prosecutors kept close track of the race of citizens during jury selection, writing "B" next to each Black person and highlighting the letter next to their names. They also made a separate list of all the prospective Black jurors and ranked them against one another, labeling them "B#1," "B#2," and so on. Other notations of N (for "No") appeared next to all the Black jurors' names. Someone had circled the race of each African American on their jury questionnaires. On a document with notes on the Church of Christ, someone wrote "NO. No Black Church."

It was obvious, then, that prosecutors paid close attention to the race of jurors, but that is not surprising. Lawyers on both sides typically did do so. The real question was whether the notes demonstrated that prosecutors had crossed the line: by removing specific jurors *because of* their race.

But first things first: Foster's lawyers had to find a judge willing to consider the new evidence. A judge in Butts County had rejected Foster's request for a new trial after this evidence came to light, concluding that the issue had been raised too late. The Georgia Supreme Court rejected review without any explanation in 2014. Finally, in 2015, the U.S. Supreme Court agreed to review Foster's trial. Bright felt that Foster had a compelling case of race discrimination if the justices could just find their way to consider the substance of his constitutional argument. But now, on the eve of argument, someone had thrown a wrench into the works by adding a procedural question. It appeared that some of the justices were trying to see if they might be able to send the case back down to the state court system and avoid addressing Foster's equality claim.

Bright worked feverishly over the weekend, reorganizing his notes and massaging new cases and arguments into his presentation. The rest of the SCHR team clicked through electronic databases in a mad hunt for useful precedent.

A PROCEDURAL THICKET

SINCE THE LAST TIME Bright had appeared before the justices, there were two additions to the Court: Sonia Sotomayor and Elena Kagan, both appointees of President Barack Obama. In 2009 Sotomayor became the first Latina on the Supreme Court. She was a former prosecutor in New York City, but unlike some of her colleagues she had trial experience as a federal judge before serving on the prestigious U.S. Court of Appeals for the Second Circuit. Kagan, by contrast, had no judicial experience, but had served as U.S. Solicitor

General and, before that, captained Harvard Law School as dean through a tumultuous period.

On November 2, the day of the argument, Bright delivered his introductory remarks with gusto: "Mr. Chief Justice, and may it please the Court: The prosecutors in this case came to court on the morning of jury selection determined to strike all the black prospective jurors."[21]

That's all that Chief Justice Roberts let Bright get out before cutting him off with a question. "Mr. Bright, maybe you could address first the question we raised Friday. Are we addressing just whether there's arguable merit to the claim or are we addressing the claim on its own merits?"

Bright replied that in past situations where a state's highest court had denied review without explanation, the Supreme Court looked through to "the last reasoned decision," and in this case it would be the state trial judge who wrote a decision denying Foster state habeas relief.

"I really don't understand that," snapped Justice Scalia. "You say we would be reversing the Georgia Supreme Court and all that the Georgia Supreme Court held is that there was no arguable basis for its accepting review." In parsing the various rules, Scalia thought that if the justices returned the case to the state system, it would just be telling the Georgia Supreme Court to accept review. That would mean that the U.S. Supreme Court should not address the substance of Foster's *Batson* claim but give the state's high court another shot at it. Doing so would show great respect for federalism.

But Bright feared such an option. He was ready to argue that, just as in *Snyder*, prosecutors in Foster's case had tried to manufacture an all-White jury. Sending the case back to the Georgia Supreme Court for a do-over would waste judicial resources, given they were all prepared to argue the federal constitutional question. If the state's high court refused to address the merits again, or did so but ruled against Foster, he would be back pleading that the Supreme Court save his client's life. Bright was also wary: the justices might get rid of Foster's appeal and then lose interest later, once the state courts took another crack at the issue. It had certainly happened in the past, and even led to the execution of a person when a chance to do justice slipped away.[22]

Bright wanted to make the most of the moment while he had the justices' attention. He pressed them to reach the substance of Foster's constitutional claim, just as they had done in previous cases. He said that in one past dispute "you had almost an identical situation where you had an intermediate appellate court that had ruled, and you had the North Carolina Supreme Court denied review." There, Justice Blackmun had noted, "We want to end the confusion about this," and the Court ultimately reached and decided the substantive legal question.

Justices Kennedy, Ginsburg, and Alito all proceeded to weigh in on the procedural issues, offering varying takes on what they believed happened in the Georgia courts, and how that might bear on the outcome. Justice Alito asked Bright whether Foster's claim might be barred by the doctrine of *res judicata*—which generally forecloses a party from relitigating an issue that has been decided. If that was the reason the state court gave for rejecting Foster's constitutional claim, then its ruling was based purely on state law and could not be second-guessed by the Supreme Court.

But Bright argued that the justices could not dodge the racial discrimination claim because the habeas court had plainly addressed the claim and rejected it. That meant the issue was properly before the Supreme Court. They shouldn't duck it even if they might want to do so.

Justice Sonia Sotomayor offered a helping hand, asking whether the state habeas court basically did step three of the *Batson* test and accepted the original trial judge's finding there was a race-neutral reason for removing the jurors? Bright agreed. "Yes, that's exactly what the court said."

"So that's a ruling on the merits."

"I think the court said the *Batson* claim is without merit," Bright replied. "That seems like a ruling on the merits to me."

Those present in the chamber were grateful for a moment of levity after the many detours into arcane matters of state and federal procedure. Yet the stakes were deadly serious. Understanding these legal rules in a manner that maximized states' rights would deprive federal courts of the power to remedy violations of the Constitution. By contrast, applying them in a more forgiving fashion would allow federal judges to bring state actors in line, but it might also encourage overly aggressive interventions.

On a Supreme Court that was becoming more conservative, some justices were hunting for any way to avoid making new law to expand constitutional rights. Strategically, Bright had to thread the needle: convince five members of the Court that they would not be doing anything novel in helping his client but rather merely enforcing already established rights, while comforting them that doing so would not interfere with the states' prerogative to control their own courts.

Justice Ginsburg implied she agreed with Justice Sotomayor: the state court "did not apply a res judicata bar." That should mean there was no reason to avoid addressing Foster's claim head on. When Bright looked up at the clock, he noticed that more than half his allotted time had been squandered on procedural issues. He needed to address the justices' concerns, but this was a bad sign.

At last, the Chief signaled that the justices had gotten all they needed on the last-minute issue. Bright launched into Foster's jury selection claim, arguing that "the prosecutors had identified the African Americans by race, they had rated them against each other in case it came down to having to select a black juror."

But the prosecutors blamed the defendant himself for making race an issue, Chief Justice Roberts pointed out, and contended that they were merely "concentrating on the black jurors" because Foster's lawyers had earlier announced they would be making *Batson* challenges.

Bright told the justices that the Floyd County district attorney had a reputation for striking every Black citizen during his criminal cases. The state's argument that it had acted in a race-neutral fashion was belied by the detailed way race was deployed in the documents, Bright argued. "They developed three strike lists. And one of those strike lists was a list headed 'Definite NO's.' These are the people absolutely who are not going to be on this jury."

"There are only six jurors on the list of 'Definite NO's,' and the first five are African-Americans": Bright wanted that detail to sink in. He wanted the justices to realize that it meant the prosecutors had already taken note of the Black jurors and decided they would all have to go. They fabricated the reasons later.

"At the time, Mr. Lanier said they weren't striking the jurors because of race," Chief Justice Roberts observed. "They were striking them because they were women and I guess three out of the four African Americans who were struck were women. How does that affect the analysis?"

The Supreme Court had not yet ruled that excluding jurors based on sex violated the Equal Protection Clause at the time of Foster's trial, Bright conceded, but sex could also be just a "pretext" for "striking on the basis of race."

When the prosecutors' notes surfaced, Lanier denied writing them and claimed that he never relied on the documents to make his strikes. But the "Definite NOs" list showed that prosecutors were lying, Bright explained. At the same time prosecutors implied that Ms. Garrett, a Black woman, would have been acceptable as a juror, their own list indicated she "was never in the running to be on this jury." Of course, when challenged, prosecutors gave a bunch of reasons for excluding her, including that "she's impudent and she doesn't respect the court."

These explanations, Bright went on, "were inconsistent, some were completely incredible, and some of the reasons applied to White jurors" were deemed acceptable by the prosecutors but not applied to Black jurors who said similar things.

Justice Sotomayor wondered what Bright thought about the practice adopted by some courts where they would reject a *Batson* challenge "if they can find one legitimate reason for striking a juror. Do you believe that's an appropriate rule?"

"I would suggest it can't possibly be," Bright replied. For support, he reached for his own victory in *Snyder* and cited Justice Alito's decision back to the justices: any strike motivated in substantial part by race could not be sustained. Bright now tried to leverage the logic of Snyder's victory—one life rescued—for another. "If this Court, as it said so many times, is engaged in unceasing efforts to end racial discrimination in the criminal courts, then strikes motivated by race cannot be tolerable."

Justice Kennedy piped up, focusing on the laundry list of explanations prosecutors gave for striking the Black jurors. How should the Court deal with a situation if some of those are reasonable and some are implausible? "I think the fact that there is a laundry list suggests in and of itself that the Court should scrutinize the reasons very carefully," Bright answered. Otherwise, indulging such a strategy "is going to encourage a party to just give as many reasons as possible and hope that one will be acceptable" regardless of the truth.

Justice Alito mused, "Suppose there's one reason that's a killer reason?" He asked Bright to assume that a juror with several felony convictions worried a prosecutor, and that the juror also behaved anxiously, looking down while answering questions. In that scenario, could a judge find that there was one clearly appropriate justification for a peremptory strike and ignore the rest of the explanations?

Bright admitted, yes, if a judge considered "all the relevant circumstances," that would be fine. But here, "We have an arsenal of smoking guns."

Justice Scalia could take no more. "A lot of those smoking guns were in the original decision by the Georgia courts." His point was that some of Foster's evidence was already known to judges who reviewed his case. What Bright needed to show for a new trial was that "the new smoking guns would tip the scale."

"The new smoking gun tells you that the prosecutor misrepresented facts and gave reasons that were absolutely false, demonstrably false," Bright argued forcefully. He also cautioned that other judges had already been fooled by the lies. The state's strike of Ms. Garrett had been allowed for two reasons: she was a social worker and her cousin had been arrested for drugs. But "she was not a social worker, and secondly, the prosecutor didn't find out until after trial about her cousin's arrest, so it couldn't possibly have been a reason for the strike." These justifications were demonstrably false. As Bright explained, the state had later slapped on extra reasons for striking Black citizens—including dirt on a juror's relative its investigators dug up later. "But you can't just add reasons on into perpetuity."

"Are you saying in answer to Justice Scalia that when you had the notes, the notes cast doubt on some of the prosecutor's justifications?" inquired Justice Ginsburg.

Bright nodded in agreement. "They do that, and that they show misrepresentations to the court, and they show the overarching goal of separating out the African American citizens, treating them differently."

Beth Burton defended the State of Georgia's position and asked the justices to leave Foster's death sentence untouched. He had already had plenty of justice, she implied. After an extended back-and-forth with several members of the Court over the procedural matters, Justice Kagan interjected. "Can I go to the merits?" she asked, looking around at her colleagues before changing the subject. "You have a lot of new information here from these files that suggests that what the prosecutors were doing was looking at the African American prospective jurors as a group, that they basically said, 'We don't want any of these people. Here is the one we want if we really have to take one.'" Such a plan was "the very antithesis of the *Batson* rule," Justice Kagan pointed out. "I'm just going to ask you: Isn't this as clear a *Batson* violation as a court is ever going to see?"

"I don't think it is," Burton responded. The notes "don't undermine any of the findings that were given by the prosecutor in his strikes." She insisted that there was a nondiscriminatory reason for tracking the race of the jurors: to prepare against the defendants' announced *Batson* challenges.

"Was this argument made before your main brief in this case?" Justice Breyer asked. "It was not," Burton admitted.

"So, if that had been his real reason, isn't it a little surprising that he never thought of it or didn't tell anybody until you raise this argument in your main brief?" Chuckles erupted from court watchers who shared Justice Breyer's incredulity.

Justice Breyer turned to the many reasons given for striking the Black jurors. He offered an analogy: "Now if my grandson tells me, 'I don't want to do my homework tonight at 7:00 because I'm just so tired, and besides, I promised my friend I'd play basketball, and besides that, there's a great program on television. And besides that, my stomach is upset, but I want to eat spaghetti. So, he's now given me five different reasons. What do I think of those reasons?"

Burton played along: "Well, they all may be valid, but they all may not be as strong as the first one." Breyer shook his head. "The point is he gave 40 different reasons." The very fact that he gave so many different reasons is problematic and suggested the true reason was being obscured. Hence, Breyer's answer to his grandchild was, "Look, you're not too tired to do your homework."

Justice Ginsburg cut in just as Justice Breyer finished his hypothetical: "Who was responsible for the definite NO list?" The only person deposed was the prosecution's investigator, who could not say, Burton responded.

"There are only three possible choices," Justice Ginsburg persisted: two prosecutors and one investigator. "We know it came from the D.A.'s office," Burton finally acknowledged.

Toward the end of her argument, Burton was asked to return to the procedural question of whether there was an adequate and independent state ground that would foreclose federal review. If the state court's reason is "ambiguous," Justice Breyer stated, "then aren't we required to assume that the judge went on the Federal ground?"

"I actually agree that it's unclear," Burton replied. "Well, that's the end of it, isn't it?" Justice Breyer opened his palms. Justice Alito followed up by inquiring about how Georgia approached res judicata, and Burton acknowledged that "if you have new facts or new evidence, then the court gets to look at the issue and go beyond."

With that, Burton made critical concessions: The Georgia habeas court didn't apply res judicata but instead addressed the merits of Foster's federal constitutional claim. That meant that it didn't rely on state law, and so the justices could, in fact, reach the equality claim.

Justice Kagan tried to close the door on the state's advocate. "That's *exactly* how the decision is framed, right?" It "lists a whole bunch of claims that are procedurally defaulted" but then addresses the *Batson* claim "in a separate section that's with all the other claims that there are merits determinations being made."

It now seemed apparent that the two factions on the Court had coalesced: a more conservative wing, committed to finding ways to restrict access to federal courts and aggressively employ older methods to stay out of criminal matters; and the liberal wing that wished to preserve what remained of precedents concerning racial equality and repel efforts to erect new obstacles to enforcing the Constitution. As Adam Liptak of the *New York Times* observed after the performance, Bright was "not at his best" when reduced to parsing last-minute technical questions. But when it came to crusading about matters of fundamental unfairness, his "elevated, almost preacher-like style" filled the chamber.[23]

The outcome would almost certainly turn on how many justices could stomach ignoring proof of blatant race discrimination.

THE CHIEF KEEPS THE CASE

SIX MONTHS AFTER THE argument, the Supreme Court issued its decision on Foster's appeal. On the morning of May 23, 2016, as Bright prepared to give a commencement address at Yale Law School, he received word that the justices had reached a decision. Chief Justice Roberts announced the ruling from the bench: "We conclude that the prosecution's purportedly race-neutral reasons for striking at least two of the black prospective jurors . . . were pretextual and that the strikes were instead based, in at least substantial part, on racial discrimination." Roberts had felt strongly enough about the stakes of Foster's case that he kept the opinion for himself to write.[24]

Foster won a new trial by a 6–1 vote. Between oral argument and publication of the decision, Justice Scalia had passed away at a resort in West Texas. Calling Bright "a force of nature" and "one of Yale's most intense and brilliant lights," Dean Robert Post congratulated Bright for a legal victory that ensures "defendants will be heard by a jury of their true peers." Attendees of the commencement ceremony gave Bright a standing ovation. During his address, Bright thanked five members of the graduating class for working on Foster's appeal, telling the audience that because of their sacrifices, "there's one less person facing execution in Georgia today," and a legal opinion from Chief Justice Roberts that says "this kind of racial discrimination in striking people from juries will not be tolerated."[25]

Justice Alito provided a seventh vote supporting the reversal of Foster's death sentence, agreeing that Bright had presented enough evidence of a *Batson* violation. Yet he wrote separately to indicate that unlike his colleagues in the majority, he would have returned the case to Georgia's Supreme Court to decide whether Foster was entitled to any remedy, given that that court had said nothing at all the first time around. He would give that court another chance to say whether Foster's claim was procedurally barred. Luckily for the condemned man, Alito's proposal did not carry the day, for it drew a road map that the state court could follow to deny relief. If the Supreme Court had returned the case below without addressing the racial discrimination claim as Justice Alito wanted, and the state court clarified its ruling to say that it was procedurally barred, Foster almost certainly would be dead because of a technicality (and the states' rights policy choice behind it).[26]

Chief Justice Roberts had more to say in his published opinion than in the chamber the day he announced the ruling. In the written decision, he quickly dispensed with the procedural issues that had so consumed oral argument and nearly derailed Foster's shot at a jury trial free of racial discrimination. Not only had the habeas judge reached the merits of the constitutional issue, Chief Justice Roberts indicated, but he also did not make clear that the claim was blocked by res judicata. So, any ambiguity had to be resolved in a forgiving way: there was no jurisdictional problem hearing Foster's new evidence of racial bias.[27]

This aspect of the case affirmed the power of the Supreme Court to address constitutional violations under certain circumstances even when a state's highest court has rejected it. The *Foster* decision brushed back the justices who would have simply deferred to a state court's perfunctory rejection of an appeal or expanded the notion of procedural default. Because Foster's motion for a new trial was based on newly discovered evidence, this part of the ruling is valuable in keeping a lifeline open to correct constitutional errors in the future—especially if that evidence concerns misconduct on the state's part.

Chief Justice Roberts then turned to Foster's equality claim. Right away he quoted *Snyder* for the proposition that the Constitution "forbids striking even a single prospective juror for a discriminatory purpose." As for the new evidence, despite some lingering questions about who authored which documents, "we cannot accept the State's invitation to blind ourselves to their existence." A decisive majority of the justices was "comfortable that all the documents in the file were authored by *someone* in the district attorney's office."

Based on those notes, Chief Justice Roberts found that prosecutors repeatedly lied about their motives in removing Black jurors. Barely able to contain his exasperation, he offered a litany of descriptions for their explanations: they had "no grounding in fact," were "false," "difficult to credit," "not true," "implausible," "not credible," and even "fantastic."

Taking a page out of the *Snyder* opinion, Roberts compared how the prosecutors treated White jurors with how they treated Black jurors as a way of assessing the credibility of their reasons for excluding them. For instance, Lanier told the trial judge that he struck Marilyn Garrett because she was divorced, but "he declined to strike three out of the four prospective White jurors who were also divorced." One of the reasons given for bouncing Eddie Hood was that he had a son around the same age as Foster. "If Darrell Hood's age was the issue, why did the State accept (white) juror Billy Graves, who had a 17-year-old son?," Chief Justice Roberts asked rhetorically. "And why did the State accept (white) juror Martha Duncan, even though she had a 20-year-old son?" Eliminating Hood because of his race "was Lanier's true motivation."

In the end, "the shifting explanations, the misrepresentations of the record, and the persistent focus on race in the prosecution's file" showed that the Georgia prosecutors had acted with discriminatory intent. Embracing Bright's portrayal of what happened, the Court found that the file "demonstrates a concerted effort to keep black prospective jurors off the jury."

Even though these constitutional errors had occurred thirty years ago, the Chief explained that the passage of time did not diminish the severity of the injustice. "Two peremptory strikes on the basis of race are two more than the Constitution allows."

Justice Thomas, the lone dissenter, would have ignored the fresh evidence of prosecutorial misconduct. He would have deferred to the state high court's refusal to consider the new evidence, insisting that states' rights encompassed the power to enforce their own courts' rules. "It is for the Supreme Court of Georgia—not this Court—to decide what new facts suffice to reopen a claim already decided against a state habeas petitioner."[28]

Justice Thomas found the notion that the "newly discovered evidence" could warrant relitigation of Foster's constitutional claim "flabbergasting." He said that the Court "invites state prisoners to go searching for new 'evidence' by demanding the files of prosecutors who long ago convicted them." Instead of appreciating the extraordinary diligence on the part of advocates in uncovering injustice, Thomas saw nothing but unfairness to the state. He would not even acknowledge what Alito did, saying that the probative value of the new documents was "severely limited."[29]

On the merits of the racial bias claim, Linda Greenhouse of the *New York Times* called *Foster v. Chatman* "not just any criminal case," but one that involved a "deep" question: "Does the court mean what it says?" She applauded the outcome for its institutional importance, and deplored Justice Thomas's "strange" and "solitary voice" in dissent.[30]

Once Foster's case returned to the trial court in Rome, Georgia, the state capital defender's office took a page from Bright's playbook, asking the judge either to dismiss the case or, if a retrial went forward, prohibit the prosecutors from seeking the death penalty because of their misconduct. The Floyd County prosecutors opposed these motions, pointing out that the lawyers found to have violated Foster's constitutional rights no longer worked in the office and insisting that the state should not be blocked from pursuing a punishment authorized by the legislature. They noted that retrials had been permitted by Georgia courts even after a *Batson* violation.

At that 2019 hearing about how to proceed, Foster's lawyers put on the stand a former Floyd County prosecutor who confirmed under oath it was "well known in the office that Stephen Lanier would not put a black person on the jury." The one occasion the district attorney allowed a black minister on the jury, that juror was the lone holdout against a death sentence and Lanier vowed never to let that happen again. The former prosecutor also testified that he overheard an argument between Lanier and an investigator during Foster's original trial. The investigator was urging him to put a black person on Foster's jury or it was "going to come back to haunt you." But Lanier would not budge.

This was the first time anyone had, under oath, contradicted the district attorney's testimony as to his jury selection tactics, i.e., that the Black jurors in Foster's trial had been excluded for reasons having nothing to do with race. The assistant district attorney stayed quiet about what he had overheard for over three decades.

Lanier served three straight terms as DA, from 1985 to 1996. After that explosive testimony finally confirming the plan to create an all-White jury for Foster back in 1987, the state capital defender's office negotiated a plea deal where he accepted a term of life without parole.[31]

Despite this favorable resolution for Foster, long-term concerns remained as to whether peremptory strikes do more harm than good. Over the course of his career, Bright twice argued cases before the Supreme Court on *Batson* issues—*Snyder* and *Foster*. That several of his other cases revealed similar problems with discretionary jury strikes and even encountered new strategies by the state to escape detection for race-based strikes suggested that judges tinkering around the edges of problems leave a lot to be desired. Concerns of democratic exclusion and the legitimacy of legal outcomes persist.

For instance, in 2020 the North Carolina Supreme Court frankly acknowledged that it had never once held a prosecutor responsible for striking a single Black juror because of race. On the other hand, that court had found Black defense lawyers responsible for violating the *Batson* rule after striking White jurors. In fact, prosecutors from around the state had even attended a training session instructing how to give judges facially neutral explanations for eliminating African Americans from jury pools. In Cumberland County, prosecutors used a "cheat sheet" for excluding Black jurors and getting away with it. Throughout North Carolina as a whole, the state's high court noted, "prosecutors strike African Americans at double the rate they strike other jurors."[32]

Back in the original *Batson* case, Justice Thurgood Marshall had gone along with the outcome but predicted that racism through peremptory strikes would continue. He was skeptical of the legal framework created, believing that an approach that relied on judges to curb misconduct on a case-by-case basis simply would not solve the problem of racial discrimination. "That goal can be accomplished only by eliminating peremptory challenges entirely," he advised at the time.

As the parade of legal challenges over the last forty years indicates, Justice Marshall was right that the rules left it child's play for lawyers to manipulate the demographics of a jury. For Marshall, tolerating this largely discretionary practice, which varied greatly from state to state, meant learning to live with some amount of racial discrimination. That seemed intolerable. He felt that judges would continue to see not just "outright prevarication" covering up intentional racism, but also reliance on outdated stereotypes when jurors were excluded.[33]

A steadfast commitment to racial equality and a fair trial by a representative jury meant forcing both sides to give up something they might find strategically advantageous. "If the prosecutor's peremptory challenge could be eliminated only at the cost of eliminating the defendant's challenge as well, I do not think that would be too great a price to pay," Justice Marshall believed. But if peremptory strikes cannot be eliminated completely, the number of strikes could surely be drastically reduced to prevent the democracy and equality problems that they pose—this is the position Bright preferred.

Some states have taken note of the continuing problems with peremptory challenges. In 2021, the State of Arizona became the first state to abolish peremptory challenges out of concerns that the practice worsens racial inequities. Instead of looking the other way, judges proved central to this turnabout. Two judges from the state's intermediate court of appeals petitioned the state supreme court to abolish the practice through a rule change, calling the peremptory strike "one of the most obvious sources of racial injustice in the courts." Other jurisdictions have begun studying whether to restrict the number of peremptory strikes or tighten regulation of for-cause exclusions.[34]

EXONERATION

Most of Bright's cases involved clients like Foster who had committed a terrible crime, and the main questions were whether the legal proceedings complied with the Constitution and whether death was appropriate. Eventually, SCHR's efforts helped lead to the exoneration of someone who was actually innocent.

For Bright, a person's guilt or innocence never mattered to his decision to get involved in their case. His radical critique of the state mobilized to kill its own citizens provided sufficient motivation to lend a hand to some desperate soul. Yet he always felt that the crush of poor lawyering, terrible funding of social services and indigent defense, and mounting jurisprudence of dread made it more likely that someone innocent would fall between the cracks. Johnny Lee Gates turned out to be one such person who wound up on death row for a crime he didn't commit.

Gates had been under a death sentence for decades for the 1977 rape, robbery, and murder of nineteen-year-old Katharina Wright, a White woman. Her body was discovered by her husband, an Army service member stationed at Fort Benning. She had been bound by neckties and a bathrobe belt, gagged, and shot in the head. There was also evidence consistent with sexual assault. A substantial amount of cash kept under a mattress was missing.

Gates, who was Black, had been arrested along with two other men for an unrelated robbery. Under severe questioning, he gave a written confession to Wright's murder. He was tried before an all-White jury in Floyd County. Gates's attorney did not call a single witness at trial. Two prosecutors brought the case against Gates: District Attorney William Smith and his assistant, Doug Pullen. Their theory was that Gates dressed up like an employee from the gas company to rob Wright, and then decided to kill her to try to get away with it.[35]

Over the years, George Kendall, Ronald Tabak, and Gary Parker represented Gates. They had nagging doubts about whether he committed the crime. Many details from his statements to the police did not match the physical evidence. His confession stated that he shot the victim on the bed, but she was found in the bathroom. There were discrepancies regarding what he said about the items used to tie up the victim. Gates admitted to dressing up like an employee from the gas company to fix a heater, but no record could be found of a heater in her apartment needing repair. A witness, one of Wright's neighbors, had reported seeing a Black man dressed as a gas company employee, but the description seemed off: instead of 5'9"–5'10" and 170 lbs. as the resident indicated, Gates stood at only 5'5" and weighed closer to 130 lbs. Nevertheless, the neighbor identified Gates in a lineup. Type B blood was found at the scene, but both Gates and Wright had type O blood.

Police found Gates's fingerprint on the victim's apartment heater, but only after they had taken the unusual step of walking him through the entire crime scene. Gates later said that officers instructed him to touch the heater.

Another person confessed to the crime before Gates did—a White man caught fondling Wright's body in the funeral home. But the police stopped pursuing that suspect. Instead, the authorities built a case against Gates. After his conviction, Gates continued to assert his innocence.[36]

It was not until after Gates lost his direct appeals that anyone had an inkling he might have been intellectually disabled. His school records showed that he failed second and seventh grades and spent time in a special education program. He tested 77 on an IQ test when he was held at a Youth Development Center and later tested at 65 as an adult while in prison. Gates's lawyers suspected that he had been pressured into making a false confession by police eager to solve a gruesome crime. Partway through a habeas hearing in 2003 on whether Gates was intellectually disabled, when his attorneys utilized many of the tactics honed by SCHR, both sides reached an agreement to remove the threat of a death sentence.[37]

SCHR attorneys worked closely with the Georgia Innocence Project on Gates's behalf. For years, the state maintained that all evidence from the case had been destroyed. But remarkably, like a scene out of a movie, in 2015 two diligent interns from the Georgia Innocence Project discovered the black ties and velour bathrobe belt used to tie up the victim. These items of evidence were kept in boxes containing the district attorney's old case files.[38]

When they had the items tested for Gates's DNA, there was no match. Based on the fresh forensic evidence, SCHR staff attorneys returned to Muscogee County and filed an extraordinary motion seeking a new trial. After the Supreme Court handed down its decision in *Foster*, Gates's lawyers added a claim alleging racial discrimination during jury selection. They asked a judge to grant them access to the county's old prosecution notes for his case as well as six other capital cases in the late 1970s involving African American defendants. Because Pullen was involved in these cases, and the Supreme Court had ruled in *Foster* that prosecution notes were relevant to jury discrimination claims, the judge granted the motion.[39]

After the prosecution notes were handed over, SCHR staff discovered that what had happened in Foster's case was more widespread than they initially believed: prosecutors in the Chattahoochee Judicial Circuit had routinely labeled prospective White jurors "W" and Black jurors with "B" or "N" when seeking a death sentence against Black defendants. In one case, prosecutors had tallied the race of the final jury panel, with twelve marks in the "white" column and no marks in the "black" column.[40]

In a stunning opinion on January 10, 2019, Judge John Allen ordered that Gates be given a new trial. He began by finding that "prosecutors clearly engaged in systematic exclusion of blacks during jury selection in this case" back in 1977. Agreeing with Gates, Judge Allen said that prosecutors had "identified the black prospective jurors by race in their jury selection notes, singled them out for peremptory strikes, and struck them to try Gates before an all-White jury."[41]

This dramatic exoneration of a wrongly convicted man resulted from creative forms of advocacy inaugurated decades ago by Bright and the first generation of SCHR lawyers—and it all came together like a symphony: proof of racial bias and exclusionary tactics curated over the years, constitutional arguments honed across cases, relentless pursuit of facts. Doing what others felt was infeasible or hopeless had paid off. Gates was not Bright's client, but it brought Bright tremendous satisfaction to see his faith in vigorous representation of the whole person carried on by the next generation of the organization's lawyers.

Judge Allen drew copiously from the record of prosecutorial misconduct gathered by investigators and presented in court by SCHR lawyers. He found the historical evidence of office-wide malfeasance persuasive: "In six of the seven cases, including Gates's case, the prosecutors removed every black prospective juror to secure all-white juries." In the seventh case, a Black defendant faced a jury with one White juror, but prosecutors failed to manufacture an all-White jury only because "the pool of prospective jurors had more Black citizens than the prosecutors had strikes." Across five of the cases, the state exercised peremptory strikes against twenty-seven of twenty-seven African Americans qualified to serve.

In a remarkable section of the opinion, Judge Allen went

beyond the constitutional defects of jury selection and denounced the kinds of arguments made by prosecutors before all-White juries. He found that the "racially charged arguments spanned across multiple cases, including Gates's case." For instance, in Jerome Bowden's case, prosecutors called the defendant, who was Black, a "wild beast" and told jurors it would take "courage" to preserve "this great nation . . . from this man and his like." The jury agreed that Bowden's life was worthless; the state electrocuted him in 1986.

During Gates's original trial, the prosecutor had similarly asked jurors, "Do you feel as free as you did ten years ago?" According to Judge Allen, this was all part of a deliberate strategy by Muscogee County prosecutors who consistently pitted all-White jurors ("us") against Black people on trial ("them") in arguments with powerful "racial overtones."

Judge Allen found this evidence of racial bias across time "overwhelming." Citing Frank Johnson's opinion in *Horton v. Zant*, another of Bright's success stories, he said that "each of the six other cases were tried by one or both of the same prosecutors who tried Gates." At last, the study of racial discrimination in jury strikes first introduced but rejected in William Brooks's case all those years ago had finally been validated by a judge. SCHR lawyers had kept at it, and were finally able to access the prosecutor's notes once the evidence of actual innocence gave them an opening.

For Judge Allen, these unconstitutional practices—race-based peremptory strikes, manufacturing all-White juries, racist arguments in open court—should not be seen in isolation. To the contrary: they were interlocking in nature, just as Bright had insisted all these years. The state's tactics were geared toward making White people fear Black people, overlook legal safeguards, and be more willing to end their lives.

The evidence of prosecutorial misconduct had apparently

shaken the judge and shaped how he viewed Gates's extraordinary motion. This aspect of Judge Allen's decision—his frank grappling with racist practices of the past and his willingness to order the state to turn over relevant evidence—promised to be most useful to people facing execution.

After spending nearly half of his twenty-seven-page opinion recounting the evidence of racial bias, however, Judge Allen indicated that he could not grant relief based on prosecutorial misconduct because of the delay in raising the matter. He clearly wanted the past practice of discrimination publicly documented. But he also wanted his ruling to stand up on appeal. An order for a new trial after so much time had passed would have to survive the gauntlet of rules worsened by the jurisprudence of dread. The exoneration ground was more likely to hold up.

For this reason, Judge Allen granted relief based on the forensic evidence, ruling that it had not been previously available to Gates because it had been lost and could not be tested in time for his original trial. That evidence, whose accuracy the state did not challenge, was "meaningful and exculpatory because it demonstrates that Gates was not the person who bound the victim's hands."

The state appealed its loss on the forensic issue, while Gates cross-appealed on the equality issue. On the very day that much of the state shut down because of COVID-19, the Georgia Supreme Court issued a unanimous decision affirming Judge Allen's order. "Had the newly discovered DNA evidence been available to Gates at the time of his trial," Justice Charles Bethel wrote, "it may well have further undermined the weight and credibility" of the state's "problematic" evidence. Gates was entitled to a new trial.

Although Justice Bethel's opinion technically did not address the equality claim, the justices went out of their way to say that "the record supports the trial court's very troubling findings" about the state's jury selection tactics in capital trials "held in the Chattahoochee Judicial Circuit between 1975 and 1979." Once again, SCHR's approach to cataloguing racism by prosecutors had paid off: that evidence had convinced the state's highest court, and record of it could forever be found in the official reports of its decisions.[42]

Shortly afterward, the district attorney offered a plea deal that credited Gates for time served, which he accepted while maintaining his innocence. On May 15, 2020, after forty-three years in prison, including twenty-six years on death row, Gates walked out of the Muscogee County Jail a free man.[43]

SHOCK THE WORLD

One of the burning questions all these years has been whether activism that emphasizes accuracy, equality, and fairness would merely lead to a more efficient killing machine, as some feared, or whether these tactics could move more people toward abolition of the ultimate punishment. Skeptics have always insisted that abstract arguments over moral desert and deterrence would be enough to win the day and that focusing on details corrodes principles. Others have found that such high-level appeals usually ended in stalemate. In Georgia at least, pragmatic arguments about the actual administration of justice convinced some citizens and civic leaders to turn away from capital punishment.

For his efforts to establish Georgia's statewide public defender system, Justice Fletcher received the Gideon's Promise Award from SCHR. In accepting the award at the organization's annual dinner, Justice Fletcher thanked Bright for an effusive introduction, wryly noting that "it's hard to believe that this is the same Steve Bright who so unmercifully derided all my decisions on the death penalty for fifteen and a half years."[44]

Fletcher continued: "Steve, I am going to shock you, and probably everyone here. For I must now admit that your criticism of my death penalty decisions was justified." Attendees exchanged surprised looks and smiles at every table. "For with wisdom gained over the past ten years," he told the audience, "I am now convinced there is absolutely no justification for continuing to impose the sentence of death in this country." Fletcher said that "it makes no business sense" because "approximately ten percent of all court resources are spent on death penalty cases." Furthermore, "over one hundred and fifty persons on death row have been exonerated, and there can be no doubt that actually innocent persons have been executed in this country."

The former jurist's speech offered potent proof that gradualist strategies could work on those who kept an open mind, adding layers of doubt to precipitate deeper reflection. He acknowledged that wrestling with the principles of equality and fairness in difficult cases helped bring him to the conviction that capital punishment "is morally indefensible." The death penalty "is not applied fairly and consistently," he said. Despite some progress made to improve indigent defense within the state, the realities of these inequities eventually pushed him toward abolition. Sadly, "funding issues, race, and political considerations all too often are factors in decisions of whether to seek the death penalty."

Fletcher was precisely the kind of person you needed to reach if you were interested in major reform: someone who believed in the rule of law, who was open to new information, a pillar of the community. "I choose to stand with those religious leaders who are calling for the abolition of the death penalty," he stated unequivocally. Invoking Justice Blackmun as a model for changing one's views about the death penalty and abandoning the jurisprudence of dread, he called upon others "to quit the tinkering and totally abolish this barbaric system," and thereby join "the vast majority of countries of this world."

A few years later, he elaborated on these themes. Fletcher recalled that when he joined the court, his colleagues warned him, "Steve will argue a lot of points, but his ultimate goal is to abolish the death penalty." Yet the accumulation of flaws uncovered by advocates eroded Justice Fletcher's belief in the possibility of fair and equitable administration of capital punishment. At the same time, it increased Fletcher's certainty that Bright's "disciples" will successfully end the practice in America, "and I hope it's in my lifetime."

Before joining the Georgia Supreme Court, Fletcher had only represented people in minor criminal matters as a small-town lawyer. He had never been involved in a death case. By the end of his first year on the Court, he felt that "we've got to do something to make the system better." Over the years, "we kept making some strides in the right direction," but in his final years he felt closer to "where Justice Blackmun was" on capital punishment toward the end of his tenure. Fletcher cited a few factors that initially held him back from confronting the immorality of the death penalty: the Oklahoma City bombing, followed by the "horrific" acts of terror on 9/11, as well as his potent sense of "sworn duty" to uphold a democratically enacted law if possible.

Now he believed that America was on the brink of practical abolition of capital punishment. Everywhere he saw the signs. "We're finding that in particular younger people on the jury actually are more inclined to give life without parole" in lieu of death sentences. This suggested a shift in public opinion toward valuing life, equality, and fairness.

Fletcher identified a second factor that put abolition within reach: the role of competent counsel. After the creation of a statewide defender's office, prosecutors in Georgia sought death only in seven cases during a single year, and experienced lawyers from the defender's office served as counsel in six of those cases. "None of them received the death penalty, the only one that did was with a private attorney."[45]

Over the years, Fletcher became such a convert to the value of the right to counsel that he came out in favor of the appointment of lawyers for postconviction lawsuits—going beyond what the U.S. Supreme Court has done. Fletcher had a very different reaction than so many other judges to the crush of criminal law cases due to policies of mass incarceration. Other judges were tempted to create new rules or harshly enforce existing ones in response to the sense that the legal system was being overwhelmed. But Fletcher recognized the evidence, so dramatically exposed in his own court, that such a reaction would merely worsen unequal justice because state high courts and even the U.S. Supreme Court were less interested in correcting legal errors. So many of the cases that cried out for review involved unconstitutional behavior that had been unearthed or carefully considered only after a person had lost a direct appeal, where an SCHR attorney or another volunteer had to step in.

But in too many cases, someone will be without legal assistance at their most desperate hour. In 2016, Fletcher lamented the pending execution of William Sallie, who missed a filing deadline in federal court by eight days. Because he did not have an attorney, he had to fend for himself from death row. "Fundamental fairness," Fletcher wrote in an editorial, required that someone in Sallie's position be given a lawyer so he can "defend his life."[46]

One of the cases from his time on Georgia's highest court that haunted Fletcher the most was that of Exzavious Gibson, who was seventeen at the time of his offense and also intellectually disabled. No volunteer lawyer was available, so while postconviction review was theoretically available, he could not realistically use that process to challenge his death sentence. Gibson lost his appeal in the Georgia Supreme Court 4–3. A majority of the justices declined to join the states that give a lawyer to individuals under a death sentence for their first habeas petition.

At the time, Fletcher penned a stinging dissent, arguing that lawyers were indispensable at that stage because courts during post-conviction proceedings found constitutional errors in 46 percent of capital cases. He also argued that the need for counsel "is even greater" after passage of the AEDPA, which imposed strict time limits and harsh rules that a poor person could not be expected to navigate without the help of an attorney. Legal issues not raised at the state court level almost certainly would have to be ignored by federal courts. Justice Leah Ward Sears also dissented, denouncing the majority for expecting "a condemned man, without counsel, to bring his claims for relief in an arcane process that he cannot possibly understand in a court of law that (most likely) will not be able to understand his constitutional concerns."[47]

Fletcher recalled his final years on the court as "a special time in my life" when he was simultaneously engaged in the project of ensuring equal justice and reevaluating his views on the death penalty. He credited Bright for having "played a big part in moving my perspective." Turning quiet for a moment, he said softly, "God has given us some people with such a great desire to right wrongs."

PART IV

INTELLECTUAL DISABILITY

McWilliams v. Dunn

IN THE SPRING OF 2017, Bright prepared to argue his fourth case in the U.S. Supreme Court. This case, *McWilliams v. Dunn*, presented some of the hardest legal and moral issues at the frontier of human rights and American law. Bright's client, James McWilliams, showed signs of brain damage, but an Alabama trial judge refused a request to furnish him with an expert to help him understand the extent of any intellectual impairment.

The timing of this dispute caught the high court and the law in some flux. On the one hand, people have never been more aware of the role that intellectual impairments can play in cognitive function and impulse control—effects that are relevant to culpability as well as appropriate punishment. Judicial decisions had started to reflect newer scientific understandings of disabilities. Yet the controversy also landed in the high court at a moment when jurists on the apex court in this country had become suspicious of technocratic solutions to social problems as well as defense lawyers who might be dragging out cases by litigating endlessly over rights. There may have been some movement in parts of the country toward rethinking War on Crime policies, but as far as the Supreme Court was concerned, efficiency and finality in capital cases were long overdue.

Bright's time in southern courtrooms taught him that race and poverty had far too much of an impact on outcomes in criminal cases. From time to time, another factor reared its head: intellectual disability. The possibility that a client charged with a serious crime might be disabled can complicate an attorney's efforts. Cognitive deficits and ongoing trauma may impede the formation of a healthy and productive relationship between lawyer and client. Special strategies might be necessary to communicate effectively and obtain information essential for a defense. Defendants who exhibit odd behavioral tics or appear impassive may be wrongly perceived by a jury as remorseless or threatening.

Yet uncovering the existence and causes of a disability may be the most effective way to save a person's life. If severe enough, it could absolve a defendant from culpability for a crime and lead to institutionalization. But that is rare. More often, it is simply relevant to the question of appropriate punishment—something that the Supreme Court made clear in its 1989 decision, *Penry v. Lynaugh*. There, Justice O'Connor rejected the argument that the Constitution categorically forbade the execution of intellectually disabled persons, even people like Penry, who had the functional mental age of a seven-year-old child. At the time, the justices hesitated to draw that line because "there are marked variations in the degree of deficit manifested." They simply held that a defendant must have a chance to demonstrate he has suffered abuse or possesses intellectual deficits so that a jury can express its "reasoned moral response" in determining the appropriate punishment.[1]

By refusing to draw a bright line in 1989, the Court left vulnerable individuals at the mercy of the states' competing legal rules. In 2002, the Court finally decided in *Atkins v. Virginia* that execution of an intellectually disabled person is barred by the Eighth Amendment because it constitutes "cruel and unusual punishment." By then, Justice Kennedy's opinion reflected a greater willingness to consult the strong consensus of jurisdictions and medical professionals against killing people with mental deficiencies.

Importantly, the Court recognized that these members of the community "face a special risk of wrongful execution." As Justice Kennedy explained, "There is no evidence they are more likely to engage in criminal conduct than others, but there is abundant evidence that they often act on impulse rather than pursuant to a premeditated plan, and that in group settings they are followers rather than leaders." The point is justice based on proportionality, not vengeance. Moreover, because of their cognitive and behavior impairments, "executing the mentally retarded will not measurably further the goal of deterrence." What we know more about now, Justice Kennedy added, is the increased "possibility of false confessions" that their own lawyers have extreme difficulty rectifying because intellectually disabled clients "may be less able to give meaningful assistance to their counsel and are typically poor witnesses."[2]

Despite articulating what seemed like a sensible constitutional baseline, the justices left it up to each state to craft rules to handle questions of intellectual disability. States often set the bar for determining a valid intellectual disability so high that few can clear it; they compound the problem by refusing to provide experts and other necessary resources to probe and document a person's mental illnesses. For example, Georgia requires that a defendant show that he has an intellectual disability "beyond a reasonable doubt," even though other states use a standard of proof that is easier to meet: "preponderance of the evidence."

In 2015, Georgia euthanized Warren Lee Hill, a Black man with an IQ of 70, through an injection of lethal chemicals. He could not satisfy the state's tough legal standard, even though three experts who originally examined him later changed their minds and testified that he met the criteria. Advocates believe that Texas has sent more intellectually disabled people to death row than any other state and has killed at least fourteen people after applying an unconstitutional standard.[3]

Not surprisingly, the quality of counsel plays a major role in determining who gets screened in for death and who gets screened out. Overworked lawyers for the poor might not perform the background investigation necessary to discover the extent or causes of an impairment. Many don't even know how to do the work. Once a death sentence has been imposed, judges and governors are loath to disturb it even when there is evidence of mental illness. In 2013, the State of Florida executed John Ferguson, a Black man, who suffered from schizophrenia and insisted that he was the Prince of God. Ferguson believed that after death he would rise again and help save America from a Communist plot.[4]

Studies show that race, poverty, and disability often intersect in ways that worsen outcomes. A Death Penalty Information Center study of 131 cases in which death sentences were overturned because of intellectual disability revealed that 80 percent involved racial minorities. Their findings were consistent with other studies showing significant levels of psychiatric, neurological, and cognitive disorders among people on death row. At one point, nearly a third of the people under a death sentence in Mississippi had a verbal IQ below 74.[5]

DONNIE THOMAS

BRIGHT'S VERY FIRST DEATH penalty case involved a mentally ill client. Thomas had been convicted of the gruesome strangulation and murder of a young boy in Atlanta. Thomas's girlfriend, who was also intellectually disabled, told police that he had confessed and showed her the body.[6]

Based on his interactions with his new client, Bright believed Thomas was schizophrenic, but nothing related to his possible mental illness made it into the record. In the courtroom, Thomas rocked back and forth at times and performed a Black Power salute. Once he proved incapable of assisting in his own defense, his original court-appointed attorney seemed to put in as little effort as possible. It was as if Thomas had no lawyer at all: his public defender stopped meeting with him, filed no pretrial motions, and gave an opening argument that took up less than two pages of a transcript. After Thomas was convicted, his lawyer gave a generic argument against the death penalty but presented no evidence to support his plea for mercy.

The first thing Bright, Kendall, and Canan did for Donnie Thomas was to petition the U.S. Supreme Court for review. The justices granted the request and sent the case back down to the Georgia Supreme Court for reconsideration.

Several weeks later, without any input from the attorneys, Georgia's high court simply issued an order reinstating its previous decision upholding Thomas's conviction. When the attorneys petitioned the Supreme Court a second time, the justices showed no more interest. That left only one course of action: trying to persuade a judge to review the record through a postconviction proceeding and grant a writ of habeas corpus if a constitutional error could be found. The odds were slim.[7]

But Bright kept at it because the moment he read Thomas's file, he had been outraged by the quality of lawyering. "If you give a person a bad lawyer at their trial, you've basically rigged the trial," Bright became convinced. "They can't possibly avoid execution if they've got a n'er-do-well lawyer who's not going to investigate, not going to put on mitigation, and not consult with experts." This list of tasks was "the most basic component" of treating an individual fairly.[8]

Bright swore not to make the same mistake. Thomas's team spent countless hours reinvestigating the case, making several trips to Atlanta to meet with their client, his family, and his friends. They even visited the crime scene, something the overworked public defender with hundreds of other cases never bothered to do. Bright came away believing that many of the state's witnesses were compromised by mental illness, intellectual disability, or alcoholism.

Bright contacted Betsy Biben, a forensic and clinical social worker, who worked at PDS. Biben taught the team how to mount a mitigation case: what to look for in their clients' behavior and profile, which kinds of witnesses to hunt down from a client's past, and how to secure the kinds of information that could be persuasive to juries responsible for making life or death decisions.

"Betsy, how do we get deeper into this client and get the stories that we need?" Bright would ask during one of their many conversations on the phone. "How do we get them to talk about the worst experiences of their lives, and then close them up again so they can still function?" Persons accused of committing a serious crime had to be treated with care because they had often themselves been traumatized in the past. Getting "inside of the soul was essential to capital work," Biben explained. Yet it was an incredibly delicate task to get what you needed from another human being without destroying the person on the inside and leaving him useless.[9]

When Thomas's new lawyers arrived for the state habeas hearing, they called fourteen witnesses who painted a vivid picture of Thomas's chaotic upbringing as well as his continuing mental health challenges. Much of the evidence that they gathered could have been easily discovered by a competent lawyer the first time around. Bright and Kendall argued that the jurors in the original trial "knew very little about Mr. Thomas' character and station in life."[10]

Despite years of work on the case, Thomas lost his postconviction challenge all the way up and down the state court system for a second time. Then, in July 1985, a federal judge ordered an evidentiary hearing. After listening to the witnesses, he declared that Thomas's original lawyer had failed to represent his interests competently, thus depriving him of his Sixth Amendment right to counsel. Judge Richard Freedman upheld Thomas's conviction for the crime but set aside his death sentence.

That ruling was affirmed on appeal in 1986. As the Eleventh Circuit panel explained, "No attempt was made to obtain possible mitigation testimony from family members or individuals who knew Thomas from school, work, or the neighborhood." There was no indication that his public defender had made a strategic choice or that Thomas had waived his constitutional rights. Therefore, the attorney's performance violated "prevailing professional norms."[11]

In fact, a little bit of work would have uncovered so much that could have been used to help plead for Thomas's life. Several witnesses could have shown that Thomas was a slow learner as a child and was raised by an alcoholic mother. A psychiatrist could have testified that he was "a pathetically sick youngster who had struggled to succeed in life . . . despite a chaotic home environment and a major mental illness." But Thomas's original lawyer had not even bothered.

Thomas was entitled to be resentenced. As his team prepared to go through all of it again to plead for his life, a surprise letter arrived in the mail. The trial judge saw no need to hold any more proceedings and just sentenced Thomas to life in prison, apparently without objection from the DA. For a single client, Bright had been able to recreate the model of zealous advocacy learned at PDS, where no expense was spared and no stone left unturned. This first major mitigation case offered a template that could be used to save other lives.

Several of Bright's subsequent clients suffered from mental illnesses. Tim Foster tested at a low and borderline IQ level and had adaptive deficits, and his father was intellectually disabled too. Johnny Luke of Alabama was born into a family in which several members had intellectual disabilities. Luke's disabilities were sufficiently severe that even Ed Carnes's own state medical expert agreed he should not be executed.

There were occasional bright spots, more proof that advocacy mattered. In 2001, Bright persuaded Paul Howard, the district attorney of Fulton County, to agree to a sentence of life imprisonment for Kimani Atu Archie, who suffered from paranoid schizophrenia. He believed that government agencies were destabilizing his brain as part of a program called "Experiment X." Archie had killed a police officer after becoming agitated during a traffic stop, the sort of crime that usually led prosecutors to seek capital punishment. He had a previous roadside encounter with police in Florida that turned into a struggle and arrest. But Bright and Ed Garland were able to show that Archie had been previously institutionalized and that he was off his meds at the time of the traffic stop.[12]

Intervening early, getting evidence of a disability in front of a prosecutor before the office got locked into a pro-execution stance, could make the difference between life and death. In Archie's case, a compassionate judge nudged both sets of lawyers toward a resolution of life in prison after serious mental health issues were raised, while giving witnesses affected by the trauma of the crime a full airing during a sentencing hearing. But where prosecutors are hell-bent on killing a person who has committed a crime and judges help speed the proceedings along, the risk of injustice increases.

GEORGIA'S TREATMENT OF INTELLECTUALLY DISABLED OFFENDERS

Based in Atlanta, SCHR staff had long been intimately aware of the state's troubled history of dealing death to people with disabilities. On June 24, 1986, Jerome Bowden—who had been called "a wild beast" by the prosecutor—died in the electric chair. State officials snuffed out his life even though his IQ tested between 59 and 65, well within the range of intellectual disability under Georgia law at the time. Nevertheless, members of the parole board refused clemency and allowed his execution to go forward because they felt he was only "mildly retarded."

Bowden, a twenty-four-year-old Black man, had been fingered by a sixteen-year-old neighbor after being arrested for robbery. No physical evidence linked him to the crime. Bowden signed a confession, but later said that he told detectives what they wanted to hear because they promised it would keep him "from going to the electric chair." His sister said it wasn't possible he understood the incriminating statement he signed because he could barely read and could not count to ten. During Bowden's trial, his lawyer did the right thing by asking the judge to order a psychological evaluation, but the judge denied the request and barred the lawyer from mentioning anything about Bowden's intellectual disability. Little wonder that the jury sentenced him to die.[13]

The year after Bowden's execution, another mentally disabled man, Jerome Holloway, came within hours of losing his life. Holloway, a Black man, had an IQ even lower—49—and according to media reports was known as "the most retarded man on death row."

Holloway had signed a confession taking responsibility for beating to death an elderly neighbor. He had even waived his rights. But while Holloway could sign his name, he could not read or write. He could not even tell time.[14]

A former girlfriend said that Holloway "always did stupid stuff." Once, he put only three lug nuts on a tire and drove the car until the tire fell off. When she broke up with him, saying that "I didn't want him no more," Holloway took her brother's rifle and shot himself through the leg. "Look what I did," he told her, displaying his bloody leg as if it was a sign of his devotion.

Holloway's lawyer sought funds to hire an expert under *Ake v. Oklahoma*, a 1985 Supreme Court case which held that due process required that an indigent defendant be afforded a state-funded psychiatrist to ensure "meaningful access to justice." However, the judge flat-out refused. During his original trial, Holloway tried to plead guilty and the trial judge said, "Obviously, he didn't understand what he was waiving" and "doesn't know his date of birth." Despite expressing doubts about Holloway's ability to understand the legal proceedings, the judge never conducted a hearing to determine whether he was competent and just said, "I think we ought to proceed with the trial."[15]

The lawyer paid out of his own pocket for an evaluation. A psychologist who examined Holloway found that less than 1 percent of the population was intellectually disabled and that Holloway was "in the bottom 10% of that 1%." Holloway had an odd sense of time and place. He believed that Mississippi was the biggest country in the world.

"All he understands is that someone is trying to kill him," SCHR attorney Clive Stafford Smith said on the eve of Holloway's appeal before Georgia's highest court. "He sits in his cell perpetually waiting for someone to come and take him away to be killed." During the argument, Justice Hardy Gregory wondered aloud how intellectually disabled a human being would have to be before the state would rule out the death penalty.[16]

No doubt cognizant of the negative press coverage around the country, the Georgia Supreme Court acted swiftly, issuing an opinion three weeks later. On November 4, 1987, the Court unanimously invalidated Holloway's death sentence. For the first time, that court saw someone who might be too mentally diminished to be killed.

The Georgia Supreme Court ordered an evidentiary hearing to be conducted. Out of fundamental fairness, Holloway was also entitled to "the kind of independent psychiatric assistance" contemplated in *Ake*. The true extent of Holloway's intellectual disability, according to the justices, was critical to "the questions of competency to stand trial, criminal responsibility, and mitigation of sentence." His mental condition "was not merely a 'significant issue,'" Chief Justice Thomas O. Marshall wrote. "It was virtually the *only* issue, at both phases of the trial." The *Atlanta Journal-Constitution* praised the court's decision granting "an independent psychiatric evaluation and a hearing on his competency to stand trial" as "decent and just." The editorial board called on the state legislature "to do more" to ensure that the law keep pace "with our growing knowledge of mental impairments."[17]

Georgia prosecutors, citing their own experts who had examined Holloway, argued that he could be executed legally because he was "only mildly to moderately retarded." After a shocking hearing conducted by Stafford Smith in which Holloway took credit for assassinating Lincoln, JFK, and Reagan, the state's lawyers finally realized the tide had turned. They agreed to spare Holloway's life. It was obvious to everyone in the courtroom that day that he was so mentally impaired he would say or do anything to please. He had little grip on what was happening in court.[18]

Momentum for reform continued to build after Bowden's execution and Holloway's near-death experience. In 1988, Georgia's legislature enacted a law that prohibited the execution of anyone found "guilty but mentally retarded" beyond a reasonable doubt. Indeed, as Justice Kennedy pointed out later in *Atkins v. Virginia*, revulsion at "the Bowden execution and our decision in *Penry*" prompted states across the country to enact laws barring the execution of intellectually disabled people.[19]

At the time, proponents hailed these moves as a progressive step. Afterward, though, people kept falling through the cracks, especially if they had borderline IQs or mental illness. In fact, in over thirty years since Georgia's law was passed, not a single individual who has gone to trial has been able to convince a jury beyond a reasonable doubt that he is sufficiently intellectually disabled to not be killed. This history suggests that, in practice, this approach is not doing enough to protect vulnerable members of the community charged with serious crimes.

Beyond having to meet tough legal thresholds, the nature of the enterprise itself no doubt increases the probability that someone with a mental impairment will wind up on death row. Unlike racist conduct, which can often be detected by observers or learned about from an individual who experiences mistreatment, an intellectual disability can be easily missed until it is too late because people feel shame about it and have learned strategies for coping with their disability and hiding it from others. Someone charged with a crime is usually the least helpful or reliable source of information about a disability. To get to the truth you need experts to evaluate the person and you also must comb through that person's background thoroughly. Anything short of that could leave someone facing a punishment that is not deserved.

SCALING THE MOUNTAIN: MCWILLIAMS'S APPEAL

At the end of 2016, Bright informed his staff that he would be retiring from SCHR. After thirty-five years at the helm of the organization, he planned to devote his energies to full-time teaching. It was time for the next generation of cause lawyers to lead the way.

Yet there was one big case left to put to bed: Bright had sought review in the U.S. Supreme Court on behalf of James McWilliams. On January 13, 2017, the Court granted a writ of certiorari and ordered briefing on the issue of whether the Due Process Clause of the Fourteenth Amendment required the state to give a capital defendant access to an independent expert.

It was fitting, if not inevitable, for Bright to tackle McWilliams's appeal to the U.S. Supreme Court. It brought him full circle on the vulnerability of mentally ill people in the criminal justice system. In Donnie Thomas's case, his lawyer had introduced no evidence of his mental illness even though Thomas was completely out of touch with reality. Since then, Bright and his staff had also seen many instances where court-appointed lawyers did not know how to secure the sophisticated expertise they needed to diagnose mental disorders. Without fail, the state's own experts are going to testify that a person is competent to stand trial and perhaps be executed. Yet a defendant's struggle to challenge the state's evidence is not merely a product of lack of diligence or knowledge: it is also evidence of a structural problem. In most jurisdictions, resources are not readily available to defendants. A defendant must ask an elected judge for funds. Because it is unpopular or may lengthen or complicate a trial, judges often deny requests for experts even when an indigent person's lawyer detects a potential mental disorder.

McWilliams's dilemma illustrated these systemic difficulties.

He had been on death row since the mid-1980s, decades before *Atkins* was decided. As with Thomas, the jury did not get an accurate picture of his mental disorders. His lawyers did what they could to introduce evidence of possible mental illness into the case by putting their client and his mother on the stand. But when the state's expert report emerged at the last minute, the judge refused the defendant's request for his own expert. If McWilliams was indeed intellectually disabled, surely it would be unconstitutional and perhaps even immoral to take his life.

Bright knew that the probability of a victory in the appeal was low. McWilliams's crimes were chilling. On the evening of December 30, 1984, he had entered a convenience store, locked the front doors, and robbed the place. He pushed the clerk working that night, Patricia Reynolds, into the back room, raped her, and then shot her dead. He was captured in Ohio driving a stolen vehicle.[20]

McWilliams was tried in August 1986. It took the jury only an hour to find him guilty. The next day, the jury voted 10–2 to recommend that McWilliams die by electrocution. But some of the records at the hospital where McWilliams was being held never arrived before the jury gave its recommendation. Because of an unusual sentencing process in Alabama at the time, a separate sentencing hearing was later conducted by the trial judge, who had to consider the jury's recommendation but could render his own judgment.

Two days before the sentencing hearing, McWilliams's lawyers received a medical report from Alabama's "Lunacy Commission" that indicated he had "genuine neuropsychological problems" and "cerebral hemisphere dysfunction." This was the same state commission whose experts found McWilliams competent to stand trial. Yet his court-appointed lawyers didn't fully understand what this new medical report meant. They did know that their client had serious head injuries as a child and was currently being treated with psychotropic drugs.

McWilliams's attorney asked for a continuance so he would have adequate time to go through the material that had just been disclosed. The judge was willing to go into a brief recess, but wanted to finish sentencing that day. Appalled, defense counsel tried to withdraw from the case in protest, telling the judge that "the arbitrary position taken by this Court" on the defendant's ability to present mitigating evidence is "unconscionable, resulting in this proceeding being a mockery." He also asked for an expert because he was "not a psychologist or psychiatrist." "Would your Honor have wanted me to file a Motion for Extraordinary Expenses to get someone?"

"I want you to approach with your client please," instructed the judge. He then sentenced McWilliams to die in the electric chair. As far as he was concerned, the case was over.

In his sentencing order issued later, the judge found three aggravating factors favoring death and no mitigating circumstances, concluding that McWilliams was "feigning, faking, and manipulative" during tests administered by the state's doctors. There was evidence in the trial that McWilliams had suffered two head injuries and had visited physicians. The judge found that he "possibly has some degree of organic brain dysfunction," but rejected the possibility that it was a "mitigating circumstance" in support of a life sentence.

Once Bright joined McWilliams's legal team, they petitioned for review in the U.S. Supreme Court. In their brief, the lawyers argued that the Supreme Court's *Ake v. Oklahoma* decision requires a defendant to be furnished with a mental health expert. They complained that the failure to provide McWilliams an expert "who works closely with the defense and independently of the prosecution" left them "unable to present any mitigating evidence."[21]

IS THERE A CLEARLY ESTABLISHED RIGHT TO AN INDEPENDENT EXPERT?

Before the U.S. Supreme Court on April 24, 2017, the questions would soon assume a surreal quality. Unlike Bright's past exchanges with the justices, this time they would spar over whether *Ake*, authored by Justice Marshall in 1985, had "clearly" established a right to independent expert assistance when someone might have an intellectual disability.

The culprit for adding this overlay of abstraction on top of the normal question of what due process required was the AEDPA, which dramatically altered federal law and severely limited the power of federal judges to apply constitutional principles in criminal cases. Enacted by a Republican Congress and signed by Democratic President Bill Clinton, the AEDPA broadly restricted access to the federal courts for all people convicted of a crime. Bright had worked so hard to ensure that the courthouse doors remained open, helping members of Congress to fend off efforts to restrict the writ of habeas corpus. But the Oklahoma City bombing changed everything. Senator Joe Biden, convinced that reform could worsen inequality and unfairness, had earlier helped strip the 1994 Crime Bill of habeas restrictions and pushed for national standards for the quality of counsel. This time, he tried to limit the damage by amending the AEDPA so it would apply only to people detained by the federal government.

But after President Clinton announced on "Larry King Live" that he supported the AEDPA without modifications, Biden lost support for efforts to limit the proposal's reach. In the end, as enacted, the AEDPA imposed a harsh one-year statute of limitations on habeas petitions. The new law also prohibited federal judges from providing relief from a criminal conviction unless it was "contrary to" or resulted from an "unreasonable application of clearly established Federal law as determined by the Supreme Court of the United States." Despite some earlier discussions about exacerbating inequality by closing the courthouse doors, Congress failed to assure competent trial counsel or fund legal assistance for habeas petitions.[22]

Bright felt that these AEDPA conditions inevitably fell hardest on marginalized populations, like the intellectually disabled. That group, more likely to confess to crimes they did not commit, and less likely to be able to help themselves, would consistently lose in what he called "death by lottery." As Bright argued in his scholarship, the byzantine legal rules would trap "people of marginal intelligence, doubtful sanity, and debilitating poverty" while the healthy and comparatively wealthy would cheat death. Because the AEDPA's habeas restrictions were not limited to capital cases, that law also prevented federal judges from addressing constitutional problems in noncapital cases.[23]

In his fourth appearance before the Supreme Court, Bright now had to find a way to navigate this additional layer of procedural obstacles. McWilliams's predicament offered a living testament to the accumulated hurdles created by legislators and judges. It was entirely possible no one would ever know the true extent of his mental condition. No federal judge could grant relief unless Bright could demonstrate that, by the time of McWilliams's trial, he "clearly" had a right to an independent mental health expert. This meant parsing Justice Marshall's *Ake* opinion, a legal text that was a product of compromise, which contained some strong and some equivocal language. McWilliams's fate would thus turn on a legal fiction: that the meaning of the case could be understood and fixed at a moment in time. Even if a constitutional principle made sense, falling on the wrong side of the timeline would mean he would get no expert and lose his life.

No less a person than Alex Kozinski, once a conservative lion of the federal judiciary, has agreed that this temporal restriction of the AEDPA is "cruel, unjust, and unnecessary." It forces judges "to stand by in impotent silence, even though it may appear to us that an innocent person has been convicted." He noted that "not even the Supreme Court may act on what it believes to be a constitutional violation if the issue is raised in a habeas petition as opposed to on direct appeal."[24]

Beyond the legal questions, there was the practical conundrum of getting to a win for a condemned man: Where exactly did philosophical consensus now lie on a Supreme Court that had tilted even more conservative over the years? After holding Scalia's seat open during President Obama's final year in office, the Republican-controlled Senate confirmed Trump's pick, Neil Gorsuch, a jurist from the U.S. Court of Appeals for the Tenth Circuit. Members of the legal conservative movement expressed confidence based on his associations and track record that Gorsuch would help complete the Reagan revolution.

On his last trip to the Supreme Court on behalf of Foster, Bright had been able to peel off Kennedy and Roberts from the rest of the Republican appointees. To prevail this time, he would need to win at least one of their votes or pick up a surprise vote from someone even more reliably conservative. He had gained Justice Alito's support in *Snyder*, but in *Foster,* where the evidence of discrimination was even more plentiful, Alito did not side with the condemned man. Furthermore, McWilliams's appeal was procedurally more complicated than Bright's earlier cases. Foster's appeal had reached the Supreme Court after the denial of state habeas, and McWilliams's case arrived collaterally through federal habeas review. For the first time in the Supreme Court, Bright would have to advocate within the exacting constraints of the AEDPA.

McWilliams's claim was also factually unappealing to most conservatives. The mere fact that a capital case had been moved along expeditiously by the trial judge was not likely to sway these justices to stop an execution, if they felt the proceedings were fair in a general sense. Unlike his other trips to the Supreme Court, here Bright was not alleging jury rigging or the use of race-based peremptory strikes.

Bright readied himself to argue that the judge's rush to punish McWilliams deprived him of a fair trial.

"Mr. Bright?" Chief Justice Roberts gestured toward the podium.

Bright took a deep breath and began: "Thank you, Mr. Chief Justice, and may it please the Court. This Court, in 1985, clearly established in its decision in *Ake v. Oklahoma* that a poor defendant whose mental health or mental issues were a significant factor in the case, is entitled to an expert—"

Justice Anthony Kennedy interrupted him right away: "Suppose we thought that *Ake* was ambiguous on this point."[25]

"Well, as your Honor guessed, we don't think it's ambiguous," Bright responded firmly. "In fact, we think it's quite clear when you look—"

Justice Ruth Bader Ginsburg chimed in. "But we're told here that the prosecution didn't have a partisan expert either, you're asking for something that the prosecution didn't have, an independent expert." She sounded doubtful that the original ruling in *Ake* could be construed to require that the state offer an "independent" expert rather than just furnish some access to someone who already worked for the state. If Ginsburg's vote was in doubt, then McWilliams's fate was really on a knife's edge.

Because of the AEDPA, people now faced the risk of temporal injustice, the possibility of being trapped between moments in the law's development as well as the public's changing sense of morality.

It was no longer sufficient to point to a Supreme Court case. Bright had done that by citing *Ake*. As the piercing questions confirmed, he had to go further and argue that the legal principle was sufficiently obvious to cover McWilliams's situation at the time of his trial rather than what it meant *today*. If he couldn't persuade five justices on this incredibly abstract point about the meaning of that case at a particular moment in time, he would lose. And even if he could do that, he would still lose if five justices decided that *Ake* clearly required only that *some* expert examine an indigent defendant but didn't have to help him prepare a defense, which was what Justice Ginsburg suggested.

Justice Kennedy wanted to know how to think about the fact that a right can be established at one moment in history and then later applications of the right began to expand it. If it became clearer only in the years after Marshall wrote *Ake* that the psychiatrist ought to consult with the defense and not with the prosecution, should the Court say that the basic right was clearly established in that case and was merely later refined, or that *Ake* was ambiguous and any later expansion was "a new right"?

Kennedy's comment suggested he might be sympathetic to the substance of McWilliams's claim, but under the AEDPA McWilliams was not allowed to litigate, much less benefit from, a new right established after his trial.

"We don't think it's ambiguous," Bright answered, sidestepping the trap. He held his ground, insisting that the best reading of *Ake* is that a person on trial for his life clearly has a right to "an independent expert."

But the judge in McWilliams's case had refused to grant him the expert assistance contemplated by Justice Marshall's opinion. The only mental health experts who tested the defendant, and then testified against him at trial, were "state experts," Bright replied.

"What do you mean by 'state experts'?" Chief Justice Roberts inquired. "They all worked for the State hospital," Bright explained.

"So you mean they were paid for work by the state as opposed to working for the prosecution for a particular result in a given case." Chief Justice Roberts was suggesting that the Alabama Lunacy Commission employees weren't "partisan" in the way that Bright was describing them, even if their paychecks were signed by a state employee. If these doctors who examined McWilliams could be deemed sufficiently "independent" in this limited financial sense, he might be willing to let Alabama continue its existing practice and not require anything more. He could then assert that the state was already keeping faith with Justice Marshall's opinion in *Ake*.

Just as the costs of furnishing a defendant with competent lawyers and experts affected how the Georgia Supreme Court addressed Jamie Weis's appeal, so the potential costs of a more robust constitutional right to a medical expert seemed to be influencing how the conservative justices were looking at this case. Keeping a constitutional right thin and easy for a state to comply with was a way to keep costs down.

In response, Bright explained that defendants could never choose their own experts in Alabama. He tried to keep the focus on the accuracy of information before a sentencing body. To do that, he stressed that a mental health expert willing to work with defense attorneys was essential to the adversary process. Otherwise, the state has complete control of scientific information. If all a person is entitled to is an expert not strictly hired by prosecutors, as Chief Justice Roberts suggested, the system couldn't work fairly when a defendant is mentally ill.

Justice Kagan, who had clerked for Justice Marshall, seemed keenly interested in this aspect of his legacy. Offering a close reading of her mentor's decision, she observed, "There's no question that when *Ake* talks about assistance over and over again, it reads like a defense expert. But the question is, did *Ake* really preclude the idea of a completely independent person, independent of both the State and the defense?"

Bright replied that "it did" preclude that "because it described what the expert *was to do*." He wanted to ensure that whatever was ultimately said about *Ake* in this case was realistic, that the right would be of practical use to a poor person on trial.

Justice Kennedy next wanted to explore whether there were any ethical constraints on an independent expert. Could such an expert meet with just the defense team and advise how to approach an issue of mental illness?

"Well, I think the ethical duty is that you can't work both sides of the street," Bright answered. He added that experts who tried to be neutral had a hard time staying that way. Because of the adversarial nature of a criminal trial, "they become experts for one side or the other, usually the prosecution." Bright was urging Justice Kennedy and his colleagues to consider constitutional rights within the legal system as it exists, not as it might be in some ideal sense if we could design it from scratch. And the most realistic perspective on the value of expertise is one grounded in a conception of a trial with clashing interests: the state which is committed to ending life and the defense which is desperately seeking to preserve life.

In the real world, the state had experts on call, and defendants should also be given access to their own set of experts. In jurisdictions with a robust public defender's office, medical expertise and other necessary resources are institutionalized within an existing program. McWilliams's case, which occurred in a place without a public defender's office, raised the question of the bare minimum we want to tolerate as a matter of basic fairness in jurisdictions still stuck with the court-assigned or contract system of representation.

Chief Justice Roberts interrupted, saying that the term "assistance" in the *Ake* opinion could mean just "diagnosis" rather than "partisan in helping shape the defense." In that case, it might be possible to say that McWilliams already got everything he was entitled to have when the state's doctors examined him.

Bright shook his head. It simply made no sense to say that the state and the defense could share experts. He argued that Justice Marshall's opinion contemplated an expert who could work more closely with a defendant, someone involved in "gathering information, organizing information, meeting with the defense about how this can be used in the defense of the case, choosing among viable defenses."

Justice Sotomayor underscored this point. What was at stake was the kind of aid to which "a defendant is entitled to mount a viable defense, correct?" The court-appointed expert employed by the state could very easily provide a lot of information that is completely irrelevant to one's defense. She emphasized that McWilliams had "a viable claim that organic brain injury exists," and that his attorneys pleaded with the judge that they needed assistance in determining the degree of his impairment.

Chief Justice Roberts then asked Bright's reaction to what Professor Wayne LaFave had written in a legal treatise about Justice Marshall's handiwork: "*Ake* appears to have been written so as to be deliberately ambiguous on this point, leaving the issue open for future consideration."[26]

"So, your position has to be that the LaFave treatise is wrong?" Chief Justice Roberts asked. "Well, I have the greatest respect for Professor LaFave," Bright replied, "but like lower courts, professors make mistakes too."

Chief Justice Roberts sounded as though he had made up his mind. "Well, they do, but your position has to be that LaFave made a mistake, the Fifth Circuit made a mistake, eight state courts made a mistake." The fact that so many judges had already reviewed McWilliams's case and found no major error seemed to satisfy him.

"I think whether a proposition is clearly established begins and ends with this Court," Bright reminded. The Supreme Court was under no obligation to defer to any other body on the meaning of the U.S. Constitution or its own legal precedent. He also said that thirty years had passed since *Ake* and that "of course" there would be judges and scholars who differed. "But I would point out the weight of the authority is certainly on our side."

Justice Alito then said during a lengthy exchange that he did not see "how an expert who is chosen by the court and paid by the court can ever function" on a defendant's behalf as Bright described. "One thing that is perfectly clear from the opinion in *Ake* is that the court will pick one expert and that's it; the defense has to live with it."

With his only set of questions, Justice Breyer threw another potential legal complication into the mix: the possibility that McWilliams's due process claim had been defaulted long ago. The rules of appellate procedure require that a person raise a legal issue at the earliest opportunity to do so or else it was deemed waived. "Did the defendant ask for an expert?" Breyer could find only record of a clear request for a continuance. If McWilliams's original lawyers had not clearly invoked his constitutional right all those years ago, then the *Ake* issue would not have been preserved. That might be a different reason to rule against McWilliams and never reach the merits of his due process claim.

Bright answered that you could almost picture McWilliams's lawyer "on bended knee" begging for help. The only kind of assistance that made sense at that moment was that of a mental health professional. Moreover, every court who reviewed this case had treated the *Ake* claim as "crisply and clearly presented."

Justice Sotomayor pointed to the place in the record where McWilliams's lawyers pleaded with the trial judge, "I needed to have somebody look at these records who understood them, who could interpret them for me." That sounded like a request for medical expertise.

Right before Bright's time expired, the newest member of the Court asked a question. Justice Gorsuch wanted Bright to confront the possibility that vindicating McWilliams's right to an expert would open the floodgates to endless requests for experts. "Where's the stopping point? Is it just psychiatry? Would we also have to apply the same rule in other kinds of medicine perhaps, forensic science?" Gorsuch was an avowed textualist and originalist when it came to interpreting the Constitution. His line of questioning implied there could be another way of limiting what due process means—and ruling against McWilliams. Perhaps by relying on "common law history," the justices should conclude that "our tradition" leaves it with the courts to appoint a neutral expert of its own choosing" and nothing more. If so, McWilliams's request for his own mental health expert would go too far. He added that experts "cost so very much."[27]

Justice Gorsuch seemed to have both historical and practical objections to Bright's position. That a right to expertise would impose additional costs on the state sounded like a reason to keep the right to expertise sharply limited. A state could always choose to provide more, but poorer states would not be forced to do so. If Gorsuch had this much trouble imagining that due process encompassed an independent mental health expert to help an indigent person, then surely he would have even more trouble concluding that such a right was "clearly established."

Then it was time for Andrew Brashear's presentation on behalf of the State of Alabama. Justice Ginsburg finally seemed to show her cards. She said that the word "assistance" as the justices have used it the most often means that "the defendant is entitled to assistance of counsel." In that context, "assistance doesn't mean neutral." An analogy to the assistance of an expert would make sense. She said that "those at least are clues that what the decision writer had in mind was assisting the defense, just as a lawyer assists the defense."

Justice Kagan added, "I started counting up the word 'assist' in this opinion and, frankly, I lost track. Every time this opinion talks about this, it talks about assisting the defense and assisting the defendant, including to cross-examine the prosecution."

In an aggressive verbal encounter with Brashear, Breyer signaled that he believed *Ake* entitled the accused to an expert that would actively assist to prepare and present a defense, and "this defendant certainly did not get that help."

Justice Kennedy gave Brashear the same question about legal meaning over time he had asked Bright. He got this response: "This Court has said that you can't extend precedent in the context of federal habeas." In Brashear's view, Bright wanted this Court to "extend the actual holding of *Ake* to embrace this new right that says that a neutral expert is insufficient." That went beyond what the case required in 1986, he insisted.

On rebuttal, Bright underscored the stakes. He knew he had to thread the needle by suggesting that deciding the appeal in his client's favor would be meaningful for him and others but would not radically transform the legal system, or else he would not get the votes he needed. Bright stressed that vindicating the right to an expert wouldn't magically change a poor person's underdog status in court. Ruling for McWilliams "certainly doesn't put the defense in an equal position with the prosecutor, not by a long shot, but it at least gives the defense a shot, at least gives them one competent mental health expert that they can talk to, understand what the issues are, present them as best they can."

The oral argument was about as rough as one might have predicted given three factors: the state of the law closing the door on habeas corpus, the ideological tilt of the Court against a defendant's rights, and the fact that it was a death case. Finally, as Adam Liptak of the *New York Times* later observed about the oral argument that day, the "AEDPA requires you to do a lot of dancing."[28]

After the argument, Bright regretted not giving Gorsuch a better answer, even though he had been pressed for time. He thought he should have noted that in Gorsuch's home state of Colorado, mental experts are freely available to public defenders who represent people threatened with capital punishment. But such resources are not available to people like McWilliams who have the misfortune of being tried in Alabama, where experts are under the state's lock and key and poor people must beg judges for what they need to put on a defense. Of course, this would not have been a direct answer to his question, which was framed as what due process required as a matter of history and tradition rather than what would be most effective.[29]

By the end, Bright felt that Justices Sotomayor, Kagan, Breyer, and Ginsburg would settle back into his camp. Yet it sounded as though he had lost Justices Alito and Gorsuch, and probably the Chief too. He had no shot at Thomas, who did not ask a single question during oral argument. If all four voted against McWilliams, then everything would come down to Justice Kennedy.

KEEPING FAITH

On June 19, 2017, eight weeks after oral argument, the Supreme Court issued its decision in McWilliams's appeal. Justice Breyer announced the outcome from the bench. To the extent that the Alabama court rejected McWilliams's due process claim because the state's medical expert had already examined him, "that reasoning of the Court is incorrect." Because the state failed to give him expertise that the defense requested, its "provision of mental health assistance fell short of what *Ake* requires."[30]

By the closest of margins, 5–4, Bright's arguments about fundamental fairness had prevailed again. A majority of the justices agreed that *Ake* had articulated a clearly established right to an independent mental health expert. Justice Kennedy had sided with the liberals, providing the crucial fifth vote. Every other Republican appointee would have closed the book on McWilliams's case and let the state proceed with the execution despite the evidence of brain damage.

The published decision explained the Court's rationale in greater detail. In an opinion authored by Justice Breyer, the Court held that an indigent defendant must be afforded "access to a mental health expert who is sufficiently available to the defense and independent from the prosecution." In parsing the original *Ake* decision, Justice Breyer emphasized that it had guaranteed "meaningful access to justice." If the mental condition of the person on trial becomes an issue, the defendant is entitled to the assistance of an expert who can "effectively" conduct an appropriate examination and assist in the "evaluation, preparation, and presentation of the defense."[31]

Justice Breyer observed that "the simplest way for a state to meet this standard may be to provide a qualified expert retained specifically for the defense team," an approach adopted by "the overwhelming majority of jurisdictions." But the state's doctor had merely examined McWilliams and furnished reports, and neither the doctor nor any other expert assisted the defense in preparing to examine witnesses or testified at the sentencing hearing on McWilliams's behalf.

The most difficult hurdles had been overcome: Bright's reading of *Ake* had prevailed. If that obligation had been met at his original trial, Breyer wrote, "McWilliams might have been able to alter the judge's perception of the case." But there was bad news too. While implying that a mental health expert could have made a difference in the outcome of the McWilliams case, Breyer did not come out and say this definitively, perhaps as the price for getting that fifth vote.

Many people do not realize that it is not enough for a court to identify a constitutional error in a criminal case; a conviction or sentence will be overturned only if it can further be established that the error reasonably altered the outcome—in legal parlance, that the error "prejudiced" a defendant. It might sound odd to the layperson that the state could violate your rights and that you might have no recourse, but this is an old rule that has long been applied to most legal errors. So McWilliams was not yet guaranteed a retrial; he had to show that the denial of a mental health expert had probably changed the outcome—i.e., that he might not have been sentenced to death.

Leaving this question open meant that when the case returned to the Eleventh Circuit, its judges would get a chance to decide whether the denial of McWilliams's right under *Ake* actually harmed him. If that court said no, and the Supreme Court refused to get involved again, his execution would be back on. The first time around, the Eleventh Circuit had rejected an appeal in cursory fashion. So Breyer's ruling was an important victory on the law, but the situation remained precarious for McWilliams, whose life still hung in the balance.

Justice Alito wrote a scathing dissent, quoting LaFave's treatise no less than three times for the proposition that *Ake* was ambiguous, and insisting that the constitutional right had not been "clearly established." Alito dwelled on the speed of McWilliams's trial not as a reason to be concerned, but rather as confirmation that giving him an expert would not have made any difference in the outcome. For the four dissenters, someone who committed a brutal slaying had already received all the process to which he was entitled. Giving McWilliams an expert and another hearing now, after all these years, was a waste of time.

Once the case returned below to the federal circuit court, judges on that court had to decide whether the violation of McWilliams's constitutional rights actually made a difference in the outcome. The Eleventh Circuit decided that the denial of an expert in a death penalty case was "a structural error" rather than a run-of-the-mill mistake. "Like the denial of counsel, the *Ake* error infected the entire sentencing hearing from beginning to end," Judge Gerald Tjoflat wrote on behalf of the three-judge panel. That grievous legal error prevented McWilliams from presenting "any meaningful evidence" based on his mental health or challenging the state's own experts. Prejudice—or harm to McWilliams's case—flowing from the violation of his constitutional right must therefore be presumed.[32]

After losing in the Eleventh Circuit, the state wanted to appeal to the Supreme Court. But the attorney general's lawyers failed to file a timely motion to stay the mandate, a legal order that dictates which court has jurisdiction over a case. Once the mandate returned below, the state was obliged to comply with the Constitution. At that point, instead of giving McWilliams the expert he was due, the local district attorney agreed to a sentence of life without parole. Thirty-three years after he was sent to death row, the long fight was over. McWilliams was permitted to live out the rest of his natural life in prison.

If we could plot the outcome in McWilliams's case in historical time, it might represent just another mark in the long arc towards ever-harsher punishment. Yet with the passage of even more time it might instead come to represent a notable point in the ebb of such destructive politics, an opening that permits a more humane sensibility to emerge. Much will depend on how advocates take advantage of the ruling, the kinds of intellectual impairments that continue to be uncovered, and how the public reacts to such revelations.

As McWilliams's odyssey illustrates, it takes incredible, painstaking efforts to vindicate one's rights in a criminal trial, even to get small changes. To truly protect the intellectually disabled more predictably, legal reforms are necessary. Policymakers should be guided by the objective of assuring an accurate and humane outcome rather than being consumed by the theoretical possibility someone might game the system to elude the executioner. Perhaps the most valuable change is for outlier jurisdictions like Georgia, Arizona, Colorado, and Florida to lower the standard for proving an intellectual disability by a "preponderance of the evidence," which is the dominant approach around the country. Alternatively, states could use a slightly tougher standard when a defendant wants to avoid a trial, but an easier test to trigger merciful sentencing decisions, as Oklahoma and North Carolina do.[33]

Another promising approach would rule out capital punishment based on specific diagnoses. In recent years, Ohio and Kentucky have prohibited the death penalty for anyone with active symptoms and a preexisting diagnosis of one or more of the following serious mental disorders: schizophrenia, schizoaffective disorder, bipolar disorder, or delusional disorder. In these states, defense lawyers would move to bar capital punishment within 120 days of trial if they believe their client had a qualifying condition; they would have a chance to present evidence and invoke the aid of experts under *Ake*, and the judge would render a decision.

There are some downsides to this approach. The requirement that a defendant already have a diagnosis is intended to prevent someone from gaming the system, but it still overlooks vulnerable people with serious undiagnosed disorders. These list-type approaches to excluding certain people from execution could be expanded, so that ongoing diagnoses of a serious mental illness would qualify. Otherwise, these laws remain in tension with cases like *Ake*, which presume that due process requires punishment to take account of ongoing intellectual deficits.

For Bright, nothing less than full public defender services, with mental health experts budgeted and placed beyond the control of tight-fisted judges and hostile prosecutors, will give poor people struggling with intellectual disabilities a fair shake. Under such structural conditions, he has faith that when "presentation of all the facts" is possible, a humane resolution can take place within the adversary system, whether it is an impartial jury that does the right thing or a prosecutor who offers a humane plea deal. But this would require political solutions in many jurisdictions because the Court has declined to require public defenders as the sole method for safeguarding the right to counsel.[34]

In the meantime, *McWilliams v. Dunn* offers a valuable weapon in the arsenal for advocates of disabled people in jurisdictions without a public defender system or where funding for mental health experts must still be approved by judges or other state officials. For people on death row who never got a hearing or a mental health expert—a continuing possibility due to disparities in funding and uneven lawyering—the decision gives them another shot at life. And for those who might face severe punishment in the future, attorneys can demand an expert who is not beholden to prosecutors and will look at the scientific evidence with a client's best interests in mind. In close cases, especially where someone has a borderline IQ and some degree of impairment, it could be the intervention that saves a life.

EPILOGUE

By the time Steve Bright returned to his family in Kentucky, he had undergone a remarkable transformation. A country boy had turned into a national spokesman for poor people and racial minorities. Bright once yearned to become like one of the progressive politicians he admired in his youth. Instead, his destiny lay in nontraditional politics and rebellious lawyering; he ultimately emerged from his legal battles as one of America's "most visible and eloquent" critics of capital punishment.[1]

As for the rest of us, we are a work in progress. We now have a vocabulary to describe what the nation has gone through over the last half century. The country is in the midst of clawing its way out of the devastating politics of mass incarceration, still searching for redemptive forms of justice. Ending the Vietnam War did not yield a generous reinvestment in society, as the most prominent proponents of peace and reconciliation had hoped. Instead, international conflicts raged on in new guises, while war was brought home against a host of common criminals and social outcasts. The generation that once aspired to lead a humanitarian revolution found themselves having to fight a mostly rearguard action.

Bright's part in this search for social transformation entailed becoming an advocate for the poor. Yet it turned out to be an epic campaign for equality and fairness in the criminal justice system that involved many allies and adversaries, forward-looking strategies, and the inventive use of resources. It became a struggle to turn the tide against political tendencies that threatened to swallow up everything else: social priorities, the economy, family relations. As with any war, even metaphorical ones, there were casualties to be tallied. Countless families, both those of victims as well as perpetrators, have been affected forever.

Fear of violent crime led to record numbers of individuals incarcerated in the United States and expanded use of capital punishment. If Louisiana, Georgia, and Alabama were countries, all three would have the highest incarceration rates in the world. Georgia, from which two of Bright's Supreme Court cases arose, continues to incarcerate just shy of 1,000 per 100,000 people. The state's rate of incarceration rose significantly through the 1980s and '90s and started to level off by 2000, beginning a slight downward trend. Bright's other two Supreme Court cases came from Louisiana and Alabama, which have experienced similar incarceration arcs of sharp incline followed by some modest decline. Pretrial detention and probation policies continue to keep people under some type of confinement, surveillance, or supervision for longer than they might otherwise need to be.

Incarceration rates and death penalty rates have often moved in tandem, as the number of new death sentences jumped sharply after the Supreme Court's 1976 *Gregg* ruling right before Bright's fateful decision to relocate to Georgia, and the number peaked at the close of the 1990s, when Americans were sending more than three hundred people each year to death row. Since then, the number of death sentences has declined steadily just as incarceration rates overall have declined slightly. Between 2015 and 2018, there have been fifty or fewer additions to the population of condemned each year.[2]

War on Crime politics has also left behind a jurisprudence of dread represented in layers of judge-made rules, legal concepts, and statutes disfigured by carceral politics. While we have begun to reconsider some of the ideas and attitudes prevalent during these decades, much of the legal infrastructure has not been dismantled. Failure to reverse the ways that the law enables the War on Crime will rob the historical moment of its promise.

None of this is to suggest that all is or was ever lost: far from it. Even in the worst of times, progress can be detected if you know where to look. As historian Sara Mayeux has documented, the battle over indigent defense has pitted two aspects of legal liberalism against each other: the associational strain, which privileges private solutions to social problems, and the public servant model, which favors the creation of new bureaucracies. Mayeux points to the consolidation of elite sentiment after the *Gideon* decision in favor of the second view, albeit incompletely, and her story ends in the 1970s. Bright's story picks up where Mayeux's account leaves off. He helped breathe life into that Supreme Court ruling promising the right to counsel through his writings, litigation strategies, and political activism. His efforts documented the effects of mass incarceration, exposed the flaws of indigent defense systems in the Deep South, and facilitated the emergence of political support for legal change.[3]

Most of the successes of the public defender movement came during the Cold War period, as elites wanted to draw sharper distinctions between America as a rights-based society and the totalitarian community represented by the Soviet Union. That urge faded with the collapse of a bipolar world. War on Crime politics may have blunted the public defender movement in the final decades of the twentieth century because so many became intensely invested in criminal justice systems with asymmetrical rules and resources. And yet, paradoxically, some elites who were committed to swift and sure executions could still be swayed to improve the quality of representation. Judges also started to give legal concepts such as equality and fairness more bite, after horrifying instances of local injustice shamed elected officials hoping to turn the page on their state's racist past. One could detect a desire to be better, to do more to ensure equal justice.

Bright played a critical role in describing what actually happens inside "the machinery of death." Through his cases, he and his colleagues shined a light on local officials rigging juries, prosecutors blocking citizens from serving on juries and making racist arguments about the individuals being punished, and judges rushing defendants to prison or the executioner's chamber.

These legal controversies, in turn, created an opening to push for more public defenders in tough-on-crime jurisdictions like Georgia. Trained as a public defender, Bright found himself in the right place at the right time to both perceive the weaknesses of the associational model of indigent defense and exploit favorable conditions to generate momentum for legal change. Bright's experience offers a welcome lesson that even in a tough-on-crime jurisdiction, structural reform is possible. While geographic inequalities persist and implementation concerns remain, the dream of equal justice survives.

After a period of trial and error, Bright discovered an approach that resonated with people who harbored doubts about policies based on vengeance. He helped unleash an insurgent discourse of dignity, fairness, and equality one case at a time, one human being at a time, one jurisdiction at a time.

The success of Bright's methods can be traced not merely in the lives saved or legal rules marginally improved but also in the altered political climate. Bright was certainly not the only one in the trenches. But his methods were distinctive, doggedly implemented, and, at times, surprisingly effective. At first, those who battled against the politics of mass incarceration made desperate pleas to an unreceptive audience. Gradually, strategies that prioritized harm reduction exposed incidents of individual mistreatment as well as systemic problems. From *Amadeo* to *Snyder*, and from *Foster* to *McWilliams*, we learn that review by federal courts remains a crucial safeguard of the right to a fair trial, but also that much more work needs to be done to restructure criminal policy so that guardians of the legal system can resist the immense pressure on them to betray fundamental values.

The drumbeat for change, once faint, has grown more audible. We do not live in the same world confronted by early opponents of mass incarceration, but one where mercy and growth have a better chance to flourish. Today Americans are actively reconsidering policing and punishment practices along a wide spectrum. Decriminalization of minor drug offenses has been taking place at one end of that continuum, while concerns about fairness and equality have led many to reject the death penalty even for heinous crimes. We do not know exactly how this conversation will turn out, but the number of people from all walks of life willing to talk about the effects of anticrime policies on their families has been a boon for reform. We can be sure that we could not have reached this point at all without cause lawyers like Steve Bright.

After a long exile, death penalty abolitionists have increased their numbers and started to turn the tide. Once he beat back a recall effort, Los Angeles County District Attorney George Gascón issued a Special Directive to all deputy district attorneys on December 7, 2020, instructing them that "a sentence of death is never an appropriate resolution in any case." In the introduction of this extraordinary memo he explained: "Racism and the death penalty are inextricably intertwined." Gascón's very first citation was to an article by Steve Bright.[4]

Even more impressive has been the number of states whose citizens have turned away from killing their own. On March 24, 2021, Governor Ralph Northam signed a bill that renounced the death penalty, marking Virginia as the twenty-third state to do so. That event represented an important repudiation of a central plank of the War on Crime. It is also historically noteworthy because the very first execution was carried out by the Jamestown colony in 1608 and from that moment on Virginia extinguished more lives than any other state in the Union. In the modern era, Virginia had executed 113 people since 1976, second only to Texas at 570 people and counting. We "can't sentence people to that ultimate punishment knowing the system doesn't work the same for everyone," Northam explained when he helped close the book on that chapter of his state's history.[5]

Virginia's decision to end a punishment practice that its citizens had long cherished offers potent proof that Americans' conscience can be pricked through a gritty form of humanistic resistance. Concerns of equality and fairness did not just end up legitimating the system so it could operate more efficiently, but instead led to a renunciation of the discredited practice itself. Scott Surovell, a Democratic state senator and sponsor of the legislation, said, "You're more likely to get charged with a capital crime and found guilty of one if you're a minority, suffer from mental illness, you're low-income, you've got diminished intellectual capacity, or if you kill a White person and you're not White." Mike Mullin, a Democrat and former prosecutor, sponsored the House version of the bill. Like his counterpart in the Virginia senate, Mullin advocated abolition on the grounds that the death penalty "is immoral, racially biased, ineffective, and costly." These arguments about punishment practices in action did not supplant more abstract concerns, but rather added to their collective moral weight—even lending more urgency to humanitarian appeals.[6]

In fact, we are closer now to another abolitionist moment than we have been since the early 1970s. One might even say that in most parts of the country, capital punishment has been practically eliminated. Fewer prosecutors demand death, knowing that the stable of experienced lawyers for the condemned has increased. Greater awareness of how juries are created has led to diversified pools, and in many places that has meant fewer racist arguments in open court and more trials by peers who are receptive to justice tempered by mercy.

The number of exonerated people also gives prosecutors pause in seeking death in close cases, for jurors may respond to a sense of residual doubt about an individual's guilt by rejecting the ultimate penalty. Today, a handful of counties, such as Harris County and Dallas County, Texas, are responsible for the most executions in the country. In most states, people seem more comfortable with having the death penalty on the books, yet are far more reluctant to inflict it upon another human being.

In a stunning step, Washington State's Supreme Court in 2018 halted further use of the death penalty under its state constitution due to an unacceptable risk of racial discrimination, issuing a decision that is the mirror image of the U.S. Supreme Court's *McCleskey* ruling. Where the Rehnquist Court had tolerated significant racial disparities, the Washington Supreme Court was unwilling to accept the demonstrated risk that Black defendants were 4.5 times more likely to be sentenced to die than White defendants. Coming after a moratorium issued four years earlier, Governor Jay Inslee praised the decision as an "important moment in our pursuit for equal and fair application of the law." He said that capital punishment was "unequally applied, sometimes dependent on the budget of the county where the crime occurred."[7]

Even in Utah, a staunchly red state, abolition is on the table. Two Republican lawmakers, Representative Lowry Snow and Senator Dan McCay, cosponsored a bill they hope will attract the support of prosecutors by retaining their ability to bargain for a sentence of forty-five years to life for aggravated murder. Some prosecutors have already signed on to the reform. These proponents of abolition believe that capital punishment "sets a false expectation for society," prolongs the anguish for families of crime victims, and increases the cost to the state in ways that can no longer be justified. A recent study revealed that the state had spent $40 million to obtain and defend death sentences against two individuals.

In Georgia, too, where Bright labored the longest, headlines appeared asking, "Can Georgia Afford the Death Penalty?" After the creation of a statewide public defender system, death sentences slowed to a trickle. The state capital defender's office is the most obvious success story. What happened in the years right after executions resumed, when some defendants were railroaded and dumped on death row, is now far less likely to occur. By law, that office takes responsibility for the defense the moment a prosecutor seeks death anywhere in the state. This new approach cuts any hanging judge out of the appointment process. The prospect of a fair fight now causes prosecutors to think hard before seeking the ultimate punishment. More often than not, they decide that finality and efficiency mean an assured conviction with a lengthy prison sentence and a chance for crime victim survivors and their families to begin the healing process.

By 2019, it was possible to say that for at least five years there had been no new death sentences in the state. This was a stunning turnabout. Georgia had long been at the center of the national debate over capital punishment. In *Furman v. Georgia*, the Court invalidated capital punishment statutes; in *Gregg v. Georgia*, the Court changed course and allowed executions to resume nationwide; and in *McCleskey v. Kemp*, the justices even announced that they would turn a blind eye to alarming evidence of racial disparities. Through decades of struggle against these headwinds, Bright and his allies have indeed made capital punishment a rare phenomenon in that state.[8]

Besides abolishing the death penalty outright, there is other work to be done to improve equal justice under law. One worthy project is to repeal the AEDPA, which not only ties the hands of well-meaning judges but also presents hanging judges too many technicalities by which to trip up poor people and frustrate justice. As law professor Larry Yackle has explained, this federal statute, once touted as the solution for bringing order to the administration of justice, ultimately became "a conceptual and practical nightmare—crippling the ability of federal courts to enforce federal rights, disserving legitimate state interests, delivering unjust and bizarre results." A fitting end to the disastrous War on Crime would be the repeal of AEDPA and a return to an older tradition of federal judges committed to ensuring equality and fairness in courtrooms across the country.[9]

Another worthwhile reform is to reverse the Supreme Court's cramped notion of racial equality through legislative solutions and reempower individuals to raise concerns about discrimination. One need not wait for judges themselves to embrace a more capacious notion of equality, which may never come. After all, many judges have come of age perfectly comfortable in applying harsh doctrines and rules without a second thought about their genesis or impact. More lasting change can be accomplished through state and local governments, which set the bulk of criminal justice policies. The key is to reject, in as many jurisdictions as possible, an impoverished sense of justice while creating mechanisms for reconsidering wrongful convictions.

States have been at the forefront of such legislative reforms. For instance, on September 30, 2020, Governor Gavin Newsom signed the California Racial Justice Act, which permits people to challenge their convictions based on race, ethnicity, or national origin, even in postconviction hearings. In October 2022, Governor Newsom signed a measure that extended the law's protections to anyone previously convicted of a felony.[10]

It is described as a civil rights law and "countermeasure to address a widely condemned 1987 legal precedent," *McCleskey v. Kemp*, which "is almost impossible to meet." The racial justice law now serves as a model for friends of equality in other states who might wish to clear away the judge-made law and other obstacles to people raising equality violations in criminal cases. Whereas the *McCleskey* decision had largely insulated prosecutorial discretion from claims of racial inequality, California's Racial Justice Act permits someone to challenge an outcome if "the evidence establishes that the prosecution more frequently sought or obtained convictions for more serious offenses against people who share the defendant's race, ethnicity, or national origin."

The law also made it easier to demonstrate discrimination during jury selection than the approach devised by the U.S. Supreme Court in *Batson*: a defendant need only show that race, ethnicity, or national origin was "a factor in the exercise of peremptory challenges," without having to show "purposeful discrimination." Of course, abolishing peremptory challenges would go further, and reduce the gamesmanship that can result in miscarriages of justice documented in Bright's cases. But if states are not going to end this practice, they must find ways to reduce opportunities for mischief.

The Racial Justice Act built on a moratorium declared in 2019, when Governor Newsom said that the death penalty "discriminated against defendants who are mentally ill, Black and brown, or can't afford expensive legal representation." Not only does it accomplish at a state level what Representative John Conyers (D-MI) and

Senator Edward Kennedy (D-MA) attempted at the federal level and failed to enact, it does so for all criminal matters, not just cases where the death penalty is on the line. We have come some distance since 1994, when the federal Racial Justice Act went down in defeat, with opponents like Senator Orrin Hatch (R-UT) who warned that it "would convert every death penalty case into a massive sideshow of statistical squabbles and quota quarrels."[11]

"Discrimination undermines public confidence in the fairness of the state's system of justice and deprives Californians of equal justice under law," the bill indicated. The law denounced the parsimonious sense of justice reflected in some of the worst rulings handed down by judges over the years, saying that citizens of California "simply cannot accept the stark reality that race pervades our system of justice." It is aimed at correcting the fact that "courts generally only address racial bias in its most extreme and blatant forms." In fact, "legal precedent often results in courts sanctioning racism in criminal trials." The law declares that racism "at any stage of a criminal trial" qualifies as "a miscarriage of justice" under the California Constitution and the state's laws. That this innovative statute even exists shows that the law can be altered to embrace robust conceptions of equality and fairness when the people's concerns are brought to bear.[12]

Forgiveness and reintegration are much harder to accomplish. These are worthy goals made all the more challenging by the adversary system, which pits accusers and offenders against each other and forces the state to choose sides. That could change, perhaps, with some imagination, but so much still needs to be done to reconcile victims and perpetrators and repair families torn apart by the jurisprudence of dread. Reconfiguring legal justice in this direction would require the formation of communal practices that, as Harvard law professor Martha Minow has pointed out, create new spaces for "mediation with victims and restitution by offenders."

From policing to punishment, a great deal of War on Crime policy was formulated in response to oversized fears of young offenders, especially Black and Hispanic men. Restorative justice would require people who break the law to take responsibility for their actions, but the rest of us to acknowledge our roles "in creating a world that can exploit the young." Today, experiments in restorative justice have taken place in communities that wish to escape from the destructive cycles of anger and retribution unleashed by violent crime. To work, the autonomy of victims and offenders must be respected in this process, but the ultimate goal is to wrest a measure of control back from the state. Not many restorative justice programs have involved violent crimes, but in a few places that have tried such experiments—notably, Alaska, Canada, and South Africa, mediation for people accused of the most serious offenses has created spaces for the expression of contrition and forgiveness, and studies suggest a reduction of fear and anger afterward. For now, restorative justice remains mostly a grassroots project. But it shows that people believe we have gone as far as possible, and already much too far, with incapacitation as the exclusive solution to crime.[13]

* * *

Of course, there will always be those who traffic in people's darkest fears and their desire for retribution. Many who profited electorally from the War on Crime made out well. Democrat Ed Koch argued in 1986 that executing murderers affirmed the value of life and that racial bias was not a reason to end capital punishment but rather a reason to expand its usage. He served three terms as mayor of New York City. Then, in a cross-partisan gesture, he endorsed Republican Rudy Giuliani, who as U.S. Attorney had touted his aggressive use of federal criminal laws to "reclaim" the Lower East Side from drug-dealing "invaders" and "win the war." As mayor, Giuliani implemented the "broken window" theory of governance, which entailed highly visible enforcement of minor crimes such as fare evasion, vandalism, and loitering, as well as aggressive stop-and-frisk policies against young Black and Hispanic men. After 9/11, Giuliani rode his reputation as "America's Mayor" to a presidential run. In 1996 Bill Clinton, who distinguished himself from other liberals in his zeal for punishment, became the first Democrat to win reelection to the White House since Harry Truman.[14]

Other crime-fighting warriors enjoyed their moments of fame but flew too close to the sun, only to hurtle to the earth. Giuliani capitalized upon his notoriety and gained entry into former New York resident Donald Trump's inner circle, but then led a humiliating, last-ditch effort to overturn the results of the 2020 presidential election. Joe Briley resigned in disgrace after twenty years as prosecutor, amid a criminal investigation for sexually harassing female staff members.[15]

Meanwhile, Bright left us with a model for overcoming cynicism and confronting unequal justice. Guido Calabresi, the former Yale Law dean who hired Bright, proclaims his campaign on behalf of the poor a triumph of gradualist strategies, reminiscent of the NAACP Defense Fund's incremental work "to undercut segregation." While Bright would "never betray a client for a cause," his persistent and pragmatic efforts contributed to the creation of "an atmosphere" where the death penalty was used far less frequently. Calabresi is confident that one day, when capital punishment is eliminated for good, Bright and others in the trenches all these years will receive due credit for moving the law toward abolition.[16]

Whatever happens next, it is undeniable that a new generation of cause lawyers has come of age, eager to carry on the work. At SCHR, a diverse and well-trained staff has integrated their labors with that of organizations around the country, provoking urgent conversations about how to reorder policing and prosecution priorities, reduce abusive pretrial practices, and end unjustifiably long sentences.

Bright left his own mark on his time, doing the best with what he had been given. When he announced his departure from SCHR, he penned a letter to his staff expressing pride in their "outstanding work" over nearly four decades—not only saving lives but also "bringing an end to unconstitutional practices and conditions in prisons and jails." Through it all, he reminded them, "we have provided a forceful voice for victims of injustices who speak in voices too faint to be heard." Bright praised the organization's recent work, which had expanded to "successfully challenging debtor's prisons" and "excessive sentences in state courts for drug offenses." These are the current fronts in the fight against the legacies of mass incarceration, half a century after Nixon ominously warned that "the brutal society that now flourishes in the core cities of America will annex the affluent suburbs" and urged citizens onward in the "national war against this enemy within."[17]

Over the years, Bright kept photos of his clients nearby to remind himself of who they were before they landed in prison, full of hope and promise. A quote from Eugene Debs, who was convicted of sedition for speaking out against the draft, hung over Bright's desk. It read: "I recognized my kinship with all living beings and I made up my mind that I was not one bit better than the meanest on earth. I said then, and I say now, that while there is a lower class, I am in it, and while there is a criminal element, I am of it, and while there is a soul in prison, I am not free."

ACKNOWLEDGMENTS

A book bears only the author's name, but it is the product of entire communities. Writing a book during a pandemic has been tricky, but one thing people are willing to do is talk. For their time and reflections, I am grateful to Betsy Biben, Emily Buss, Guido Calabresi, Russ Canan, Angela Davis, Norman Fletcher, Christine Freeman, Ruth Friedman, Sarah Geraghty, Bernard Harcourt, George Kendall, Harold Hongju Koh, Sally Katzen, Ellen Kreitzberg, Carol Lee, Andy Lipps, Adam Liptak, Bob Mosteller, Patrick Mulvaney, Charlotta Norby, Victoria Nourse, Leah Ward Sears, Mary Sinclair, Palmer Singleton, Victoria Sloan, Clive Stafford Smith, Sheryl Snyder, Bryan Stevenson, and Sara Totonchi. Steve Bright generously answered my intrusive questions and pointed me in the right direction of long-forgotten documents. Too many of the incredible stories I heard ended up on the cutting room floor, but I vow that they will be told again someday.

Workshops at Boston University School of Law, Fordham University School of Law, New York Law School, University of Colorado Law School, University of Utah Law School, and University of

Connecticut Law School allowed me to test and refine arguments, as well as to tighten the narrative structure. So did the chance to interact with attendees of the Constitutional Law Schmooze, based these days at the University of Maryland and organized by Mark Graber. Conversations with these additional colleagues proved invaluable: Bethany Berger, Debby Denno, Del Dickson, Jim Fleming, Brandon Garrett, Erika George, Aya Gruber, Aziz Huq, Gary Lawson, Benjamin Levin, Jessica Lowe, Justin Murray, Sachin Pandya, David Seipp, Matt Tokson, and Mark Tushnet. Generous support from Dean Angela Onwuachi-Willig, Stacey Dogan, Anna di Robilant, and Stefanie Weigmann were crucial to the completion of this book. Gail Ross and Shannon O'Neill of Ross Yoon Agency were invaluable from conception through acquisition of the project. My brilliant Norton editors Matt Weiland and Huneeya Siddiqui gently pushed me to rewrite the manuscript so that Bright's story might reach a broad cross-section of the reading public. Nancy Green provided excellent copyediting.

I am also grateful to Nathan G. Jones, an archives specialist at the National Archives in Atlanta, who helped me access crucial legal documents the moment that archives reopened two years into the COVID-19 pandemic. As always, the staff of the Manuscript Division of the National Archives in Washington, D.C., offered superb assistance in chasing down documents in the files of individual Supreme Court justices. Mary Sidney Harbert, operations manager at SCHR, went above and beyond in retrieving old case files.

To my research assistants, I owe my deep gratitude, especially Victoria Gallerani, Catherine MacCarthy, Colin Wagner, Katherine Thomas, and Allie Wainwright.

Without my family—Tammy, Graeme, Nora, and Pie—nothing would be possible.

I hope I have accurately captured the work of the Southern Center for Human Rights and the philosophy of Steve Bright, a humble and fascinating figure who spanned periods of optimism and pessimism in American legal history. My goal has been to tell a true story about the development of the law as a set of ideas based on justice and order, propelled not just by lawsuits but also political advocacy. If there's one thing that I hope stays with readers, it is that the Constitution is not a faded parchment kept behind glass in Washington, D.C., to be venerated, but rather something that is constantly given meaning through the inspired actions of people around the country. Even in the darkest of days, commitment and creativity can still lead to course corrections that point the way toward a better world.

NOTES

INTRODUCTION

1 *Gideon v. Wainwright*, 372 U.S. 335 (1963).

2 *Amadeo v. Zant*, 486 U.S. 214 (1988); *Snyder v. Louisiana*, 552 U.S. 472 (2008); *Foster v. Chatman*, 578 U.S. 488 (2016). For roughly thirty years, the median justice on the Supreme Court was Byron White. From 1994 to 2005 it was Justice Sandra Day O'Connor. From 2006 to 2018 the median justice was Anthony Kennedy, and since the addition of Trump's appointees it has been either Roberts or Kavanaugh. *See* Kalvis Golde, "On a New, Conservative Court, Kavanaugh Sits at the Center," SCOTUSBlog, May 13, 2021, www.scotusblog.com/2021/05/on-a-new-conservative-court-kavanaugh-sits-at-the-center/, accessed Jan. 5, 2023; Andrew D. Martin and Kevin M. Quinn, "Dynamic Ideal Point Estimation via Markov Chain Monte Carlo for the U.S. Supreme Court, 1953–1999," *Political Analysis* 10, no. 2 (2002): 134–53; Andrew D. Martin, Kevin M. Quinn, and Lee Epstein, "The Median Justice on the United States Supreme Court," *North Carolina Law Review* 83 (2005): 1275–322; Jeffrey A. Segal and Harold J. Spaeth, *The Supreme Court and the Attitudinal Model Revisited* (2002).

3 Interview of Bernard Harcourt, Feb. 20, 2021.

4 James Forman, Jr., *Locking Up Our Own: Crime and Punishment in Black America* (2017); James Forman, Jr., "Racial Critiques of Mass Incarceration: Beyond the New Jim Crow," *New York University Law Review* 87 (2012): 21–69.

5 Jonathon Simon, *Governing Through Crime: How the War on Crime*

Transformed American Democracy and Created a Culture of Fear (2007); Michelle Alexander, *The New Jim Crow: Mass Incarceration in the Age of Colorblindness* (2010).

6 John Hope Franklin and Alfred A. Moss, Jr., *From Slavery to Freedom* (1988), 115; Stuart Banner, *The Death Penalty: An American History* (2002), 139.

7 *Furman v. Georgia*, 408 U.S. 238 (1972).

8 *Gregg v. Georgia*, 428 U.S. 153 (1976). In *Gregg*, the justices rejected the argument that the death penalty could never be administered because it always constituted cruel and unusual punishment. Upholding Georgia's rewritten death penalty statute, the Court praised the fact that the guilt and sentencing phases were now bifurcated and that jurors were required by law to consider the circumstances of the crime and offender before they [jurors] recommend sentence. *Gregg v. Georgia*, 428 U.S. at 187.

9 Carol S. Steiker and Jordan M. Steiker, *Courting Death: The Supreme Court and Capital Punishment* (2016); Certiorari sheet and notes, *Amadeo v. Kemp*, No. 87-5277, Oct. 19, 1987, in John Paul Stevens Papers, Box 503, folder 6, Supreme Court Case File O.T. 1987, *Amadeo v. Kemp*, No. 87-5277.

10 Mark V. Tushnet, *The NAACP'S Legal Strategy Against Segregated Education, 1925–1950* (1987), 32–33; Juan Williams, *Thurgood Marshall: American Revolutionary* (2000). Megan Francis contends that the NAACP's receipt of resources from the Garland Fund put an end to the organization's primary concerns about racial violence, which she describes as movement capture by funders. Megan Ming Francis, "The Price of Civil Rights: Black Lives, White Funding, and Movement Capture," *Law & Society Review* 53 (2019): 275–309.

11 James E. Fleming and Linda C. McClain, *Ordered Liberty: Rights, Responsibilities, and Virtues* (2013); Ronald Dworkin, *Sovereign Virtue: The Theory and Practice of Equality* (2000); Ronald Dworkin, *Taking Rights Seriously* (1977); interview of Stephen Bright, Apr. 25, 2020.

12 Paulo Freire, *Pedagogy of the Oppressed* (1994), 32.

13 Bright interview, Apr. 25, 2020.

14 Transcript, Steve Bright, Feb. 1, 1977, Louie B. Nunn Center for Oral History, University of Kentucky Libraries; interview of John W. Oswald, Aug. 11, 1987, Nunn Center for Oral History.

15 Robert A. Caro, *The Years of Lyndon Johnson: The Passage of Power* (2012), 562–70; Kyle Longley, *LBJ's 1968: Power, Politics, and the Presidency in America's Year of Upheaval* (2018).

16 "Why Not?," *Kentucky Kernel*, Apr. 8, 1969, 4; "Bright, Althoff, Are The Best Qualified Candidates," *Kentucky Kernel*, Apr. 6, 1970, 4; "Steve Bright to Serve as Page," *Advocate-Messenger*, Aug. 12, 1968; "Boyle Boys Team Up In Taking Smashing Election Win at UK," *Advocate-Messenger*, May 7, 1968, 1; Bright interview, Apr. 25, 2020.
17 Interview of Steve Bright, Feb. 13, 2020.
18 Dale Matthews, "Greeks Told to Integrate: Bright Speaks to IFC," *Kentucky Kernel*, Oct. 13, 1970, 1.
19 Louie B. Nunn, Address Concerning University of Kentucky Campus Disorder, Lexington, May 6, 1970, in Robert F. Sexton (ed.), *The Public Papers of Governor Louie B. Nunn, 1967–1971* (1975), 352; Louie B. Nunn, Statement, May 7, 1970; Frank Ashley and Phil Norman, "Guard, Police Enforce Curfew on UK Campus," *Courier-Journal*, May 7, 1970; Mitchell K. Hall, "A Crack in Time: The Response of Students at the University of Kentucky to the Tragedy of Kent State," May 1977, *Register of the Kentucky Historical Society* 83, no. 1 (Winter 1985), 62.
20 Associated Press, "Judge Refuses to Disarm Police and Guard at UK," *Courier-Journal*, May 8, 1970; James M. Miller, "Board Upsets Ruling Against Bright," *Courier-Journal*, Nov. 24, 1970; interview of Sheryl Snyder, May 6, 2020.
21 Frank Ashley and Richard Wilson, "UK Trustees Adopt Stiffer Student Code," *Courier-Journal*, Aug. 14, 1970.
22 Bright's first real mentor in the law was John M. Rosenberg, director of AppalReD, who became a hero to working-class people in Appalachia for helping to end strip mining and securing redress for black lung disease. Will Wright, "Attorney Escaped the Holocaust, Changed Eastern Kentucky," *Kentucky Today*, May 4, 2019; Oral History interview of John and Jean Rosenberg by David P. Cline, Aug. 15, 2013; "Michael Winerip, What's a Nice Jewish Lawyer Like John Rosenberg Doing in Appalachia?," *New York Times Magazine*, June 29, 1997.
23 Interview of Bob Mosteller, Mar. 19, 2020.
24 Interview of Ellen Kreitzberg, Apr. 10, 2020; interview of Russ Canan, Apr. 13, 2020.
25 Peter Cooper, "Will Campbell: A Bootleg Preacher Who Tried to Love Them All," *Tennesseean*, Mar. 1, 2017. The model for SPDC was the Mississippi Prisoners' Defense Committee, organized in 1975, first led by L. C. Dorsey, a civil rights leader and colleague of Fannie Lou Hamer.
26 Interview of Bryan Stevenson, Sept. 14, 2020; Bryan Stevenson, *Just Mercy* (2014), 5–6; interview of Charlotta Norby, Apr. 10, 2020; interview of Christine Freeman, Apr. 16, 2020.

27 Interview of Clive Stafford Smith, May 5, 2020.
28 Stafford Smith interview.
29 Interview of Steve Bright, Feb. 13, 2020.
30 *Gamble v. State*, 257 Ga. 325, 328-29 (Ga. 1987); Stafford Smith interview; interview of Steve Bright, Mar. 14, 2020.
31 Duane Riner, "Court Asked to Overturn Nightclub's Closing; Another Appeal Cites Jurors Struck for Race," *Atlanta Journal-Constitution*, Apr. 7, 1987; Joe Dolman, "Ensuring That Justice is Color Blind," *Atlanta Journal-Constitution*, Apr. 20, 1987; Stafford Smith interview.
32 *Gamble v. State*, 357 S.E.2d 792 (Ga. 1987).
33 Steve Bright interview, Feb. 16, 2020.
34 Canan interview.
35 Maura Dolan, "Executions: The South—Nation's Death Belt," *LA Times*, Aug. 25, 1985.
36 Stevenson interview.
37 Interview of Leah Ward Sears, Mar. 20, 2020; interview of George Kendall, Mar. 23, 2020.
38 Mark Tushnet, "Abandoning Defensive Crouch Liberal Constitutionalism," *Balkanization*, May 6, 2016.
39 Lyndon B. Johnson, Special Message to the Congress on Law Enforcement and the Administration of Justice, Mar. 8, 1965; Richard Nixon, Remarks: "Toward Freedom from Fear," New York, May 8, 1968.
40 Remarks of Stephen B. Bright, Georgetown University Law Center Commencement, May 17, 2015.

PART I: SMOKING GUN

1 William S. McFeely, *Proximity to Death* (2000), 134–37.
2 *Bailey v. Vining*, 514 F. Supp. 452 (M.D. Ga. 1981).
3 *Amadeo v. State*, 243 Ga. 627 (1979)Interview of Palmer Singleton, Mar. 17, 2020.
4 John Adams, *The Revolutionary Writings of John Adams* (2000), 55.
5 *Amadeo v. Kemp*, 816 F.2d 1502 (11th Cir. 1987).
6 Anthony Downs, Preliminary Memorandum for Oct. 16, 1987 Conference, No. 87-5277-CFH, *Amadeo v. Kemp*, Oct. 7, 1987, in Harry Blackmun Papers, Supreme Court Case Files, O.T. 1987, Opinions, Box 508, folder 3: *Amadeo v. Zan*t, No. 87-5277, Manuscript Reading Room, Library of Congress, Washington, DC.
7 Interview of Emily Buss, Aug. 11, 2021. Buss used the shorthand "J3" for "join three" other justices if they showed interest in granting review.

8 Evan J. Mandery, *A Wild Justice* (2013); Carol S. Steiker and Jordan M. Steiker, *Courting Death* (2016).

9 Buss told Blackmun, "This is both a very hard and a very easy case." If the issue is "whether a conviction and capital sentence can ever be upheld when it is discovered that they rest on a blatantly unconstitutional, state-sponsored act of intentional discrimination . . . the answer to this question has to be no. . . . What makes this case at the same time a hard one, is that . . . [i]t seems incongruous to give pet[itione]r the benefit of a constitutionally sound petit and grand jury which he might have sought to avoid." Emily Buss, Memo for Justice Harry Blackmun, *Amadeo v. Kemp*, No. 87-5277, Mar. 25, 1988, in Harry Blackmun Papers, Box 508, folder 3.

10 Brief of the NAACP Legal Defense and Educational Fund, Inc., as Amicus Curiae in Support of Petitioner, *Amadeo v. Zant*, 1987 WL 881161, Dec. 14, 1987; Buss, Memo.

11 Justice Harry Blackmun, Notes, *Amadeo v. Kemp*, No. 87-5277, Mar. 26, 1988, in Harry Blackmun Papers, Box 508, folder 3. My thanks to Harold Koh, who helped decipher Blackmun's handwriting.

12 Oral argument, *Amadeo v. Zant*, No. 87-5277, Mar. 28, 1988.

13 *Swain v. Alabama*, 380 U.S. 202 (1965).

14 *Strickland v. Washington*, 466 U.S. 668, 685 (1984).

15 *Shepherd v. Florida*, 341 U.S. 50 (1951).

16 *Amadeo v. Zant*, 486 U.S. 214 (1988). Memo from Chief Justice Rehnquist to Thurgood Marshall, *Amadeo v. Zant*, No. 87-5277, May 26, 1988, in Thurgood Marshall Papers, Box 451, folder 5, Supreme Court Case File O.T. 1987, *Amadeo v. Zant*, No. 87-5277.

17 McFeely, *Proximity to Death*, 140–41; interview of Ruth Friedman, Mar. 10, 2020.

18 *Harris v. Superior Court*, 567 P.2d 750 (Cal. 1977).

19 Jeanne Cummings, "Lawyer's Experience a Factor in Capital Cases," *Atlanta Journal-Constitution*, Oct. 7, 1989.

20 Mark Curriden, "The Changing Faces of Southern Courts: Some Call Them Progressive: Others Say They're Becoming Downright Liberal," *ABA Journal* 79, no. 6 (June 1993), 68–70, 72, 74.

21 Brief of Amicus Curiae Ad Hoc Committee of Lawyers in Support of Motion to Disqualify Prosecuting Attorney, *State v. Amadeo*, Ind. No. 88CR-25-11 (Putnam County).

22 Interview of Clive Stafford Smith, May 5, 2020.

23 Mark Curriden, "Fees for Pleas Called Improper," *ABA Journal*, May 1993; McFeely, *Proximity to Death*, 141; interview of Steve Bright, Feb. 29, 2020.

24 Formal Advisory Opinion No. 93-3, State Bar of Georgia, Supreme Court, Sept. 17, 1993.

25 Bill Rankin, "This Low-Paid Atlanta Lawyer is One of the Best," *Atlanta Journal-Constitution*, Apr. 20, 2017.

26 Larry W. Yackle, "The Habeas Hagioscope," *Southern California Law Review* 66 (1993): 2331–432, 2331; James S Liebman, "More Than 'Slightly Retro': The Rehnquist Court's Route of Habeas Corpus in *Teague v. Lane*," *NYU Review of Law and Social Change* 18 (1990): 537–635. Efforts to restrict access to habeas corpus have continued as part of the War on Terror. Amanda L. Tyler, *Habeas Corpus: A Very Short Introduction* (2021); Richard H. Fallon, Jr., "The Supreme Court, Habeas Corpus, and the War on Terror: An Essay on Law and Political Science," *Columbia Law Review* 110 (2010): 352–98.

27 Larry W. Yackle, "The Reagan Administration's Habeas Corpus Proposals," *Iowa Law Review* 68 (1983): 609–66, 614, 617; Attorney General's Task Force on Violent Crime, Final Report (1981).

28 Office of the Attorney General, U.S. Department of Justice, Combatting Violent Crime: 24 Recommendations to Strengthen Criminal Justice, 37–39, 145 (1992), in Yackle, 66 *Southern California Law Review* at 2352; *Pennsylvania v. Finley*, 481 U.S. 551 (1987); *Murray v. Giarratano*, 492 U.S. 1 (1989).

29 *Ex Parte Merryman*, 17 Cas. 144 (C.C.D. Md. 1861).

30 Interview of Victoria Nourse, Sept. 30, 2020.

31 Hearings Before the Committee on the Judiciary, U.S. Senate, 1001 Congress, 1st and 2d Sessions on S.88, S.1757, and S.1760, Nov. 8, 1989, and Feb. 21, 1990. The Democratic position was a "very pragmatic thing," said Victoria Nourse, then Special Counsel to the Judiciary Committee. Nourse interview.

32 Statement of Steve Bright, Director, SPDC, Hearings Before the Committee on the Judiciary, 400–3.

33 Stephen B. Bright, "Death By Lottery—Procedural Bar of Constitutional Claims in Capital Cases Due to Inadequate Representation of Indigent Defendants," *West Virginia Law Review* 92 (1990): 679–95, 688.

34 Statement of Ed Carnes, Assistant Attorney General, State of Alabama, Hearing Before the Committee on the Judiciary.

35 Nourse interview.

36 Nourse interview.

37 *McCleskey v. Zant*, 499 U.S. 467 (1991); *Coleman v. Thompson*, 501 U.S. 722 (1991).

38 Liliana Segura, "Gutting Habeas Corpus," *The Intercept*, May 4, 2016.

39 Memorandum on Proposed Habeas Legislation from Chris Cerf to Abner J. Mikva and James Castello, May 5, 1995.

40 Segura, "Gutting Habeas Corpus,"; Larry W. Yackle and Mark Tushnet, "Symbolic Statutes and Real Laws: The Pathologies of the Anti-Terrorism and Effective Death Penalty Act and the Prison Litigation Reform Act," *Duke Law Journal* 47 (1997): 1–86. According to a new restriction on evidentiary hearings, a prisoner would have to show that the Supreme Court had created a new constitutional rule and made it retroactive or that the failure to develop certain facts could not have been discovered earlier *and* that "no reasonable factfinder" would have found the person guilty. 28 U.S.C. Sec. 2254(d)(1) (1996).

41 Associated Press, "Anti-Terrorism Bill Passes," *Chillicothe Gazette*, Apr. 19, 1996.

42 *Washington v. Davis*, 426 U.S. 229 (1976); *Village of Arlington Heights v. Metropolitan Housing Dev. Corp.*, 429 U.S. 252 (1977); *McCleskey v. Kemp*, 481 U.S. 279 (1987); *U.S. v. Armstrong*, 517 U.S. 456 (1996).

43 *McCleskey*, 481 U.S. 279; John Charles Boger, "*McCleskey v. Kemp*: Field Notes from 1977–1991," *Northwestern University Law Review* 112 (2018); 1637–88.

44 *McCleskey*, 481 U.S. at 344 (Brennan, J., dissenting); *Gregg v. Georgia*, 428 U.S. 153, 188 (1976); Robert L. Tsai, *Practical Equality: Forging Justice in a Divided Nation* (2020) 80–92; EJI's Bryan Stevenson Pays Tribute to SCHR's Steve Bright, July 25, 2013, www.youtube.com/watch?v=3HmU0t68vE0, accessed Mar. 13, 2023.

45 Interview of Bryan Stevenson, Sept. 14, 2020; Robert L. Tsai, "After *McCleskey*," *Southern California Law Review* 96 (forthcoming 2023).

46 Stevenson Tribute to Bright; Tsai, "After *McCleskey*."

47 Stevenson interview, Sept. 14, 2020.

48 Stevenson interview.

49 *Berryhill v. State*, 249 Ga. 442, 446 (1982); *Berryhill v. Zant*, 858 F.2d 633 (11th Cir. 1988).

50 *Brooks v. Kemp*, 762 F.2d 1383, 1414–15 (11th Cir. 1985). The Eleventh Circuit reversed Brooks's conviction because the prosecutor's closing arguments had the likely effect of reversing the presumption of innocence in the minds of the jurors. "The Reminiscences of Stephen B. Bright," The Rule of Law Oral History Project, May 24 and 26, 2009.

51 "Reminiscences of Stephen B. Bright"; interview of George Kendall, Mar. 23, 2020.

52 Capital Cases Involving African American Defendants Tried in the Chattahoochee (Ga.) Judicial District Since 1973, *State v. Brooks*, Def. Ex. 2A; Tsai, "After *McCleskey*."

53 Wade Lambert and Martha Brannigan, "Death Penalty Case Challenged on Grounds of Racial Discrimination," *Wall Street Journal*, Aug. 14, 1990.

54 Steve Bright, Closing Argument, *State v. Brooks*; McFeely, *Proximity to Death*, 162–75.

55 Sonji Jacobs, "Where Cases Diverge," *Atlanta Journal Constitution*, Sept. 24, 2007, A8; Maura Dolan, "Executions: The South—Nation's Death Belt," *LA Times*, Aug. 25, 1985; Katya Lezin, *Finding Life on Death Row* (1999), 139–40.

56 *Horton v. Zant*, 687 F. Supp. 594 (M.D. Ga. 1988); interview of Andy Lipps, Mar. 5, 2020.

57 *Horton v. Zant*, Civil No. 88-46-1-MAC, Hearing Before Honorable Wilbur D. Owens, Jr., Transcript, Oct. 18, 1989, 61–62.

58 Interview of Mary Sinclair, Mar. 17, 2020; Lezin, *Finding Life*, 149–50.

59 *Horton v. Zant*, hearing transcript, 85–86.

60 *Horton v. Zant*, hearing transcript, 95, 108–9; Lipps interview.

61 *Horton v. Zant*, hearing transcript, 205–14.

62 Order of the Court, *Horton v. Zant*, No. 88-46-1-MAC (WDO), Apr. 12, 1990.

63 Jack Bass, *Taming the Storm: The Life and Times of Judge Frank M. Johnson, Jr. and the South's Fight Over Civil Rights* (1993), 194, 212.

64 Lezin, *Finding Life*, 153–55.

65 In *Allen v. Hardy*, 478 U.S. 255 (1986), the Supreme Court held that *Batson v. Kentucky* would not be applied retroactively because it announced a new constitutional rule of criminal procedure."

66 *Horton v. Zant*, 941 F.2d 1449 (11th Cir. 1991).

67 *Horton v. Zant*, 941 F.2d at 1457.

68 *Horton v. Zant*, 941 F.2d at 1462, 1465.

69 Katie Wood, "Briley Handpicks Another Defeat," *Fulton County Daily Report*, Sept. 5, 1991; David Goldberg, "Verdict in D.A.'s Slaying Voided," *Atlanta Journal-Constitution*, Sept. 4, 1991.

70 Lipps interview.

PART II: POVERTY AND REFORM

1 James C. Forman, *Locking Up Our Own* (2017); President Bill Clinton, Remarks on Signing the Violent Crime Control and Law Enforcement Act of 1994, Sept. 13, 1994.

2 Transcript, *State of Louisiana v. Snyder*, No. 95-5114 (Aug. 20, 1996), *Snyder v. Louisiana*, No. 06-10119, Joint App. Vol. I, JA 54–55.

3 *Batson v. Kentucky*, 476 U.S. 79 (1986).

4 Shari Seidman Diamond and Joshua Kaiser, "Race and Jury Selection:

The Pernicious Effects of Backstrikes," *Howard Law Journal* 59 (2016): 705–38.

5 *State v. Snyder,* 750 So.2d 832 (La. 1999).

6 Interview of Harold Hongju Koh, May 1, 2020; interview of Charlotta Norby, Apr. 10, 2020.

7 Interviews of Guido Calabresi, May 5, 2020; Carol Lee, May 30, 2020; Sally Katzen, June 23, 2021; Harold Koh, May 1, 2020.

8 Stephen B. Bright, "Counsel for the Poor: The Death Sentence Not for the Worst Crime but for the Worst Lawyer," *Yale Law Journal* 103 (1993–94): 1835–83. In 2012, "Counsel for the Poor" was tied for fourth place as "most-cited law articles" with "The President's Power to Execute the Law" by Steven G. Calabresi and Sakrishna Prakash, and just behind articles authored that year by Akhil Amar, Lawrence Lessig, and Cass Sunstein, and Edward Rubin and Malcolm Feeley. See Fred R. Shapiro and Michelle Pearse, "The Most-Cited Law Review Articles of All Time," *Michigan Law Review* (2012): 1483–520, 1493.

9 Bright, "Counsel for the Poor"; Katya Lezin, *Finding Life on Death Row* (1999), 101–27.

10 Bright, "Counsel for the Poor," 1844.

11 Bright, "Counsel for the Poor," 1841.

12 Bright, "Counsel for the Poor," 1879.

13 Justice Scalia called himself a "faint-hearted originalist," but others have claimed he is not even an originalist. Antonin Scalia, "Originalism: The Lesser Evil," *University of Cincinnati Law Review* 57 (1989): 849–65; Randy Barnett, "Scalia's Infidelity: A Critique of 'Faint-Hearted' Originalism, *University of Cincinnati Law Review* 75 (2006): 7–24.

14 *Callins v. Collins*, No. 93-7054, Feb. 22, 1994 (Blackmun, J., dissenting from denial of cert.); Linda Greenhouse, "Death Penalty is Renounced By Blackmun," *New York Times*, Feb. 23, 1994.

15 Interview of Patrick Mulvaney, Aug. 28, 2020.

16 Brief of Petitioner, *Snyder v. Louisiana*, No. 06-10119, Sept. 5, 2007, at 44.

17 *Holmes v. South Carolina*, 547 U.S. 319 (2006).

18 Oral Argument, *Snyder v. Louisiana*, No. 06-10119, Dec. 4, 2007.

19 Announcement of opinion in *Miller-El v. Dretke*, No. 03-9659, June 13, 2005, www.oyez.org/cases/2004/03-9659, accessed Mar. 18, 2023.

20 The leading cases setting for the "death-qualified jury" include *Witherspoon v. Illinois*, 391 U.S. 510 (1968); *Lockhart v. McCree*, 476 U.S. 162 (1986); and *Wainwright v. Witt*, 469 U.S. 412 (1985).

21 Interview of Adam Liptak, Mar. 10, 2020.

22 *Snyder v. Louisiana*, 552 U.S. 472 (2008).

23 Paul Purpura, "Kenner Man Sentenced to Life for Second-Degree Murder," *Times-Picayune*, Mar. 2, 2012; Purpura, "Kenner Man Again Is Convicted of Killing a Man Who Was Dating His Estranged Wife," *Times-Picayune*, Feb. 4, 2012.

24 As of 2021, Louisiana had an incarceration rate of 1,094 per 100,000 people, making it the state with the highest confinement rate in the country that has the highest incarceration in the world. Emily Widra and Tiana Herring, "States of Incarceration: The Global Context 2021," *Prison Policy Initiative*, Sept. 2021, www.prisonpolicy.org/global/2021.html#methodology. On the Orleans Public Defender, see Richard Drew, "Louisiana's New Public Defender System: Origins, Main Features, and Prospects for Success," *Louisiana Law Review* 69 (2009): 955–87; Albert Samaha, "Indefensible: The Story of New Orleans' Public Defenders," *BuzzFeed News*, Aug. 13, 2015.

25 Sharon E. Crawford, "Justice on Hold: Legislators Seek $44 Million for Revamped Indigent Defense Program," *Macon Telegraph*, Mar. 14, 2004.

26 Bill Rankin, "'I Felt Like I Was Just Nothing' Suspect Held Months After Charges Dropped," *Atlanta Journal-Constitution*, Dec. 20, 2003.

27 "A Sampling of Indigent Defense Complaints," Southern Center for Human Rights.

28 Letter from Stephen Bright to Charles Morgan and Members of the Georgia Supreme Court Commission on Indigent Defense, Apr. 2, 2001.

29 Adam A. Gershowitz, "Raise the Proof: A Default Rule for Indigent Defense," *Connecticut Law Review* 40 (2007): 85–124.

30 Gershowitz, "Raise the Proof."

31 Amy Bach, "Justice on the Cheap," *The Nation*, May 21, 2001; Bill Rankin, "Public Defender System's Approval Called 'Giant Step,'" *Atlanta Journal-Constitution*, Apr. 26, 2003.

32 Robert L. Tsai, "The Public Defender in the Age of Mass Incarceration: Georgia's Experience," *Journal of American Constitutional History* 1 (2023): 85–114.

33 Bill Rankin, "'This Is Fast-Food Justice, and It's No Justice at All," *Atlanta Journal-Constitution*, Jan. 25, 1998, 65.

34 Rankin, "'This Is Fast-Food Justice," 65.

35 Stephen B. Bright, "Neither Equal Nor Just: The Rationing and Denial of Legal Services to the Poor When Life and Liberty Are at Stake," *Annual Survey of American Law* 1997 (1999), 783.

36 Nat Hentoff, "A New Form of Slavery," *Village Voice*, Oct. 9, 2001.

37 Marc Bookman, "This Man Sat in Jail for 110 Days—After He Already Did His Time," *Mother Jones*, Aug. 6, 2015.

38 Press release, "Justice Department Applauds Settlement to Improve Juve-

nile Right to Counsel in Georgia," *U.S. Department of Justice Office of Public Affairs*, Apr. 22, 2015; Carrie Johnson, "Georgia Settles Case Alleging Assembly-Line Justice for Children," NPR, May 2, 2015.

39 "Georgia Supreme Court Justice Advocates Better Indigent Care in Annual Address," *AccessWDUN*, Jan. 18, 2002; Rankin, "This is Fast-Food Justice"; Tsai, "The Public Defender," 101–6.

40 Interview of Norman Fletcher, Mar. 16, 2020.

41 Interview of Sara Totonchi, Mar. 17, 2020; interview of Angela Davis, Apr. 14, 2020.

42 Guido Calabresi interview, May 5, 2020; Carol Lee interview, May 30, 2020; Sally Katzen interview, June 23, 2021.

43 Governor Sonny Perdue Signs Indigent Defense Legislation, May 22, 2003, https://sonnyperdue.georgia.gov/00/press/detail/0%2C2668%2C78006749_91290006_91665626%2C00.html, accessed Mar. 17, 2023.

44 Bill Rankin, "Indigent Defense Funding Wins House Passage," *Atlanta Journal-Constitution*, May 5, 2004.

45 Bright, "Neither Equal Nor Just."

46 Trisha Renaud, "Angry Man of Indigent Defense," *Daily Report*, Dec. 3, 2003.

PART III: DEMOCRACY AND RACE

1 Rhonda Cook, "Nichols' Defense Cost $3.2 Million," *Atlanta Journal-Constitution*, July 22, 2009.

2 Robbie Brown, "Long Held in Capital Case, Man Sues to Get a Lawyer," *New York Times*, Jan. 2, 2009.

3 Harry R. Weber, "Ruling to Replace Attorneys Protested," *Atlanta Journal-Constitution*, Dec. 23, 2007, D17; Bill Rankin, "Pike County Defendant Sues Judge," *Atlanta Journal-Constitution*, Feb. 10, 2008; A.P., "Accused Killer Files Suit Against System," *Ledger-Enquirer*, Jan. 2, 2009; Bill Rankin, "Without a Lawyer, Indigent's Case Stalls," *Atlanta Journal-Constitution*, Jan. 6, 2009.

4 Bill Rankin, "'Travesty of Justice' Prompts Protest," *Atlanta Journal-Constitution*, Jan. 28, 2008, B1, B6.

5 Bill Rankin, "Can Georgia Afford the Death Penalty?," *Atlanta Journal-Constitution*, Nov. 11, 2009, A1, A12.

6 Rankin, "Can Georgia Afford the Death Penalty?"

7 Rankin, "Can Georgia Afford the Death Penalty?"

8 *Weis v. State*, 694 S.E.2d 350 (Ga. 2010).

9 *Weis v. State*, 694 S.E.2d at 359–363.

10 Bill Rankin, "Ruling Allows Death Penalty," *Atlanta Journal-Constitution*, Mar. 26, 2010, B1, B7; Rankin, "Speedy-Trial Ruling Stands in Capital

Case," *Atlanta Journal-Constitution*, May 26, 2010; John Schwartz, "Murder Case May Proceed in Georgia," *New York Times*, Mar. 25, 2010.

11 Petition for Certiorari, *Weis v. State*, Oct. Term 2010.

12 Interview of Patrick Mulvaney, Aug. 28, 2020; interview of Sarah Geraghty, Mar. 18, 2020.

13 Bill Torpy, "Court Mess Turns Messier," *Atlanta Journal-Constitution*, May 16, 2010, https://thecitizen.com/2010/04/22/caldwell-file-which-judges-knew-what-and-when/.

14 Sheila A. Marshall, "Pike Murder Defendant Makes Blind Plea After Judge Hankinson Says He Can Changed His Mind," *Thomaston Times*, July 18, 2011.

15 Marshall, "Pike Murder Defendant Makes Blind Plea."

16 Bill Rankin, "Killer Denied Counsel Gets Life," *Atlanta Journal-Constitution*, July 15, 2011: B3.

17 Letter from Scott S. Harris, Clerk of the U.S. Supreme Court, to Stephen B. Bright and Beth A. Burton, Oct. 30, 2015.

18 Mulvaney interview.

19 *Foster v. State*, 258 Ga. 736 (1988), cert. denied, 490 U.S. 1085 (1989); *Foster v. State*, 272 Ga. 69 (2000), cert. denied, 531 U.S. 890 (2000).

20 O.C.G.A. Sec. 50-18-72(a)(4) (2020).

21 Oral Argument, *Foster v. Chatman*, No. 14-8349, Nov. 2, 2015.

22 In *Williams v. Georgia*, for instance, the Supreme Court sent a capital case back down to the Georgia Supreme Court to take a second look at a condemned man's constitutional claim. The state court refused, and when the man's lawyer sought a writ of certiorari again, the U.S. Supreme Court denied the appeal. He was executed. *See Williams v. Georgia*, 349 U.S. 375 (1955); *Williams v. State*, 88 S.E.2d 376 (Ga. 1955), cert. denied, 350 U.S. 950 (1956); Del Dickson, "State Court Defiance and the Limits of Supreme Court Authority: *Williams v. Georgia* Revisited," *Yale Law Journal* 103 (1994): 1423–81.

23 Interview of Adam Liptak, Mar. 10, 2020.

24 Opinion announcement, *Foster v. Chatman*, No. 14-8349, May 23, 2016, www.oyez.org/cases/2015/14-8349, accessed Mar. 20, 2023.

25 Steve Bright, Commencement Address, Yale Law School, Mar. 23, 2016.

26 *Foster v. Chatman*, 578 U.S. 488 (2016).

27 *Foster v. Chatman*, 578 U.S. at 515 (Alito, J., concurring).

28 *Foster v. Chatman*, 578 U.S. at 524 (Thomas, J., dissenting).

29 *Foster v. Chatman*, 578 U.S. at 534.

30 Linda Greenhouse, "Justice Clarence Thomas's Solitary Voice," *New York Times*, June 8, 2016.

31 Bill Rankin, "Judge Asked to Toss Death Penalty Case Due to Illegal Jury Selection," *Atlanta Journal-Constitution*, May 13, 2019.

32 *State v. Robinson,* 846 S.E.2d 711, 716 (N.C. 2020); Order Granting Motions for Appropriate Relief, *State v. Golphin*, 97 CRS 47314-15 (Superior Court Dec. 12, 2012).

33 *Batson v. Kentucky*, 476 U.S. 79, 102 (1986) (Marshall, J., concurring).

34 Paul Davenport, "Arizona Supreme Court will be first state to end peremptory challenges to potential jurors," *AZ Central*, Aug. 29, 2021.

35 Bill Rankin, "Motion: Prosecutors Excluded Black Jurors in Seven Death-Penalty Cases," *Atlanta Journal-Constitution*, Mar. 19, 2018.

36 Tim Chitwood, "Hearing on DNA Testing Delayed in 1976 Rape, Murder," *Ledger-Enquirer*, Aug. 25, 2015.

37 Ronald J. Tabak, "Representing Johnny Lee Gates," *University of Toledo Law Review* 35 (2004): 604–16.

38 Gates was represented by Patrick Mulvaney, who succeeded Bright as Director of Capital Litigation at SCHR. Katherine Moss served as co-counsel.

39 Interview of Patrick Mulvaney, Aug. 27, 2021.

40 *State v. Gates*, 308 Ga. 238 (2020).

41 Order on Defendant's Extraordinary Motion for New Trial, *State v. Johnny Lee Gates*, Case No. SU-75-CR-38335 (Muscogee County, Jan. 10, 2019).

42 *State v. Gates*, 308 Ga. at 457 n.22.

43 Tim Chitwood, "Gates Set Free After Accepting Plea Deal in 1976 Slaying," *Ledger-Enquirer*, May 16, 2020.

44 Norman S. Fletcher, Remarks, Reception at Southern Center, May 12, 2015.

45 A similar phenomenon unfolded in Virginia, where capital defenders "managed to grind Virginia's machinery of death to a halt by disrupting death at every turn." Corinna Barrett Lain and Douglas A. Ramseur, "Disrupting Death: How Dedicated Capital Defenders Broke Virginia's Machinery of Death," *University of Richmond Law Review* 56 (2021): 183–304, 300.

46 Norman S. Fletcher, "Georgia's Dangerous Rush to Execution," *New York Times*, Dec. 5, 2016.

47 *Gibson v. Turpin*, 513 S.E.2d 186 (Ga. 1999) (Fletcher, P. J., and Sears, J., dissenting).

PART IV: INTELLECTUAL DISABILITY

1 *Penry v. Lynaugh*, 492 U.S. 302 (1989); Deborah Denno, "Testing *Penry* and Its Progeny," *American Journal of Criminal Law* 22 (1994): 1–75.

2 *Atkins v. Virginia*, 536 U.S. 304, 319–21 (2002); Robert L. Tsai, *Practical Equality* (2019), 153–54.

3 Staff Writer, "Georgia Executes Intellectually Disabled Man," *Bartlesville Examiner-Enterprise*, Jan. 28, 2015.

4 David Ovalle, "Miami Killer John Errol Ferguson Executed," *Miami Herald*, Aug. 5, 2013.

5 "DPIC Analysis—Intellectually Disabled Defendants of Color, Foreign Nationals Disproportionately Subject to the Death Penalty," Dec. 4, 2020; D. O. Lewis, J. H. Pincus, M. Feldman, L. Jackson, and B. Bard, "Psychiatric, Neurological and Psychoeducational Characteristics of 15 Death Row Inmates in the United States," *American Journal of Psychiatry* 143 (July 1986): 838, 840–44; Mark D. Cunningham and Mark P. Vigen, "Without Appointed Counsel in Capital Postconviction Proceedings: The Self-Representation Competency of Mississippi Death Row Inmates," *Criminal Justice and Behavior* 26 (1999): 293–321.

6 *Thomas v. State*, 247 Ga. 233 (1981).

7 Interview of George Kendall, Mar. 23, 2020.

8 Interview of Stephen Bright, Feb. 29, 2020.

9 Interview of Betsy Biben, Apr. 20, 2020.

10 Katya Lezin, *Finding Life on Death Row* (1999), 49–62.

11 *Thomas v. Kemp*, 796 F.2d 1322 (11th Cir. 1986).

12 Steve Visser, "Suspect's Plea of Guilt Averts Death Penalty," *Atlanta Journal-Constitution*, May 3, 2001; Jay Croft, "Suspect Once Arrested for Assaulting Florida Cop," *Atlanta Journal-Constitution*, Apr. 2, 1991, 32.

13 Alan Judd, "30 Years Later, Details of Disabled Man's Execution Still 'State Secrets,'" *Atlanta Journal-Constitution*, Oct. 19, 2016.

14 Joe Parnham, "Condemned Man Called 'Most Retarded Man on Death Row,'" *UPI*, Oct. 12, 1987; Amy Wallace, "Death Row Inmate with IQ of 49 a 'Calculating Killer'?," *Atlanta Constitution*, Oct. 18, 1987.

15 *Ake v. Oklahoma*, 470 U.S. 68, 77 (1986).

16 *Holloway v. State*, 361 S.E.2d 794 (Ga. 1987); Wallace, 18.

17 *Holloway v. State*; Editorial, "Jerome Holloway Gets Justice," *Atlanta Constitution*, Nov. 6, 1987, 14.

18 Interview of Stafford Smith, May 3, 2020.

19 *Atkins v. Virginia*, 536 U.S. at 315.

20 *McWilliams v. State*, 640 So.2d 982 (Ala. Crim. App. 1991).

21 Brief of Petitioner, *McWilliams v. Dunn*, No. 16-5294 (Feb. 27, 2017).

22 28 U.S.C. Sec. 2254(d)(1) (1996); Radley Balko, "Joe Biden Fought This Destructive Law. 25 Years Later, He Can Help Repeal It," *Washington Post*, Apr. 27, 2021.

23 Stephen B. Bright, "Death by Lottery—Procedural Bar of Constitutional Claims in Capital Cases Due to Inadequate Representation of Indigent Defendants," *West Virginia Law Review* 92 (1990): 679–95, 683.

24 Alex Kozinski, "Criminal Law 2.0," *Annual Review of Criminal Procedure* 44 (2015): i–xliv, iii–2, xli–xlii; Emily Bazelon, "The Law That Keeps People on Death Row Despite Flawed Trials," *New York Times*, July 17, 2015.

25 Oral Argument, *McWilliams v. Dunn*, No. 16-5294, Apr. 24, 2017.

26 Wayne LaFave, *Criminal Law* §8.2(d) (5th ed., 2010): 449.

27 Neil M. Gorsuch, "Why Originalism Is the Best Approach to the Constitution," *Time*, Sept. 6, 2019.

28 Interview of Adam Liptak, Mar. 10, 2020.

29 Conversation with Bright, June 17, 2022.

30 Opinion announcement, *McWilliams v. Dunn*, No. 16-5294, June 19, 2017, www.oyez.org/cases/2016/16-5294, accessed Mar. 19, 2023.

31 *McWilliams v. Dunn*, 137 S. Ct. 1790, 1794 (2017).

32 *McWilliams v. Commissioner*, 940 F.3d 1218 (11th Cir. 2019).

33 Lauren Sudeall Lucas, "An Empirical Assessment of Georgia's Beyond a Reasonable Doubt Standard to Determine Intellectual Disability in Capital Cases," *Georgia State University Law Review* (2017): 553–608, appendix.

34 Emails from Bright to Tsai, June 20, 2022; from Bright to Tsai, June 18, 2022.

EPILOGUE

1 Carol S. Steiker and Jordan M. Steiker, *Courting Death* (2016), 197. Bright was an early presenter at rebellious lawyering conferences first organized at Yale Law School in 1994, originally inspired by Gerald Lopez's 1992 book, *Rebellious Lawyering: One Chicano's Vision of Progressive Law Practice.*

2 Emily Widra and Tiana Herring, "States of Incarceration: The Global Context 2021," Prison Policy Initiative, www.prisonpolicy.org/global/2021.html#methodology; "History of the Death Penalty," Death Penalty Information Center, https://deathpenaltyinfo.org/facts-and-research/history-of-the-death-penalty.

3 Sara Mayeux, *Free Justice* (2020); Robert L. Tsai, "The Public Defender Movement in the Age of Mass Incarceration: Georgia's Experience," *Journal of American Constitutional History* 1 (2023): 85–114.

4 George Gascón, Special Directive 20-11, Dec. 7, 2020.

5 Veronica Stracqualursi, "Virginia Governor Signs Historic Bill Abolishing Death Penalty into Law," *CNN*, Mar. 24, 2021; Brandon Garrett, "The Decline of the Virginia (and American) Death Penalty," *Georgetown Law*

Journal 105 (2017): 661–729; Corinna Barrett Lain and Doug Ramseur, "Disrupting Death: How Specialized Capital Defenders Ground Virginia's Machinery of Death to a Halt," *University of Richmond Law Review* 56 (2021): 183–304.

6 Stuart Banner, *The Death Penalty: An American History* (2002), 150–53; Austin Sarat (ed.), *Is the Death Penalty Dying?: European and American Perspectives* (2011).

7 *State v. Gregory*, 427 P.3d 62 (Wa. 2018).

8 Katie McKellar, "Should Utah Abolish Its Death Penalty? These Utah GOP Lawmakers Are Going to Try," *Deseret News*, Sept. 8, 2021; Bill Rankin, "Can Georgia Afford the Death Penalty?," *Atlanta Journal-Constitution*, Nov. 11, 2009; Rankin, "Death Penalty on the Wane in Georgia," *Atlanta Journal-Constitution*, Jan. 11, 2019.

9 Larry Yackle, "AEDPA Mea Culpa," *Federal Sentencing Reporter* 24 (2012): 329–33; James S. Liebman, "An 'Effective Death Penalty'? AEDPA and Error Detection in Capital Cases," *Brooklyn Law Review* 67 (2001): 411–28.

10 The original Racial Justice Act applied to cases after January 1, 2021. See Michael Levenson, "Judge Overturns Murder Convictions, Citing Use of Rap Lyrics at Trial," *New York Times*, Oct. 4, 2022.

11 "Governor Newsom Signs Landmark Legislation to Advance Racial Justice and California's Fight Against Systemic Racism & Bias in Our Legal System," Office of Governor Gavin Newsom, Sept. 30, 2020; "Governor Gavin Newsom Orders a Halt to the Death Penalty in California," Office of Governor Gavin Newsom, Mar. 13, 2019; William J. Eaton, "Senate Opposes 'Racial Justice' Measure," *LA Times*, May 12, 1994, A19.

12 Assembly Bill No. 2542, ch. 317 (2020).

13 Martha Minow, *When Should Law Forgive?* (2019), 68; Elizabeth Beck et al., *In the Shadow of Death: Restorative Justice and Death Row Families* (2007), 20–23.

14 Ed Koch, "Death and Justice," *New Republic*, Apr. 15, 1986, 12–15; Rudolph W. Giuliani, "Traffic in Drugs Lowering the Lower East Side," *New York Times*, Dec. 17, 1983, 23.

15 Don Schanche, Jr., "GBI: Briley Harassed Employees," *Union-Recorder*, Oct. 28, 1994; Emily Heller, "The Briley File," *Fulton County Daily Report*, Nov. 7, 1994.

16 Interview of Guido Calabresi, May 5, 2020.

17 Richard Nixon, Remarks: "Toward Freedom from Fear," New York, May 8, 1968.

INDEX

abolition of death penalty
Blackmun's changing view, 81, 143–44
Fletcher's belief in, 143–46
freeing resources, 116, 143
Marshall and Brennan supporting, 32
in most countries, 143
progress toward, 183–87
public opinion shifting, 144
for specific diagnoses, 177
Utah proponents of, 186
by Virginia as 23rd state, 184–85
by Washington State, 185
access to justice, 5, 23, 48, 49, 156, 174
Adams, John, 30
adversarial process
culture of respect and, 9
experts for one side, 168
ideal of justice in, 93
making reintegration difficult, 189
O'Connor on effective representation, 35
AEDPA (Anti-Terrorism and Effective Death Penalty Act). *See also* access to justice; War on Crime
habeas restrictions in, 56–57, 203n40
McWilliams case and, 162–63, 164, 165–66, 173
need for counsel and, 146
signed by Clinton, 56–57
working for repeal of, 187
Agnew, Spiro, 11
Ake v. Oklahoma
holdings of, 156
specific diagnoses and, 177
Ake in *McWilliams* case
Eleventh Circuit decision, 176
Supreme Court argument, 161, 162–73
Supreme Court decision, 173–75
Alito, Samuel
appointed to the Court, 80
Foster decision and, 164
in *Foster* oral argument, 122, 128
McWilliams dissent, 175

Alito, Samuel (*continued*)
  in *McWilliams* oral argument, 170, 173
  separate *Foster* opinion, 130, 132
  Snyder opinion, 90–92, 125, 164
  in *Snyder* oral argument, 82–83, 84, 86, 89
Allen, John, 139–41
Amadeo, Tony
  new lease on life, 46–47
  trial of, 28–29
Amadeo v. Zant, 23, 183. *See also* jury-rigging scheme
  appeal to Supreme Court, 31–33
  Bright's national reputation after, 76
  decision in Supreme Court, 41–43
  discovery of jury rigging, 27–28
  habeas suit in federal court, 29–30
  oral argument in Supreme Court, 33–40
  reindicted by Putnam County, 43–45
  retrial appealed, 30–31, 35, 37, 42
  stay of execution, 31
  surprise plea deal, 45–46
  as valuable precedent, 70
Appalachian Research and Defense Fund, 13, 199n22
Archie, Kimani Atu, 154
Atkins v. Virginia, 149, 158, 160. *See also* intellectual disability

bail, inability to afford, 94, 96
Baldus, David, 58, 66
Baldwin, James, 24–25
Ballard, Scott, 115
Batson v. Kentucky. *See also Foster v. Chatman*; *Snyder v. Louisiana*
  applied by Georgia Supreme Court, 20
  California Racial Justice Act and, 188
  Foster's murder trial and, 121, 122–25, 127–28, 130, 133–34
  not retroactive, 68, 204n65
  requiring judge's active role, 87–88
  Snyder's murder trial and, 73–74, 75, 84, 89, 134
  strategies to get around, 134
  striking of White jurors and, 134
Benham, Robert, 102, 113
Bethel, Charles, 141
Biben, Betsy, 152
Biden, Joe, 50, 54, 55, 162
Birch, Stanley, 67–68
Black and Hispanic young men, 190, 191
Black citizens. *See also* racial discrimination
  encouraged to serve on juries, 59–60
Black Leadership Forum, 101
Blackmun, Harry
  in *Amadeo* oral argument, 36
  becoming abolitionist, 81, 143–44
  clerk's input on *Amadeo*, 31–33, 201n9
  on ending judicial confusion, 122
Blecker, Robert, 110
Boleyn, Susan, 39–40
Bolton, John R., 49
Bork, Robert, 32, 37
Boudreaux, Terry, 89–90
Bowden, Jerome, 140, 155, 157–58
brain damage. *See also* intellectual disability
  Clinton's denial of clemency, 56
  likely suffered by Weis, 116
  McWilliams's signs of, 147

Brashear, Andrew, 171–72
Breathitt, Edward "Ned," 10
Brennan, William
assigning *Amadeo* opinion, 41
McCleskey v. Kemp and, 58
opposed to death penalty, 32
on "unimpaired" habeas review, 52
Breyer, Stephen
constitutional death penalty and, 81
in *Foster* oral argument, 127–28
McWilliams opinion, 173–75
in *McWilliams* oral argument, 170, 172, 173
Bright, Stephen. *See also* Southern Center for Human Rights (SCHR)
as "agitator of the year," 107
becoming a cause lawyer, 4, 25
on "death by lottery," 52, 163
defibrillator implanted in, 75–76, 81, 90
early life through college, 9–12
embracing his life's mission, 7–9, 15
gradualist approach of, 191
litigation strategy, 2–3, 17–18, 70
methods of, 182–83
neglecting his health, 14–15
personality of, 8
pragmatism of, 78–79
as public defender in D.C., 13–15
as student activist, 11–13
taking cases no one else wanted, 3
at University of Kentucky, 10-13
at Yale Law School, 76, 103, 129–30
Bright's oral arguments
in *Amadeo v. Zant*, 33–40
in *Foster v. Chatman*, 121–26
in *McWilliams v. Dunn*, 1, 3–4, 163–71, 172–73
in *Snyder v. Louisiana*, 81–89
Briley, Joe. *See also* jury-rigging scheme
admonished by Georgia Bar, 46
Horton case and, 63–67, 69
memo attributed to, 27–28, 29–30, 38, 41, 63–64
motion to disqualify, 45
offering plea deal for Amadeo, 45–46
Owens's ruling on scheme of, 34–35, 45
secret plan of, 36, 37
sexual harassment investigation of, 191
Brooks, Jeffrey, 73–74, 86–87, 89, 91
Brooks, William Anthony, 15, 60–62, 70, 81, 140, 203n50
Brown, Pless, Jr., 62–63
Brown v. Board of Education, 2, 11
Burton, Beth, 126–28
Bush, George H. W., 5, 80, 82
Buss, Emily, 31–33, 200n7, 201n9

Calabresi, Guido, 103, 191
Caldwell, Johnnie, Jr., 110–12, 113–14
California Racial Justice Act, 188–89. *See also McCleskey v. Kemp*
Campbell, Will, 16
Canan, Russell, 15, 151
capital defender
in Georgia, 106–7, 110, 112, 133, 186
in Virginia, 209n45
capital punishment. *See* death penalty

Carley, George, 112
Carnes, Ed, 54, 154
"cause and prejudice" rule, 52
cause lawyering, 7, 8–9, 22, 103, 191
Chief. *See* Roberts, John
Civil Rights Act of 1964, 10
civil rights movement, 10, 16, 25
Clinton, Bill, 5, 56–57, 71, 162, 191
Coates, Christopher, 27–28, 29, 42
Coleman, Terry, 102
conflictioneering, 18
Constitution. *See also* Eighth Amendment; Fourteenth Amendment; originalism; Sixth Amendment
  habeas corpus in, 50
  right to jury trial in, 30
constitutional law, 23
contract defense lawyers, 94, 96, 98, 99–100, 168
Conyers, John, 188
"Counsel for the Poor" (Bright), 76–80, 93, 96
COVID-19, 141
crime. *See also* War on Crime
  fear of, 5, 180, 190
  restorative justice and, 190
cruel and unusual punishment, 198n8

death penalty. *See also* abolition of death penalty; executions
  Bright as visible critic of, 179
  Bright on "death by lottery," 52, 163
  Clinton's 1996 campaign and, 56
  conservative reformers in 1980s and, 47–48
  constitutional errors and, 146
  as costly practice, 184, 186
  declining number of sentences, 181
  for drug offenses, 50–51
  expanded in 1980s and '90s, 5, 180
  Gascón on racism in, 183–84
  Georgia public defenders and, 144–45
  Georgia's capital defender, 106–7, 110, 112, 133, 186
  intellectual disability and, 148–50
  Marshall's experience as defense lawyer, 41
  new offenses in 1994 crime bill, 71
  Newson on discrimination in, 188
  O'Connor's support for, 35
  quality of counsel and, 79, 144–45, 150, 153
  reinstated in 1976, 6, 32
  temporarily halted in 1972, 6
  as tool of racial control, 5–6
  Virginia capital defenders, 209n45
Debs, Eugene, 192
debtor's prisons, 192
defense lawyers. *See also* contract defense lawyers; inadequate representation; indigent defense; public defenders
  basic tasks required of, 152
  Bright's advice to be aggressive, 79–80
  compensation for, 77, 79
  needed for habeas petition, 145–46
demanding the impossible, 24–25
dignity, 8, 9, 14, 21, 22, 114, 182
Dred Scott, 53

drug offenses. *See also* War on Drugs
death penalty and, 50–51
decriminalization of, 183
excessive sentences, 192
Dubina, Joel, 67–68
due process, and expert witness, 156, 159, 162, 170, 171, 173
Due Process Clause, 159
Dukakis, Michael, 56
Duke, David, 72
Duncan, Martha, 132
Dungee, George, 54

Edelman, Marian Wright, 76
Edelman, Peter, 76
Eighth Amendment, 149
Eisenhower, Dwight, 2
Eleventh Circuit
appeal of *Amadeo v. Zant*, 30–31, 35, 37, 42
appeal of *Horton v. Zant*, 67–70
McWilliams retrial decision, 175–76
Thomas's death sentence set aside and, 153
equality and fairness, 24–25, 80, 143, 182, 184, 187, 189. *See also* fairness
"equal justice under law," 1
Equal Protection Clause
peremptory strikes in Foster's trial and, 117, 124
race-based removal of a juror and, 20
sex-based removal of a juror and, 124
Snyder's *Batson* claim and, 75, 91, 92
executions. *See also* death penalty
attended by Bright, 21
Georgia law on "mentally retarded" and, 158
of innocent persons, 143
intellectually disability and, 150, 155, 177
Supreme Court decisions allowing, 186–87
Texas responsible for most, 184, 185
Williams v. Georgia and, 208n22
exoneration of death row inmates
of Gates, 136, 138–39, 141, 142, 209n38
giving pause to prosecutors, 185
over 150 persons so far, 143
Ex Parte Merryman, 49
experts. *See* mental health experts

fairness. *See also* Due Process Clause; equality and fairness
Blackmun on appearance of, 81
Bright's arguments and, 78, 79, 129
Fletcher's concern for, 143–44, 145
judges reacting to politics of, 182
McWilliams decision and, 174
presiding judge as guardian of, 92
false confessions, 136–37, 138, 149, 155, 156, 163
Farmer, Millard, 18
Fay v. Noia, 52
fear of violent crime, 140, 180, 190. *See also* War on Crime
Ferguson, John, 150
fines, jail for nonpayment of, 96, 98
Fletcher, Norman, 102, 103–4, 105, 142–46
forgiveness, 189, 190

Foster, Timothy
intellectually disabled, 118, 119, 154
sentenced to death by all-White jury, 117–18
Foster v. Chatman, 24, 183
Batson issues in, 121, 122–25, 127–28, 130, 133–34
decision in 2016, 129–33, 164
explosive 2019 retrial testimony, 133–34
Georgia Supreme Court rejections, 119, 120
oral argument in, 121–29
procedural issue in, 117, 120, 121–22, 123, 130–31
Fourteenth Amendment. *See also* Due Process Clause; Equal Protection Clause
Bright's litigation and, 25, 107
Snyder's claim under, 91, 92
Francis, Megan, 198n10
Franklin, Pink, 7
Freedman, Richard, 153
Freire, Paulo, 8
Friedman, Ruth, 43–44, 61
Furman v. Georgia, 6, 186

Galloway, Carol, 62
Gamble, Willie, Jr., 19–20
Garland, Ed, 99, 110, 154
Garrett, Marilyn, 124–25, 126, 131
Gascón, George, 183–84
Gates, Johnny Lee, 136–42
exoneration of, 136, 138–39, 141, 142, 209n38
false confession, 136–37, 138
forensic evidence, 137, 138, 141
intellectually disabled, 137–38
maintaining his innocence, 137, 142
plea deal making him free, 142
racial discrimination in trial, 138–42
Georgia criminal justice system
legislative action, 102–7
mass incarceration in, 104, 180
SCHR actions against, 96–101
standard for intellectual disability, 150, 158, 177
Georgia Innocence Project, 138
Georgia Supreme Court
Amadeo case and, 29, 44–45
applying *Batson* for first time, 19–21
execution in *Williams v. Georgia* and, 208n22
Foster case and, 117, 119, 120, 121–22, 130, 132
granting Gates a new trial, 141
intellectual disability and, 145–46, 150, 156–57
upholding Thomas's conviction, 151
Weis's appeal to, 111–14, 167
Geraghty, Sarah, 110–11
Gibson, Exzavious, 145–46
Gideon's Trumpet (Lewis), 77
Gideon v. Wainwright, 2, 77, 93, 103, 181
Gingrich, Newt, 56
Ginsburg, Ruth Bader
in *Foster* oral argument, 122, 123, 126, 128
in *McWilliams* oral argument, 165–66, 171–72, 173
in *Snyder* oral argument, 85, 87

Giuliani, Rudy, 5, 190–91
Gorsuch, Neil
conservative record of, 164
in *McWilliams* oral argument, 171, 173
Grant, Sherrell, 62–63
Graves, Billy, 132
Great Writ. *See* habeas corpus
Greenhouse, Linda, 133
Gregg v. Georgia, 6, 32, 81, 180, 186–87, 198n8
Gregory, Hardy, Jr., 20, 156–57

habeas corpus. *See also* access to justice; AEDPA
"abuse of the writ," 55
in actions against Georgia counties, 99
Amadeo case and, 29–30, 31, 42, 47
Bright's role against changes in, 23, 51–52, 55
denied to Foster, 121, 122, 128, 130, 132
Gates hearing, 138
getting Brooks a new trial, 60
history of, 29
in *Horton* case, 63–64
one-year statute of limitations, 162, 164
restricting access to, 29, 47–57
restrictions signed by Clinton, 56–57, 162–63, 172, 203n40
states providing lawyer for, 146
Supreme Court restrictions on, 55
in Thomas's case, 151, 152–53
War on Terror and, 56, 202n26
Haney, Judy, 76–77
Hankinson, Tommy, 115–16
Harris v. People, 44
Hatch, Orrin, 189
Hearst, Patty, 44
Hentoff, Nat, 99
Hill, Warren Lee, 150
Holloway, Jerome, 155–58
Hood, Eddie, 131–32
Horton, Jimmy Lee, 62–63
Horton v. Zant
appeal to Eleventh Circuit, 67–70
cited in Gates appeal, 140
habeas petition, 63–67
plea deal giving life sentence, 69
Howard, Paul, 154
human dignity, 8, 9, 14, 21, 22, 114, 182
Hunstein, Carol, 113
Hunt, Willis B., Jr., 44

inadequate representation. *See also* defense lawyers
Bright's advice to defense lawyers, 79
Bright's Judiciary Committee testimony, 50–55
by Horton's court-appointed lawyers, 63, 69
judges' role in, 77–78
Judy Haney's death sentence and, 76–77
limited compensation and, 77
pervasive in death penalty cases, 6–7, 79
incarceration rates. *See also* mass incarceration
declining slightly, 180–81
exploding in 1980s and '90s, 5
highest in Louisiana, 93, 206n24
U.S. highest in the world, 206n24
War on Crime and, 50

indigent defense, 181–82. *See also* public defenders; right to counsel
Ake v. Oklahoma and, 156
indigent defense in Georgia
Bright's reform project, 96–101
broken system, 94–96
Commission on, 104–5
Fletcher on progress in, 143
funding issues, 105–6, 109–10, 111–14, 116
legislative action, 101–7, 116
inequality, worsened by AEDPA, 163
Innocence Project, Georgia, 138
Inslee, Jay, 185
intellectual disability. See also *McWilliams v. Dunn*; mental health experts
AEDPA falling hard on, 163
Bright's clients with, 62, 118, 119, 153–55
Bright's preferred policies, 177–78
Clinton's denial of clemency and, 56
Eighth Amendment bar of execution, 149
executions of persons with, 150, 155
of Exzavious Gibson, 145–46
of Gates, 137–38
Georgia standard for, 150, 158, 177
Georgia's treatment of offenders with, 155–58
law currently in flux, 147–50
legal reforms proposed for, 177–78
reactions of judge or jury, 3–4, 24, 148
state laws on execution and, 158
states' competing legal rules, 149–50, 177
state's witnesses compromised by, 152

Johnson, Frank M., Jr., 67–69, 140
Johnson, Lyndon, 23
judges
denying requests for experts, 77–78, 159–60
duty regarding jury selection, 92
exhibiting racial bias, 59
indifferent, 9, 23, 53, 78, 87–88, 89–91
mistreating the poor, 77–78
opposed to Georgia reform, 102–4
recusal motion in Brooks case, 60–61
responses to mass incarceration, 145
in unequal justice system, 97, 98, 103, 113
Judiciary Committee hearings, 50–55, 202n31
jury discrimination claims. See also *Batson v. Kentucky*; jury-rigging scheme; peremptory strikes
Marshall's 1951 experience, 41
prosecution notes relevant to, 138–39, 140
Swain v. Alabama and, 34–35
jury-rigging scheme, 27–28, 29–30. *See also* Briley, Joe
Bright's committee testimony about, 51
Bright's oral argument about, 34–40

Briley's explanation, 63–64
cited by Johnson in *Horton*, 69
jury trial, constitutional right to, 30

Kagan, Elena
experience of, 120–21
in *Foster* oral argument, 127, 128
in *McWilliams* oral argument, 167–68, 172, 173
Katz, Joseph, 66
Kavanaugh, Brett, 197n2
Kendall, George, 15, 137, 151, 153
Kennedy, Anthony
in *Amadeo* oral argument, 36–37, 38
appointed to the Court, 80
as deciding vote in *McWilliams*, 173, 174
Foster decision and, 164
in *Foster* oral argument, 122, 125
in *McWilliams* oral argument, 165, 166, 168, 172
as median justice from 2006 to 2018, 197n2
opinion on intellectual disability, 149, 158
Kennedy, Edward, 189
Kent State massacre, 11
King, Catherine, 109, 115
King, Martin Luther, Jr., 16
Koch, Ed, 5, 190
Kozinski, Alex, 164
Kreitzberg, Ellen, 14–15
Kunstler, William, 4, 13

LaFave, Wayne, 169–70
Land, John Henry, 60–61
Lanier, Steve, 117–18, 124, 131–32, 133–34
Lawson, Hugh, 61
legal liberalism, 4, 22, 181
legislative reforms, 187–89
Lewis, Anthony, 77
Liberson, Gary, 66
Lincoln, Abraham, 49
Lipps, Andy, 63, 67–68, 69
Liptak, Adam, 129, 173
literacy tests, 60
Lopez, Gerald, 211n1
Louisiana Supreme Court, 75, 81–82
Lowery, Joseph, 59, 101
Luke, Johnny, 154
lynching, 7, 61

mandamus, writ of, 111, 113
Marshall, Thomas O., 157
Marshall, Thurgood
Ake decision authored by, 162, 163, 166, 167, 169
in *Amadeo* oral argument, 40–42
experience with rigged juries, 41
opposed to death penalty, 32
peremptory challenges and, 134–35
replaced by Thomas, 80
writing *Amadeo* opinion, 41–42
mass incarceration. *See also* incarceration rates
battling against politics of, 183, 192
Bright's exposure of effects of, 25, 97, 18
devastating politics of, 179–81
judges' responses to, 145
legacy of slavery and, 2
overwhelming Georgia's legal institutions, 104
two-thirds Black, 101
Weis's ordeal and, 116

Mayeux, Sara, 181
McCay, Dan, 186
McCleskey v. Kemp, 57–58, 66, 185, 187, 188. *See also* equality and fairness
McGlasson, Robert, 29
McGovern, George, 13
McVeigh, Timothy, 56
McWilliams, James, 1, 3
McWilliams v. Dunn, 24, 183. *See also Ake v. Oklahoma*
  decision of Supreme Court, 173–74
  dissent by Alito, 175
  ending in life without parole, 176
  expert refused by trial judge, 147, 159–61, 175
  federal habeas review and, 164, 172
  oral argument in, 1, 3–4, 162–73
  retrial not guaranteed, 175
  timing of law's development and, 165–66, 172
  value for the future, 176–78
Melton, Harold, 113
mental health experts. See also *Ake v. Oklahoma*; intellectual disability; *McWilliams v. Dunn*
  of Alabama, 154, 173
  for capital cases in Colorado, 173
  for defense in most jurisdictions, 174
  denied for Weis by Georgia, 110
  funds necessary for, 79, 167, 171
  Georgia execution in 2015 and, 150
  in Holloway case, 156, 157
  judges denying requests for, 77–78, 159–60
  of state testifying to competency, 159, 160
  at Weis sentencing hearing, 116
mental illness. *See* intellectual disability
mental retardation. *See* intellectual disability
Metzenbaum, Howard, 49
Miller-El v. Dretke, 83–84, 86
Minow, Martha, 189
Miranda rights, 47, 53
Moore, Samuel, 94–95, 96
Morris, John B., 15
Morris, Patty, 15
Moss, Katherine, 209n38
Mullin, Mike, 184
Mulvaney, Patrick, 209n38

NAACP
  hailing new defense strategies, 61
  in lawsuits against Georgia counties, 101
  racial violence and, 7, 198n10
NAACP Legal Defense Fund
  friend-of-the-court brief in *Amadeo*, 33
  incremental work of, 191
  Marshall in founding of, 41
  poor people charged with capital crimes and, 16
  statistics on death penalty bias, 57–58
Nahmias, David, 112
Newsom, Gavin, 188
Nichols, Brian, 110
Nixon, Richard
  defeating McGovern, 13
  Kent State massacre and, 11
  mass incarceration and, 192

Supreme Court appointees of, 33, 80
War on Crime and, 23
Northam, Ralph, 184
North Carolina Supreme Court, 134
Nourse, Victoria, 55, 202n31
Nunn, Louie B., 12

Obama, Barack, 120, 164
O'Connor, Sandra Day
in *Amadeo* oral argument, 35
intellectual disability and, 148
as median justice from 1994 to 2005, 197n2
replaced by Alito in 2005, 82
role in Amadeo's appeal, 32, 33
Oklahoma City bombing, 144, 162
originalism, 80, 82, 171, 205n13
Owens, Wilbur, Jr.
AEDPA and, 57
Amadeo's habeas petition and, 30, 35, 37
Horton's habeas petition and, 63–67
jury-rigging scheme and, 28, 34–35, 41–42, 45
reversed on *Horton*, 68

paranoid schizophrenia, 154
Parker, Gary, 137
Penry v. Lynaugh, 148–49, 158
Perdue, Sonny, 102, 105, 114
peremptory strikes. *See also Foster v. Chatman*; *Snyder v. Louisiana*
abolished by Arizona, 135
backstrikes, 74, 84–85, 86–87, 91
Bright's position on, 135
in Briley's career, 64–67, 69
California Racial Justice Act and, 188
easily manipulated, 134–35
in Foster's trial and, 117
in Gates's original trial, 139, 140
Roberts's *Foster* decision on, 132
SCHR approach to racism and, 60, 61
Snyder and, 24, 74–75, 81–87, 91
poor people. *See also* inadequate representation; indigent defense; public defenders
AEDPA falling hard on, 163
of Appalachia, 13, 199n22
Bright as advocate for, 180
death penalty and, 52, 118
excluded from juries, 59
harsh criminal justice policies and, 5
with intellectual disabilities, 178
marked for punishment by the system, 8
Post, Robert, 129
Powell, Lewis F., Jr., 32, 49–51, 53, 55, 58
pragmatism, 78–79
pretrial detention, 94–95, 104, 180
prisons. *See also* mass incarceration
construction in 1994 crime bill, 71
in Gingrich's Contract with America, 56
proportionality, justice based on, 149
public defenders. *See also* right to counsel
Cold War impetus for, 181
vs. court-appointed system, 104–5, 106

public defenders (*continued*)
Georgia's new system, 105–6, 110, 142, 144–45, 186
inadequate resources for, 93–94
for juveniles, 101
medical experts and, 168, 177–78
not required by Supreme Court, 178
Public Defender Service (PDS), 13–15, 63, 152, 154
Pullen, Doug, 45, 61–62, 117, 136, 138
Punishment. *See also* War on Crime
humane approach to, 8, 9
zeal for, 23
Putnam County, Georgia, 28, 33, 34, 43, 57

racial discrimination. *See also* jury discrimination claims
Bright's doubling down on proving, 58–59
McCleskey v. Kemp and, 57–58, 66, 185, 187, 188
Washington ending death penalty and, 185
Racial Justice Act, 189
racism
Bright's testimony on, 53–54
in Brooks case, 60
death penalty intertwined with, 183–84
in manipulating jury pools, 60
McCleskey v. Kemp and, 57–58
peremptory strikes and, 134–35
of prosecutors in open court, 54, 140, 185
SCHR's cataloguing of, 142
shaming of elected officials and, 182
rape of White women
Marshall's winning of retrials for, 41
mostly Black men executed for, 6
Raulerson, James David, 15, 21
Reagan, Ronald
habeas corpus and, 48, 49, 56
Supreme Court appointees, 33, 36
rebellious lawyering, 179, 211n1
Reconstruction Amendments, 60
Rector, Ricky Ray, 56
Rehnquist, William
Amadeo case and, 31, 41
habeas reform and, 49, 55
McCleskey v. Kemp and, 185
Wainwright v. Sykes decision by, 52–53, 54
remorse
of Jamie Weis, 116
of Tony Amadeo, 47
of William Brooks, 62
Republican Party, and David Duke, 72
res judicata, 122–23, 128, 130
restorative justice, 190
Reynolds, Patricia, 160
right to counsel. *See also* public defenders
abdicated by Georgia Supreme Court, 114
Bright's speaking out about, 76
Fletcher on value of, 145
Gideon v. Wainwright and, 2, 77, 93, 103, 181
habeas reform and, 48–49, 50
lawsuits against Georgia counties and, 98
in Sixth Amendment, 77, 107, 111, 153
right to speedy trial, 111, 112–13

Roberts, John
  appointed as chief justice, 80
  Foster decision by, 129–32, 164
  in *Foster* oral argument, 121, 123–24
  in *McWilliams* oral argument, 1, 165, 167, 169–70, 173
  as median justice, 197n2
  in *Snyder* oral argument, 84, 90
Rosenberg, John M., 199n22
rule of law, 78, 116, 143

Sallie, William, 145
Samuel, Don, 110
Scalia, Antonin
  in *Amadeo* oral argument, 36, 37–38, 40
  death before *Foster* decision, 129
  in *Foster* oral argument, 121, 126
  as originalist, 80, 205n13
  replaced by Gorsuch, 164
  Snyder dissent by, 91–92
  in *Snyder* oral argument, 85–87, 89
  voting to deny *Amadeo* review, 32
schizophrenia
  in Bright's first death penalty case, 151–54
  Florida execution and, 150
  paranoid, 154
  ruling out execution in Ohio and Kentucky, 177
SCHR. *See* Southern Center for Human Rights (SCHR)
Scott, Elaine, 74, 85, 91, 92
Sears, Leah Ward, 22, 146
Shaw, J. C., 15, 21
Simon, Jonathan, 5
Simpson, O. J., 24, 72–73, 75, 82, 89–90, 92
Sinclair, Mary, 61
Singleton, Palmer, 29
Sixth Amendment, 77, 107, 111, 153. *See also* right to counsel
slavery
  Georgia indigent defense as, 101
  mass incarceration and, 2
Smith, Paula, 65–67
Smith, William, 136
Smith, William French, 48
Snow, Lowry, 186
Snyder, Allen, 72
  murder trial of, 72–75, 94
  retrial and sentence, 92–93
Snyder, Mary, 72
Snyder v. Louisiana, 24, 183. *See also Batson v. Kentucky*; *Foster v. Chatman*
  backstrikes and, 74, 84–85, 86–87, 91
  Batson issues in, 73–74, 75, 84, 89, 134
  Bright asked to plead, 75–76
  opinions of the justices, 90–92
  oral argument in, 81–90
  peremptory strikes and, 24, 74–75, 81–87, 91
  prosecutorial misconduct and, 75
  Roberts's *Foster* decision and, 131
Sotomayor, Sonia
  in *Foster* oral argument, 120, 122–23, 125
  in *McWilliams* oral argument, 169, 170–71, 173
Souter, David, 83, 89–90
Southern Center for Human Rights (SCHR), 1–2
  abuses in Georgia system and, 94–95
  Bright's retirement from, 159, 192

Southern Center for Human Rights (SCHR) (*continued*)
cataloguing racism by prosecutors, 142
colleagues sharing challenges of, 21–22
early days of, 18–19
exoneration of Gates and, 136, 138–39, 141, 142, 209n38
first win involving jury selection, 19–20
Fletcher honored by, 142–43
growth of, 103
initial group of lawyers, 17
legislative reform in Georgia and, 103
new approach after *McCleskey*, 58–60
ongoing work of, 191–92
revived by Bright, 8, 15–17
shaming Georgia public officials, 96–101
welcoming women lawyers, 17
Southern Christian Leadership Conference, 16
Southern Prisoners' Defense Committee, 16, 17
speedy trial, right of, 111, 112–13
Stafford Smith, Clive, 19, 20, 156, 157
states' rights
Foster case and, 130, 132
O'Connor's support for, 35
Stephens, Lawton, 103–4
Stevens, John Paul
in *Amadeo* oral argument, 38, 39–40
in *Snyder* oral argument, 89
unequal death penalty and, 32
Stevenson, Bryan, 4, 17, 58, 59–60
stop-and-frisk policies, 191
Strickland v. Washington, 35
Supreme Court, U.S.
conservatives and liberals in 1980s, 33
decisions allowing executions, 186–87
intellectual disability and, 147–49, 156
legal papers hand delivered to, 19
limiting the principle of equality, 57–58
median justice on, 197n2
moving to the right in 1990s, 80–81
two factions apparent in *Foster*, 128–29
wanting finality in capital cases, 148
Warren Court, 2, 33, 45, 78
Surovell, Scott, 184
Swain v. Alabama, 34–35
Amadeo's case and, 34–35
Horton's habeas petition and, 65, 67, 68–69
Symbionese Liberation Army, 44

Tabak, Ronald, 137
Team Defense, 16, 17, 18, 19. *See also* Millard Farmer
terrorism on 9/11, 144, 191. *See also* War on Terror
textualists, 171
Thomas, Clarence
Foster dissent by, 132–33
Snyder case and, 80, 91–92
Thomas, Donnie, 15, 151–54, 159
Thompson, Don, 63
Thompson, Hugh, 112, 113
Thurmond, Strom, 49–50, 51, 55

Tjoflat, Gerald, 176
Trump, Donald, 164, 191, 197n2
Tushnet, Mark, 23

Utah, proponents of abolition in, 186

Violent Crime Control and Law Enforcement Act (1994), 71
Virginia
  abolition of death penalty, 184–85
  capital defenders, 209n45
Vivian, C. T., 59
voting rights, 2, 59, 60

Wainwright v. Sykes, 52–53, 54
Walker, Loretta, 74
Wallace, George, 68
War on Crime, 4–5. *See also* AEDPA; mass incarceration
  crime bill of 1994, 71
  fear and, 5, 180, 190
  habeas corpus restrictions in, 23, 29, 47, 49
  indigent defense broken by, 95–96
  legal system corrupted by, 97, 181
  Nixon on "enemy within," 192
  politicians profiting from, 4–5, 23, 190–91
  in prosecutor's closing argument, 60
  public defender movement and, 181–82
  Supreme Court's role in, 148
War on Drugs, 5, 33, 190. *See also* drug offenses
War on Terror, 5. *See also* AEDPA; terrorism on 9/11
  habeas corpus and, 56, 202n26
Warren, Earl, 2
Warren Court, 2, 33, 45, 78
Washington Supreme Court, 185
Weinglass, Leonard, 13
Weis, Jamie, 109–16, 167
Wheeler, Bill, 99–100
Whisnant, Mullins, 60
White, Byron
  in *Amadeo* oral argument, 40
  death penalty and, 32
  as median justice, 197n2
  Swain opinion, 68
Williams, James, 72–73, 75, 88
Williams v. Georgia, 208n22
women jurors
  excluded by prosecution, 124
  rigged jury lists and, 27, 30, 34, 37, 41, 45, 51, 69
Wright, Katharina, 136–37
writ of mandamus, 111, 113

Yackle, Larry, 48, 187
Yale Law School, 76, 103, 129–30, 211n1